ON THE ROAD
TO MANDALAY

ASIAN PORTRAITS

VISAGES D'ASIE

ON THE ROAD TO MANDALAY

TALES OF ORDINARY PEOPLE

MYA THAN TINT

Translated from Burmese by
Ohnmar Khin and Sein Kyaw Hlaing

Illustrated by
U Win Pe

White Orchid Press
Bangkok 1996

Mya Than Tint
On the Road to Mandalay
Tales of Ordinary People
First English edition 1996

First appeared in Burmese in Kalya monthly magazine, Rangoon 1987–1991 and subsequently published in two volumes by Ah-man Thit Sar-pay, March 1993, Rangoon

Publication supported by an Open Society Institute project

Published by
White Orchid Press

98/13 Soi Apha Phirom, Ratchada Road,
Chatuchak, Bangkok 10900 Thailand.

ISBN 974-89219-9-9

CONTENTS

PART 1
KALEIDOSCOPE

1

THE AUTHOR

Mya Than Tint is probably Burma's most prolific contemporary writer. His original fiction, translations and essays appear in numerous magazines each month. As a young boy he read anything he could get his hands on, from classical poetry to modern fiction, through love stories to thrillers before realising that his heart lay with realism. In his own fiction writing, he has always drawn both on his own experiences and those of others. 'Portraits of Ordinary People', his first series of profiles takes this one step further, and records real lives. The series first appeared in the monthly literary magazine, Kalya, *in 1987, and continues a tradition of profiling ordinary Burmese begun by Ludu U Hla in 1958 with his collection of stories about prisoners, '*The Caged Ones' *(also published in the* Asian Portraits Series*). Since then, Mya Than Tint has continued the series with 'Contemporary Portraits'.*

I first met him in 1981 when we shared a platform at a literary lecture; in January 1995 I met him again in Rangoon and briefly turned the tables so that interviewer became interviewee . . .

—Anna Allott

I was born in Myaing, a town in the Pakokku district of Upper Burma, in May 1929. Myaing is a small upcountry town, about five thousand people at the time, quite out of the way on the west side of the Irrawaddy, far from the railway, not even near the river. I was sent to an Anglo-vernacular school where we studied in both languages so I started learning English when I was quite young, seven or eight years old.

No, we didn't have any English teachers, they were all Burmese. I think we were the first generation of children to learn English in the town. I was the oldest of seven brothers and sisters. My father used to tell me I was the stupidest! He was a lawyer, a higher-grade pleader and my mother was the daughter of a lower-grade pleader, so you could even say that we were provincial intellectuals. My father had attended a private school where he had learned English including the legal English he needed for his work. I completed my schooling in Pakokku, passed the tenth standard examination and went on from there down to Rangoon University, where I spent four years doing a Bachelor of Arts degree, majoring in Philosophy, English Literature and Political Science. After graduating I went on to take a second degree, this time in law, which I obtained in 1955.

When the war broke out in 1942 I was thirteen, nearly fourteen. Yes, we lost three years' schooling during the war, but I was lucky because I had the chance to go and read with a *hpongyi* in a monastery with a big library. I studied Burmese literature and read the classical works, the famous *pyo* and *mawgun* poems; the library was full of old books and palmleaf manuscripts and folded paper *parabaik*. I used to go there every day. When the anti-Japanese resistance movement started, I joined in — I was about fifteen at the time. The Japanese Kempetai came after me so I left home and joined the resistance fighters who were based in Mandalay. That was when I became left-leaning. All of us young people were influenced by left-wing ideas at the time, first through books from the *Nagani* Red Dragon publishing house.

Later in the Japanese period we made contact with communists. Two of the earliest victims of the Japanese were communists in Upper Burma. One was Thein Dan, elder brother of Colonel Saw Myint, and the other was a leader from the oil-fields. The communist cells in Upper Burma collapsed and moved down to our area and that was when I first made contact with them. Then, when the Japanese pursued me, I ran away from home to Mandalay, to the Resistance Headquarters which were led by Colonel Ba Htu. Once the British Army arrived in 1945, we met British leftwingers such as Captain Mackenzie, [Mya Than Tint refers to him as a 'British communist'] and another gentleman who had fought in the Spanish Civil War. So that was my early political career.

After the war ended I finally went to university in 1948, the same year that Burma obtained her independence. That was when I really read

English widely. No, my university teachers were all Burmese. As far as I remember, David Morgan was the first teacher sent by the British Council, and he didn't arrive till 1953, after I had graduated.

I started writing when I was at university in Rangoon because I wanted to write about what happened during the war, to put on record in poem or story form my experiences of the Japanese regime and the anti-fascist movement. The first pieces were published in 1949, in *Ta-ya* magazine edited by Dagon Ta-ya. My first story was about an old peasant woman whose son was killed by the Japanese and my second story was about the civil war between the Karen and the Burmese.

At the time I had no difficulty getting published because *Ta-ya* magazine was the meeting place for all young leftwing writers. I wasn't paid much for my stories, but that wasn't important, the main thing was being published. I was a sub-editor on a newspaper so I had a regular income, even if it wasn't much. And I wasn't married yet.

. . . Yes, I've been abroad once. I went to Stockholm, Moscow and Peking to attend the World Peace Council meeting in 1961. At the time I was the General Secretary of the World Peace Council. The delegation from Burma that time wasn't very big. Earlier ones had been bigger. Only Council members were invited and at the time the Council members were myself, Dagon Ta-ya and U Aung Hla, Professor of Mathematics at Rangoon University. The three of us went to the Council meeting in Stockholm where I met some of the leading activists of the peace movement, such as Professor Bernal.

I got married in 1957, and our first child was born in 1959. We have four children. From 1949 to 1960, part of my time was spent as a writer and part as a peace activist. No, at the time we had no problems with censorship, we wrote whatever we liked. There was no censorship at the time but there was a certain Act, I don't remember the name and that was the reason that Ludu U Hla was jailed in October 1953. He published an article in his newspaper in Mandalay which was regarded as seditious and was charged under Section 124(a) of the criminal law. He served 3 years and 3 months in prison, but it was not a case of censorship.

Was I involved in politics? Not in any particular party but in organisations such as the World Peace Council, and as an individual member in the *Pa-ma-nya-ta*, the National United Front, in the 1950s and why was I sent to jail? I don't know why, to this day I don't know. I went to jail for the first time in 1958 under the first military government, the so-called 'Caretaker Government'. They thought I was a communist although at the time I wasn't a member of the Communist Party, I was only a member under the Japanese regime. I left the Party, before 1948, because most of my colleagues were going to university and because my family put very strong pressure on me to continue my education and not to go underground. But I still believed in the ideology of the Communist Party. In 1958, as I was the General Secretary of the World Peace Council, they thought I was pro-communist and a leftist and they put me in jail.

At the time there was an Act, 'P.O.P.A.', the Public Order Preservation Act and they detained me under Section 5(e) of that Act. It is the same Act that is still being used today. I was in prison for two years, first in Insein where we were very well treated as B-class prisoners and later, in May 1959, I was sent to the Coco Islands. I wasn't released until the end of 1960 when U Nu's government came to power. During this time in Insein prison I was allowed to read and write, to send out letters and articles, to listen to the radio and mix freely with the other inmates, common criminals as well as political prisoners, of whom there were about five or six hundred. It was a so-called 'model' jail, life there was as good as in a hotel.

The second time was in 1963 when the country was once again under military rule. Peace negotiations between the Revolutionary Council and opposition groups broke down, and we were all arrested again and detained without trial at Insein. This time our conditions were quite different; no visits, no books, no letters, not even interrogations, from 1963 to 1966 I was in continuous solitary confinement. Some detainees went mad, some died there for lack of medical treatment. And then in 1968 we were sent to the Cocos Islands again. I stayed there for over four years. At the time it was an open jail with no barbed wire, we could go wherever we liked. I knew every stone on the island. The authorities told me that I was quite free to leave if I dared to swim across the sea. The seas around the island are infested with sharks, but three people did set out in a boat. That was where I got the idea for my novel, *Da taun-go kyaw-ywei Mi-pin-leh-go hpyat-ywei* ('Climb the mountain of swords and cross the sea of fire'), It is the story of those three people.

After my release in 1972 I started writing novels and short stories. By 1972, the Press Scrutiny Board was already in existence and we could no longer write quite freely. Sometimes books were banned, sometimes passages were painted out by the censors. Strange to say, even some of my translations have been banned; for example, up until now, two of my translations, a novel by Maurice Collis, *'She was a Queen'* and a book by Louis Allen, *'Burma: the Longest War'*, are still refused permission for publication. Yes, you're right, about a quarter of the translation appeared in the 1980s in *Pe-Hpu-Hlwa* magazine but when I wanted to publish the full-length book it was banned without any reason. I asked the Board why but they wouldn't tell me. But I found out unofficially that it was because this book glorified the 14th army, the British Army, that is. *'She was a Queen'* had already been serialised in *Sanda* magazine, but when

11

I applied for the whole book to be published, it was banned. They told me that it wasn't historically accurate. For example they said that Queen Saw is depicted as having a romance with a Chinese lord, or something like that. I said it was just a romance, it was only meant to be fiction. But they wouldn't allow it, and it is still banned.

Why did I start doing interviews and writing profiles? One day I read a book by the American writer Studs Terkel who wrote 'American Dreams: Lost and Found' and 'Working', two very famous books about American society. That was what gave me the idea. He used to interview the man in the street. When I go on literary lecture tours, (sar-pay haw-pyaw-bwe) all over the country, I take the opportunity to interview the people I meet, on the train, in teashops, by chance, informally. I write their stories down when I get back home. For example last year I went to Bhamo, Tigyaing, Katha, Myadaung and some very out of the way towns and villages. There I encountered some exceptional young women — Burmese teachers who had been sent out to teach in this remote minority area.

The lecture tours are a unique phenomenon in our country. After Independence in 1948, we set up the Writers Association. We used to have an annual celebration on 'Writers' Day' in December and put on plays about the lives of famous classical writers. In 1956, when we became executive members of the Burma Writers Association, we decided that staging plays in Rangoon was not enough and we resolved that we should go out into the countryside with lecture tours to reach the mass of the ordinary people. So we've been holding these literary lecture tours since 1956. When we started, we had very small audiences, only fifty or a hundred people. We would go at our own expense, or the organisers might give us some financial help, if they could afford it. In the 1960s, the lecture tours started to attract bigger audiences and that has remained the case up to now. The lecture tours just before 1988 were attracting larger and larger audiences of people eager to listen to us. We were making history. Pop-music shows, and Chinese cultural shows couldn't compete with us.

My interviews are intended to let Burmese people know about the contemporary life of our country, the life of people from every class. Ours is a closed society, we don't understand enough about one another. We in Rangoon do not know how people suffer in the countryside, how hard they have to work because we have to rely on the official media which says nothing about this. And people in the country don't know about life in Rangoon, in the towns, for instance about how a karaoke machine works and so on. I am not writing for the outside world but for Burmese people. I think my interviews are popular with the readers, especially younger ones. Sometimes we have letters from readers offering themselves up to be profiled. Sometimes I accept them, but first I listen to their stories.

I am still doing interviews. I wanted to stop the series because I had done so many but the editor of *Kalya* magazine urged me to carry on writing them. But I do other kinds of other writing as well, sometimes under pen-names. Readers know some of them are me, because I admitted to it in an interview, and the editors and publishers know which ones are mine. I have five or six. I write important articles and fiction under my own name. I translate modern English essays for example from such journals as the *Times Literary Supplement* or *Time* magazine under the name of Htet Aung. I also translate articles on military history, for example about D-Day and the Second World War, under the name of Saw Yun. And I am writing a novel at the moment — about the 60s, not about the present day.

I enjoy life. I am an atheist, I don't believe in an after-life. So I look on this life in a very optimistic way. That's all.

2

CONSULTATION WITH
A ROAD-SIDE FORTUNE-TELLER

You what? You want to interview me? Well, I dunno. Nowadays, this interview lark is all the rage isn't it? Interviews with writers; interviews with movie stars; interviews with pop stars—everyone's brother and sister and granny and grandpa, they reckon they can flick open a notebook and do an 'interview'. Well if you want to interview me, go on then. I won't stop you. I suppose reading it'll keep someone from being bored.

Ah—so you're a writer are you? I suspected as much judging by the looks of you. Those glasses, the hair, not too short, not too long, that shoulder bag, the umbrella. That jacket, which is looking a bit shabby. You've got a couple of books in your bag, and a few handwritten pages tucked inside one of them. Probably a draft of your next story, or your next article. And of course, the cheroot in your hand. Well you may be a writer, but I'd say you're not a very successful one. You're not famous yet—either that, or you write about the real world . . . .

That's a fortune-teller for you—we tell a lot about a person from his appearance. Also, I read a bit myself. So I reckon I know what a writer looks like.

There was a time when I'd never seen a writer. When I was a child. Once the war was over, we had all those left-wing writers, you know, scrubby hair, short *longyis*, clasping those weighty tomes to their chests. Those shoes, and their *pinni* jackets, or some kind of grubby army ones. I never saw those writers myself, but I've read about them. If you'd said 'writer' to me then, that would have been the sort of person who'd have sprung to mind.

Nowadays though, the new writers are a different kettle of fish, what with their long hair, T-shirts, jeans, shoes, denim jackets and everything. You see them sometimes, riding around in the latest model of car. Some people tell me though, that they've just hired those cars for the day. I don't know if that's true or not. So nowadays, if you said 'famous writer' to me, that's the kind of person I'd picture—half the time, you can't tell the difference between them and filmstars.

Well, sir, you're hardly the picture of the modern writer are you? That's why I've got you down as a not very successful writer. Or if you're not that, then you're a hand-to-mouth writer, writing about real life. I'm sorry sir, I'm taking liberties. Please don't take what I'm saying personally.

So..my life, eh? Well, it's hardly been unusual. I'm just like the rest of the world. I'm forty. Born the year that Aung San was killed. You might have heard of villages called Kyauk-ywa and Pakantan in Henzada township? Well, that's where I was born. My father was a paddy-farmer, he had his own land. But he only had a few acres. I reckon he couldn't have grown more than two or three hundred baskets of paddy a year

When I was four or five, my father disappeared. They said he'd gone underground. I haven't seen him since. Later we heard that he'd been killed in the jungle. I don't remember much of him. So we were left in Kyauk-ywa to fend for ourselves, me and my mother and my younger sister. My mother sold fried snacks to support us.

Did I get an education? How could I? I had no father. My mother sold fried food for a living. I had to go to the monastery for my education, and you know what that means. I learnt about religion and not much else. At dawn, we would have to follow the monks when they went out to collect alms in the nearby village. We would sneak down to the stream behind their backs and catch frogs and fish and crabs for roasting when we got hungry in the afternoon.

When I was about ten, my mother remarried. She must have been about thirty then. Her husband was from a nearby village called Pakantan. He wasn't even a farmer—he was only a coolie. Later on, when our village was attacked by rebels[1], we had to escape to Henzada. We stayed in Tarkalay ward. In Henzada, my stepfather started to pedal a trishaw. He was a decent man. He treated us like we were his own. He put both of us into primary school. To begin with, I wanted to leave. I was already over ten years old, but I had to start off with the five and six-year olds in kindergarten. My mother and stepfather forced me to stay in school and eventually I got as far as fourth standard. I was quite clever and my mother wanted her smart son to get ahead in life.

Well, that was all very well. I did enjoy school. I always came third and fourth in class, even though I didn't have all the school books. After fourth standard, though, I hit adolescence. I transferred to middle school because my mother wanted me to continue my education. Our family's finances were improving a little. My father now owned three trishaws, which he'd either pedal himself or rent out. My mother had a *mohinga* stall in Tarkalay market. Things were looking up.

But it was then that I started to go to pot. You writers are always talking about the diseases of affluence—well, you've got a point. My mother's *mohinga* stall was doing well, and she was earning enough to put some aside, which I used to dip into. In those days, drug addiction wasn't a particular problem, but as they say, easy come, easy go. My mother had a bit of an inferiority complex so she used to do everything she could to make sure she could feed and clothe her children properly, and she'd give us anything we wanted. She'd cover up her inferiority

---

[1] A number of insurgent groups were active in the delta in the late 1940s and early 1950s including the Red and White Flag Communists, the Karen National Defence Organisation (KNDO) and the People's Volunteer Organisation ('White Band' PVO). In 1949, the People's Democratic Front, comprising Red and White Flag Communists and the PVO captured the towns of Henzada and Tharawaddy for a few months.

complex by boasting. It's quite a common phenomenon. I'm sure you'll know what I'm talking about, since you're a writer. A psychologist would have something to say about it, no doubt.

So that's why I went off the rails, spending money recklessly, on women and so on. To tell you the truth, I married too young. I wasn't much more than sixteen. After that, I couldn't stay on in school.

There wasn't anything particularly remarkable about how I married Tar Kyi, my wife. Her family owns a mill. They process beans, rice, chillies . . . . Since my family had a *mohinga* stall, I used to go there often for my mother and that's how I met Tar Kyi. She must have been about sixteen too. We ran away together. I had been steadily dipping into the shop profits which my mother kept in a cash-box and we ran off to A-htaun and Thaungyi. When our money run out, we came back to Henzada. Her family refused to have anything more to do with her, so we had to go and live with my mother.

My mother took us in fairly reluctantly. In our house, we were all expected to pull our weight. My stepfather no longer rode a trishaw himself. By now he'd bought another two, and just stayed home. My mother and younger sister, Khin Than, were working on the *mohinga* stall in the market, but my wife Tar Kyi said she would be ashamed to go out and sell things at the market like that—after all, she was a miller's daughter. So she just stayed at home, while my mother and sister went out to work. This started to cause problems between them, and every day, if it wasn't one thing they were arguing about, it was another. After a while, it got me down and it got Tar Kyi down too—and my mother and sister.

So about that time, I started to drink because I was depressed, and then when I'd got drunk, I'd get into arguments with my wife. We'd hit and beat and kick each other, and after a while it all got too much and she said she couldn't stand it any more and was leaving me. I went after her to get her to come back, but she told me she couldn't stand living with her in-laws, having to eat our food out of the same pot. But she was asking too much—I had no job, so how could we afford to live on our own? I had to depend on my mother for money.

Since she wouldn't come home with me, I drank even more. I'd meet up with friends every afternoon to get drunk and make it home at about seven or eight o'clock. To start off with I drank because I was depressed, like that song by U Thuka: 'I drink because I'm down; I'm down because I drink'. But I've got to say, I don't agree with the second line. I don't mean U Thuka necessarily got it wrong. But the way it happened to me, I drank because I was down, but once I'd got drunk, all the things that got me down disappeared, it was like an escape. But you can't escape for long—once the drink wears off, it's back to the real world.

I think this often happens in families when one member of the family starts to go off the rails. When I started to drink, my mother's *mohinga* stall started not doing so well. She sold plain country *mohinga*. In those days, the people selling in the market were genuine traders but then later on, people with money started opening up shops too, and competing. Take *mohinga* stalls for example—they used to be run by proper *mohinga* sellers, but nowadays anyone with a brick building is opening a *mohinga* stall in their house. Retired people are opening tea-shops. Officials' wives are running restaurants. People like my mother with her plain *mohinga* stall don't have the money to invest to keep up with these copy-cats. So she got put out of business. Then my sister Khin Than, who'd got married, split up from her husband. They say bad luck never comes singly.

By that time, I was becoming a hardened alcoholic. My stepfather had to sell off his trishaws one by one and then he got a stroke and was laid up in bed. That was when I got fed up and decided to take off for Rangoon. I did have a job, but it wasn't much of a job, going out in a motor boat and catching *hilsa* fish. But I wasn't making much from it so I went off to Rangoon. I had a relative who was a monk there, so I was able to stay in his monastery. I could eat what was left over of the alms for my morning meal, but in the evening I had to make do with what I could find. But I didn't have a job.

After about four or five months I had a stroke of luck. Thanks to a friend, I got a job in the Textile Factory in Thamaing. It was just a labourer's job, pushing a trolley with the bales of cotton from place to place all day. I enjoyed it to start off with, because of the bright lights on the factory floor, and all the girl workers.

While I was working there, I got married to a girl called A-thein who use to push a trolley around like me. Her father worked in the Railway Workshops in Insein. We rented a small hut near Oke-kyin-than-lan ward but while we were living there, I got caught stealing from the factory and was charged with Section 6(1)—that's the Public Property Protection Law. It was bound to happen. We'd move the cotton bales from place to place, and sometimes they would never make it to where they were supposed to be going.

So, to cut it short, I went to jail on this 6(1) case and while I was there I met a rich businessmen who was there on 6(1) too. He ran a long-distance trucking business, but he told me that when he was young, he'd only been a car 'spare'. Little by little he'd worked his way up.

When I got out of jail, I discovered my wife Ma Thein had got a new man. She told me that she'd married me because she'd thought she could rely on me, but if she couldn't rely on me, she wasn't interested in hanging around. Initially I was angry with her for being so disloyal, but when I thought about it I realised she was right. Without me around, she'd had to do whatever she could to survive.

My rich friend offered me a job as a 'spare' on one of his trucks. One day we were taking a fully-loaded long-distance truck to Mandalay. On the road between Yamethin and Pyawbwe, where the trucks have to go quite slowly, there's a gang of bandits who climb on board trucks, break in and steal the goods. One time it happened to us and we lost a lot of cargo. The owner though it was us who had stolen it, so the driver and I got the sack. I had to go back to the monastery. Then I worked as a gardener, and a dish washer, and well, lots of different jobs.

How did I get to be where I am today? Well, in the monastery where I was living there was one monk who was very good at fortunes. If he had some free time, he'd teach me how to do it. I learnt about the elements, horoscopes, how to construct a horoscope, the planetary positions. I also read the books by Cairo on palmistry. And when the people came to the monastery to have their fortunes told by the monk, I would write down what he said for them.

After that I went and told fortunes at the pagoda festivals in places like Mogaung, Mehlamu, Kyaikkalo, Bohtataung and Kyaikkauk. It wasn't a bad life, I earned enough to make a living. Then I came back to Rangoon and told fortunes in the shade of the trees in the zoo, or in Bandoola and Bogyoke Parks.

How do people come to me to get their fortunes told? What do you mean exactly? For starters, anyone who has their own car isn't going to stop off and visit a roadside fortune-teller like me. My customers are the sort of people who travel by bus and truck. Some of them are quite poor. They can only pay two *kyats* to have their fortunes told.

Oh, I see, you want to know what kind of people they are? All sorts. Trishaw-peddlers, drug addicts, scruffy looking couples, women off to market carrying baskets on their heads, people who've got love troubles, people who've split up, people who are having problems making ends meet. People who want to know about exams, who want to know where they can find lost things. You know, one of you writers should come by and spend a day listening. 'Tales of a Fortune-teller's Slate': it would make a good book.

You've got to be smart to be a fortune-teller. Smart enough to be able to size a person up, and tell whether he's come to see you because he's wondering if something's going to happen. He might be worried, or there might be something he just can't make up his mind about, or maybe he's just having his fortune told for a laugh.

If they're coming to you because they're expecting something to happen to them, then you've got to confirm it for them. If they're coming to see you because they're depressed, you've got to say something which will cheer them up. If they're confused or can't make up their minds, then they'll be wanting some advice from you. And if they're coming for fun, then they'll want to hear something which will amuse them.

So you have to know the nature of your audience. What was that you just mentioned—oh yes, that's right—you've got to be a 'psychiatrist'. I've heard about them, and read about them in magazines. They're professionally trained people that cure mental illness, in the West. Here in Burma, I reckon we don't need that kind of a professional—we've got fortune-tellers!

I've got training in horoscopes and fortune-telling, which is the basic theory we use. But I don't just rely on that. Like I was saying just now, you also need to know how to size a customer up. And you need kindness too, you need to empathise with people. You've got to show the sort of kindness to people so that when they come and see you, they go away happy. On top of the knowledge, you've got to have that sense of kindness.

What about me? Well, I still live in hope. Right now, I'm telling fortunes in the shade of this tree, but I hope that one day I'll have a house and a phone and a signboard and advertisements in the magazines.

To go back to the sort of people that come and see me, I'd say you can divide them into two types. One sort is worried that their present situation is going to get worse. Take that teashop owner, the one who's squatting over there, for example. He arrived here at the same time as me. The whole day long, he never sold more than ten cups of tea. But now he's doing a bit better, can you see? His wife's the one wearing all that jewellery. They were barefoot when they first got here. Now he's doing fine. It's people like that, who are worried that things are going to get worse for them—they're the first type. The second type are the ones who can't see a way forward.

Fortune-telling is a vast subject. You can never know it all, because it's the science of people's lives. But you can't just make a living from pure knowledge and following rules. You've got to keep your audience satisfied—just like you writers in fact. You can't be a successful writer if you stick to writing pure literature. As that writer Aung Myin says, you've sometimes got to stretch the truth to earn an honest crust. If you think about it, writing and fortune-telling are very similar ways of making a living. If you like what a writer writes, you'll read it, and if you don't, you won't. The same goes for fortune-tellers. If you like what he says, you'll consult him, if you don't, you won't. No one's going to force you to listen. You writers can't always write brilliant prose. Sometimes you just knock off whatever trash you can. So you know, you writers shouldn't try and make out you're a cut above us fortune-tellers—we're all in the same boat.

Is that it then? OK. Well, if the writing's not going well, you know where to come for advice. I won't charge you anything for this, don't worry.

[October 1987)

3

HEY MR COMPOSER, OVER HERE!

Though he might have been light-skinned once, you could only describe him now as dark, a sort of dirty grey colour. He can't have been more than thirty, skinny, with mid-length hair which revealed a high temples and deep-set eyes. He was wearing a vest and cheap faded dirty brown cotton longyi. *I met him in the typesetting room at a printing press. He washed the ink from his hands with petrol, and showered vigorously before changing into a freshly laundered shirt and a* longyi *which was a bit newer but still the same dirty brown colour as the other one. His name was Maung Myint, Typesetter.*

I almost always read your 'Tales of Ordinary People', *Saya*. We com positors are interested in them because we've heard you plan to write about one of us. Yes, I've heard of your piece 'Hey Mr Composer, Come Over Here'. It's a line from that song 'The Garuda Pounces on the Elephant'.

When I first heard a comedian in an *a-nyeint* announcing that he was going to sing a song entitled 'The Garuda Pounces on the Elephant' I thought it must be some kind of a joke. One comedian was saying 'Give me a break! A Garuda pouncing on an elephant! What kind of rubbish is that?' When the other comedian started to sing, the first one started beating him about the head shouting 'Why are you still singing when I've told you to stop?' I often used to see this kind of sketch in *a-nyeints* but I only realised that it was an old song after I'd heard it sung by Win Oo and Thu Maung.

You see, 'East Palace' *Saya* Tin was famous for writing modern songs. But some old-fashioned songwriters accused him of not being able write grand old classical songs. *Saya* Tin got fed up of them telling him that he only wrote piddling little songs, so he turned round and composed 'The Garuda Pounces on the Elephant'. As he pointed out to them, you can't get a bigger song than that.

That's what I've heard—well, actually, that's what I've read. I remember all this from an article I read while I was typesetting at a magazine house.

When *Saya* Tin talked about composers, what he meant was musical composers. When we're called composers, what that really means is type-setters. How are the two different? There's a big difference. Where shall I begin? Well for starters, the other kind of composer gets to write his name at the bottom of the piece, like East Palace *Saya* Tin. For us, on the other hand, there's no chance of putting 'Typeset by Maung Myint' at the bottom of our stories and articles. So while they achieve fame and fortune, we achieve anonymity. *Saya* Tin drew attention to our having the same title. Beyond that there are no similarities at all. Our jobs are quite different. They're famous and important, we're not.

Yup, I've been doing this job since I was sixteen years old, so that's fifteen or sixteen years now. My father was a typesetter like me. He worked on the newspapers and magazines which started after the end of the war like *'Journal-gyaw'*; *'Fish Owl Journal'*, *'Complete News Magazine'* and *'Progress'* newspaper. His name was U Maung Ngeh. He became assistant foreman when I was about ten and by the time he died, he was a foreman. At that time we lived on Rose Hill in Tamwe. You couldn't even call it a suburb then, it was more like a village—mango and banana plantations everywhere, all watercress ponds and cauliflowers. There was no power or electricity or anything and the houses were just shacks made out of palm leaves and woven bamboo.

As far as I know, we moved to that mango plantation between Rose Hill and Bauktaw at about the time I was born. That's where I grew up. My father had been a farmer and fisherman when he was young. He came from Ye-le-galay village near Ma-U-Bin in the delta, and he used to work in the paddy fields in season, and out of season he'd fish in the lakes.

He was still quite young when the English came back after the war. In those days he'd go with his father to the fields or to fish in the streams. One of our relatives in the village was a monk who had been to India to study. Soon after the war was over he returned to our village and spent the rest of his life running the monastery.

He enjoyed reading and before the war he had written articles for 'Dagon' magazine and 'Fish Owl'. He asked my grandparents whether they wanted my father to grow up to be only a fisherman or whether they wanted him to go to school. Then he called my father into the monastery to teach him reading and writing.

After the war, he sent my father to Rangoon to live in the monastery of one of his followers and helped him find a job as a typesetter. It was easy enough for him to get my father fixed up since he had good contacts in all the printers and publishers in Rangoon.

His first job was to watch over the presses and make sure that the papers stayed flat as they were churned out. When the print run was completed, he unloaded the papers from the press. After that, he moved on to learn how to typeset. First he had to learn the containers and how to pick up the type and set it. Then he had to learn how to take a forme[1] apart and put the pieces back in their containers. You can only start to type-set once you've mastered the order of the containers, because otherwise your text will be full of mistakes.

It takes you a while to set the text, and the other typesetters have to wait for you to finish so that they can put the formes together. This means that the forme handler doesn't earn as much as he should, and everyone else's wages are affected too. So a new boy won't be given the chance to set type when he starts work. He's told to take apart the old boards, which gives him the chance to learn the order of the containers properly. It's just the same now as it was in my father's day.

When my father first arrived in Rangoon, the monk arranged for him to work in a printing house which printed *pitaka* and prayer texts. That was where he came across the *Pali* text proof-readers. He learnt a lot from them about setting *Pali*. He said that the foremen were very meticulous.

---

[1] A forme is a body of type, secured in a chase or frame, for printing at one impression. Sixteen pages of a Burmese novel comprise a forme.

After that he typeset in either a magazine or a newspaper printers, I'm not sure which. At that time he was living in the monastery, but he told me that once he'd married my mother, he had to leave. My mother was the daughter of a machine operator in one of the presses where my father worked. She got to know my father because she would come to the press to bring her father his lunch. Once they were married they moved to where she lived, between Rose Hill and Bauktaw. At that time, the area was full of squatters, including my mothers' family. I think the land, which was mostly mango and jackfruit trees, belonged to a rich Indian. My father put up a shack not far from his in-laws. In those days the area had no electricity and buses stopped running at six so no-one wanted to come and live there because commuting was too difficult. There were no buses or taxis at night so people tended to avoid the area.

I was born on Rose Hill. I don't know if you know it. Between Thingangyunn and Bauktaw. In those days I think there was a Chinese noodle factory nearby, but the rest was fields and plantations and squatters huts.

I was the oldest. There were five born after me. After four or five of us had been born, my father transferred to work in a newspaper printing press as a foreman. In his previous jobs he'd only been a typesetter. A friend of his who worked as a machine operator got him a job there as an assistant foreman on account of his previous experience putting together formes. But he wasn't too happy because he was only getting a typesetter's wage. His friend told him that there was a vacancy for a foreman with a journal which used to come and get printed on his machine, but set their type themselves, as they were quite poor. He suggested my father apply for the job. He'd put in a word and tell them my father could do everything, including formes. So my father ended up leaving the job on a typesetter's salary at the newspaper and moving across to be foreman at the journal.

On my days off from school I used to go along with my father to the press. The journal was quite poor and its premises weren't grand. They consisted of a little bamboo hut squashed between two tall buildings on the middle block of 37th Street. At the front of the hut were the three small desks for the editor and manager, and the proof readers. Behind them was the desk where the formes were put together, and in the back room, the typesetter's desk. It was a tiny building, about twelve and a half feet wide and fifty foot from back to front. They didn't even have the entire fifty feet because the owner was living in the back twenty feet, and only renting out the front thirty. It was a noisy neighbourhood with an Indian family on the right. They were Coringee Indians. Every lunch time the women would be out pounding turmeric and the smell would fill the office. On the left were more Indians. An Indian teacher had opened up a private tuition school for Indian kids. What with the teacher declaiming the lessons and the kids shouting them out loud, it was amazing the editors could ever manage to get any work done.

What's more, in the back room where the typesetters were, there was no electricity and the room was dark during the monsoon. They'd opened up a skylight to let the light in, and they had to set type by that. On really rainy days, they had to set the type by lamplight. You can tell how poor the journal was by the fact that sometimes they ran out of kerosene for the lamps and had to close the office.

But my father was happy working there. He had finally made it as a foreman and was handling the formes. Since he was paid by the forme, this meant that he could work the hours he liked. If a publication was important, he worked night and day typesetting. Although it was tiring, he earned more than working for a monthly wage. At the newspaper he'd been on a monthly wage and no matter how many pages he typeset, he always got the same amount. Also, at the newspaper, there had been no chance to take a break. There was no question of sloping off.

At the paper, as soon as he arrived at work, he'd have to stay at his desk until he'd finished setting type for his share of the copy, so that the edition would get out on time the next day. The foreman would curse the typesetters who lagged behind because they would hold up the putting together of the formes. At the paper, when you were on nightshift, you just wanted to finish setting your formes as quickly as possible, so you could go home. And all for a fixed wage which you couldn't do anything to increase.

At the magazine publishers, it was a different arrangement. There they paid him by the forme. Of course it wasn't as grand as the newspaper, but the magazine came out once a week, so it was regular work. When I turned ten years old, my father started bringing me to work, and I would go out and get tea and run errands for him and the other foremen and typesetters.

I think you remember how they used to sell tea to take away in those days. You didn't get it in a plastic bag like you do now. They'd put it in an old condensed milk tin. If you topped up the tin with plain tea from the pot there'd be enough for both my father and me.

If I went to work with my father, there was nowhere for me to perch so I would just have to sit between the typesetting benches. That was how I started to pick up the order of the type containers without hardly trying. If the typesetters didn't feel like taking the formes apart, they'd get me to do it. If their backs were aching, they'd call me over from where I was squatting between the benches. 'Hey kid, come and take my formes apart for me!' I would painstakingly put the type back into the boxes.

To start off with I was slow. Although my brain had picked up the position of the boxes, my hands hadn't got the habit yet. But after a while I picked it up and my hands started sticking the type back into the right box almost automatically, just like an experienced typist can find the keys without thinking.

I must have been about fourteen or fifteen by then. I could take the formes apart, but I still couldn't set the type properly. I had problems picking up the letters from the boxes. You have to practice to get it right.

I was sixth or seventh standard then, I think. Yeah, that's right, seventh standard. Seventh standard was the year I failed my exams. If you failed twice, you had to leave. After that, I hung out with my friends, smoking cigarettes and stuff and chatting up girls. I had no proper job, and was living off my parents and just killing time, hanging out. I met my girlfriend about that time. She'd failed eighth standard twice and been thrown out of school. She worked over in Bauktaw for a woman who'd set up a whole lot of sewing machines and used to employ girls to make bras which she'd then sell wholesale down in Theingyi Market.

I met her when she was working there and chatted her up and she became my girlfriend. She was really fed up with living at home with her parents and was always trying to persuade me to elope with her. I was forever pointing out to her that I had no job and was hardly in a position to run off and get married. But one day she had an argument with her stepmother and left home anyway. She told me in tears that we could elope if I wanted, and if I didn't want to then she'd just go wherever her feet took her. That night I didn't go home. Instead we stayed the night at a friend's house. We were both about seventeen at the time.

It was OK just to elope to my friend's house. But we could hardly live there permanently. I didn't have a job and my friend was living off his parents. He'd only let us stay there because his parents were away. We were going to have to leave before they got back.

I'd not finished school. I'd not got a job of any description. My wife knew how to sew on cloth buttons and bows and that was about it. And what's more, she couldn't even go back to her old job because it was in the same quarter as her parents' house and she was afraid to go near there. So I went over to my father's printshop. He was furious with me and refused to speak to me when I got there. He just stayed hunched over his bench, scowling.

But the boss, U Ye Aye, and the assistant editor U Mun Aung were fond of me seeing as I'd always been willing to run errands for them. When I turned up, they bombarded me with questions. 'Hey kid, so you went and got married did you? How are you going to feed yourself and your lovely new lady wife?'

I said to the boss, 'Saya, that's why I'm here. I was wondering if you'd got any jobs going . . .'

U Ye Aye turned to my father and called out 'U Maung Ngeh, your son may as well prepare some formes. There's a worker who hasn't turned up'. My father just stayed hunched over the table, and said 'Boss, you own the place. If that's what you want..'.

That's how I got a a job as a typesetter. Well, as an apprentice. But since I'd already learnt how to take formes to pieces and knew a bit of typesetting already, I didn't have to serve for long. I soon learnt how to set the galleys as quickly as the other typesetters. After a while my parents relented and took us back and things started going OK.

I stayed working in that magazine house for a couple of years, until it closed down. After that I went and set formes in magazine and book publishers. Working in the magazine houses was hard work. The pages sometimes have two, sometimes three, sometimes four columns and if you have to set all three sorts it creates a lot of work. The foremen have to work even harder. But you pick up a lot of general knowledge, working for a magazine. It's good typesetting an article because you get a sneak preview. When you do a novel, though, you only get to read the bits you get given for typesetting so you can only read half the story.

You get to find out some strange things working as a typesetter. For example, there are these 'ghost' writers. Some of these famous women writers, you get their manuscripts sent into the magazine house, and the handwriting isn't the same from one manuscript to another. I can think of at least one case, with a woman writer who's quite famous. She sent in her novel and in the first month's instalment the writing was quite different from the second. Sometimes it looks more like a man's writing, sometimes it looks like a woman's. Sometimes you get the same handwriting coming from two different authors.

So we typesetters can all tell you who really writes these stories, and who the ghosts are. Just like that 'East Palace' Saya Tin song 'Hey Mr Composer come over here—you don't know anything about classical music'. But someone can know a good song when he hears one even if he does not understand the theory. We typesetters are the same. We may not be particularly up on our literature and we may not be writers ourselves, but we can all tell you who's writing what for whom and who's behind the big names. There's this famous writer, he's going on seventy, and he's ghost-writing. You'd be shocked if I told you who it was.

Nowadays? Nowadays I've got four children. I don't know, maybe one day I'll make it as a foreman. I'll certainly try my best. I like working as a typesetter. It's an interesting job. But it does for your health and that's the one problem I have with it.

Yes, I've heard about occupational diseases. In fact I've more than heard of them, I've had personal experience of one. My father spent his whole life working as a typesetter and then as a foreman. He died of TB. When they did the autopsy, they said they found about fifty *pyas* of lead inside his stomach. He'd been handling lead type all his life, and I don't know, maybe he'd got lead on his hands, or maybe he'd been breathing it in or something. But anyway, it couldn't have been good for him.

By now I may already have ten or even twenty-five *pyas* of lead inside me. My father did forty years typesetting and acquired fifty *pyas*. I've already been doing it for over ten years so I must have at least ten *pyas*. Whenever a typesetter dies, you're bound to discover he's saved at least ten *pyas* in his stomach.

[June 1989]

4

ANY OLD NEWSPAPERS?

I still don't know his name, even though we must have known one another for over ten years. I call him 'Old Man', and so does my wife. It's not a particularly dignified name for someone approaching eighty. We really should use a more respectful name, but we never seem to have got round to finding one out, so Old Man it is. He doesn't seem to mind. He's never suggested he thinks it's too familiar, or seemed irritated. It's not just us who call him that—everyone does. No-one seems to know his real name, so Old Man he will remain.

He comes round our way once every two or three days. He's a dark-skinned Indian, with white hair and a white moustache. Tall and sturdy, he carries a gunny sack on his head for old paper, books and newspapers, and his weight-scales. Whenever we have books or old newspapers to sell off, we wait for the Old Man to visit. Sometimes, if he's tired, he comes inside for a chat. I have great admiration for this old man, approaching eighty, yet still healthy and independent, and working hard for a living.

I'm seventy-six. I've been buying and selling paper since I was a nipper. I take bottles and glass too sometimes. My whole life I've been dealing with old glass and paper. I don't bother with anything else. Some kids collect the lot—powder compacts, condensed milk cans, milk powder tins, biscuit tins, plastic containers. That's not for me. I only do the two types, paper and glass, just paper and glass, my whole life long. I don't touch the other stuff. Why should I try dealing in stuff which I don't know anything about, when I can survive on the stuff I know?

There's so much stuff around nowadays. So many varieties. Nail varnish, powder compacts, old X-ray films, biscuit tins. I don't know anything about that kind of thing. Also, it's heavy to lug around, you need a big sack. Biscuit tins and that, you only need ten or so and you've filled a sack. It's difficult to carry those things around, but paper and glass are easy. Anyway, I've been selling paper and glass all my life, and it's what I know. I don't know how to sell the other stuff.

I'm a Tamil, but I've been living in Burma for a long time, since I was young, before the War. My parents brought me here. My father was a *jardoowallah*, a street-sweeper, with Rangoon Municipality. I'm the oldest of ten. My father went on to pull a rickshaw. You'll know what a rickshaw looks like, but young people nowadays have probably never seen one. In those days, they used to be pulled by the Coringees and the Tamils.

When I first came to Burma, I must have been about five years old. Those days, the place was full of English. Not many cars, just dog-carts. In the evenings, the rich used to go out in dog-carts to take the air. You'll know what I mean by dog-cart, I think. Traps, pulled by horses, that only the rich could ride in. People who didn't have that kind of money had to go by rickshaw.

Pulling a rickshaw is tiring work, so my father used to drink *gazaw* liquor every day. He liked to get drunk on *gazaw* and once he was drunk he would sing songs from the Indian film '*Dasangyi*' and do the Pharisee dance.

We were happy in those days, *Saya*. My mother had us, one after the other, but she still kept working, pounding spices, turmeric, garam masala. We'd help her, even though we only kids. We were a big family, but we always had enough to eat, not like India, where there's not enough food to go round. In Burma there's plenty for everyone. Paddy, rice, beans, chillies, tamarind, potatoes. Enough for us to eat fish curry, rice and beans every day. We're Hindu, you see, so we don't eat meat. There's loads to eat in Burma. We can eat bean stew and *bhajis* almost for free.

My father died when I was about twenty. He'd pulled a rickshaw all his life, in the heat, and in the monsoon, without any problem, then he came home one day for a rest after pulling his rickshaw, went to bed and died peacefully in his sleep. You'd have thought if he was going to die, he would have done it out on the street, lugging the rickshaw around, in all weathers.

In those days, though, he was coughing up blood. One time, while he was pulling the rickshaw, he did collapse in the street, from exhaustion. But he didn't die. Next day, he was back on the streets again. And even when he was bringing up blood, he was still OK to work. One time he coughed up enough blood to fill almost an entire spittoon. He told us that it wasn't blood, it was betel juice. But how could it have been? We knew it was blood. It was bright red, like the blood that I used to get when I had a nosebleed. Scarlet. The whole day he was coughing it up. But the next day, he was back on the streets, no problem, and drinking booze to keep his strength up. By then he'd given up *gazaw*, and was on to country spirit made out of sticky rice, the sort that you can light with a match and it goes whoosh. He'd start off with a glass in the morning, go out and pull the rickshaw, and then when he was tired, he'd have a bit more to drink, pull the rickshaw a bit more. It didn't cause him any problems. Then one day, when he was quietly resting at home, Buddha called him to heaven.

When he died, I was twenty, maybe not even that. I had to start taking care of my mother and brothers and sisters. We still had the rickshaw which my father had owned, so I took it on. My mother carried on pounding spices and I started pulling a rickshaw. But I couldn't manage. Look at me *Saya*. I'm tall, I've got a good build, I'm strong, too. But I couldn't pull a rickshaw. I couldn't cope with the running either. My father was skinny, but he could run. He never tired. He'd been pulling a rickshaw all his life. I tried it for a month, and had to take to my bed for ages to recover. I couldn't get up for days. In the end I went to the doctor and he told me I shouldn't pull rickshaws ever again, or it'd kill me. So I gave up, and my little brother tried, but he couldn't do it like my father could either. One month did for him too. Straight to bed. After that, we were amazed that my father had managed it.

After I gave up the rickshaw, I started selling newspapers down on Pansoedan Street. Not Burmese ones, English ones. I became an agent for the foreign English-language newspapers which were published by the City Book Club and came from India and England. I used to go down to the High Court to sell them. The newspapers in those days were enormous and I would hang them over my arm, with about a foot trailing down on either side. I used to go down to the High Court because that was where the foreigners were, the Indian court clerks, lawyers, and barristers. They were all Indians, so I always did good business down there. You know how Pansoedan Street was full of courts. Well the Indian clerks all wanted to buy my newspapers. In the evenings, I used to go and sell them in the bars and liquor shops.

Then the war happened. I was already married then. My wife was an *ayah*. I suppose today's young people wouldn't know what that was either. But you do, I'm sure. My wife worked as a nanny for an Indian barrister on 40th Street. I used to go and take newspapers to his house which is how I met her.

By the time the war started, we'd had one kid. A son. We couldn't go on living in Rangoon because of the bombs. We left Rangoon during an air-raid and set off for Prome. There were no trains, so we had to take a bus. It broke down on the way and we had to walk from there. I couldn't believe the roads, how full of people they were. Lots of Indians like us were crossing the Irrawaddy at Prome to get to India. From there, we headed for Taungup. We got very hungry along the way. Some people got cholera and died by the roadside. There were a lot of rotting corpses. By the time we had crossed the Arakan Yoma, my mother and my son had died of cholera too. We had to leave them by the road. From Taungup we moved up through Arakan State, and from there to Bengal. We stayed briefly in Calcutta but since there wasn't anything to eat there, we set out into the country side. By the time we got there we were starving. India was full of people dying of hunger.

In the three years we were in India, I turned my hand to whatever jobs I could find. I was an oddjobman, a waiter, a *jardoo-wallah, chaprassi* messenger boy. After the war, we came back to Burma. It had always been our home. We'd always had enough to eat here, a job, a way to earn money. That's why we came back. The British sent a boat for us, and we left for Rangoon as soon as the shipping routes re-opened.

Back in Rangoon, we found our house had been bombed. Still, it was better than the village we'd lived in in Bengal which hadn't got any proper houses. We'd had to build our own hut.

I had no job left in Rangoon, so I went off and worked as a *jardoo-wallah* for the Gurkhas in the British army. I used to wait on the English soldiers too. The pay was good. I got given rations, canned fish, cheese, cigarettes, tinned meat. Since I was a Hindu and I only ate vegetarian curries and *bhajis*, I used to sell my rations.

When the British left, I lost my job. They left behind loads of books in the barracks, English books. I took them and sold them in front of Scott Market. After that I went and worked for a paper merchant on 27th Street. I used to go out and collect old newspapers and bottles for him. I would walk all over Rangoon buying paper and glass, one day to Pazundaung, the next day to Thingangyunn, then Kokine, then Sanchaung, walking all over Rangoon, buying up paper and glass.

I've been doing it now for over forty years. In all that time it's been paper and glass. Sometimes I'd collect English books. I'd buy them by the *viss*. I had no idea what books I was buying. One day I had four or five thick ones in my gunny sack. I'd bought them from a house over in Kokine. By the *viss*. I was weighing them out in 27th Street when this man came along and offered a hundred *kyats* for them. I couldn't believe my ears!! How much had they weighed? Three or four *viss* maybe. In those days, a *viss* of paper was worth about twenty-five *pyas*. I'd only paid a *kyat* for the lot, so it must have been about four *viss*. And here was this man offering a hundred *kyats* for books which had cost me one *kyat*! I had never come across anything like it in my life. So after that, I would go round buying English books. You could make a lot of money if you bought them by weight and then re-sold them.

Later on I rented a room in Myenigone and used it to store as much paper and glass as I could, rather than selling it straight away. I would hold on to the books. Kids used to come and buy from me. These were kids who could read. They knew something about books. They'd buy them cheap from me and sell them for a profit.

So that's how I became a paper merchant. Later, I hired another room down on 27th Street. Now I send other Indians off throughout Rangoon with money to buy paper and glass for me and bring it back to the shop in the evening. I'm getting old and I can't walk the whole city myself any more. I get my son to look after the shop in 27th Street, and I cover the streets around Myenigone. I can cope with Myenigone, seeing as it's nearby, but I have to send other people off to the areas which are further away. They bring the stuff back to 27th Street or Myenigone.

How old am I now? Seventy-six. But I'm still fit. I can still pound the streets for scrap paper. I can't sit down like this for long, though, I get sick. I've got gout. My legs start to ache if I don't keep walking. As long as I'm walking, I'm OK.

My wife died about ten years ago. Now she's gone, I look after myself. I've got children, but they're all grown up and married. I used to have a grandson living with me, one of my daughter's sons. I brought him up. My daughter died and her husband married again. Her son came to live with me and I put him through school. And do you know what? He went on to attend medical school. Now he's a doctor working in the Department of Health. He's married to another doctor. They've asked me to come and live with them.

I don't want to though. They keep telling me that if I come and live with them, I won't need to go and collect paper and glass. They keep saying how comfortable I'd be. But I wouldn't be happy doing nothing, and that's what they seem to want for me. I'd rather keep on living on my own in Myenigone. I avoid visiting their house too often. With them being doctors, they're probably ashamed of me. They don't say so of course. They just tell me to stop collecting old paper and come and live with them.

Why give up a job I've been doing all my life, that's what I say? So long as I know I'm sitting on a big pile of old newspapers, I know I'll eat properly and sleep happily. If I don't have a big pile of papers, I don't feel quite right. Newspapers have been my only companion since my wife died.

If you're free some time, you should come over. You'll be able to see how my whole house is full of paper. I've got a lot of old books, goodness knows what they are. But so long as I've got books and papers keeping me company, I'm a happy man.

[January 1990]

5

THE PARAKEET

His name was Aung Yin but most people didn't call him that. They called him by his nickname, Kyet Taw, the Parakeet. He was a man of few words and those few words came out hesitantly. I met him in Insein Jail. He must have been about thirty. He was tall and stooping with long limbs. As well as being tongue tied, he moved clumsily too. He was brown-skinned and had round eyes and thick eyebrows. Like the other prisoners, his head was shorn. He was inside for pickpocketing. I was told that this was his third time in jail for the same offence.

I'm from Rangoon, North Okkalapa. That was where I was born and brought up. My father was a bus driver for a private bus line. He started off as a spare and worked his way up to become a driver. In his day, the buses didn't have numbers, they had symbols. Buses running between Kemmendine and Pazundaung used a prawn, Tamwe buses had a yacht, Insein buses had wings, Mingaladon had an aeroplane, Kaba Aye was an elephant, Htaukkyant buses used rhinos, Thingangyunn and Bauktaw used a full moon and a crescent moon, buses which ran along Bogyoke Street had a train, the ones which went to the university had dragons and so on. I can remember him telling me all this.

Where was he from? Yelegalay village near Ma-U-Bin. He used to be a farmer-cum-fisherman. Then he moved to Rangoon and got a job as a spare's assistant. His job was to help the spare. In the old days, only the spare could sell tickets. The assistant would climb down from the bus and drum up business. For example, if the bus was running along Insein Road or Prome Road, he would get off near the bus-stop and shout 'Rangoon . . . Rangoon!' and check down the side-streets to see if any potential customers were on their way. If he spotted any he would run over to them and bring them back to the bus and give them a hand with their luggage and their baskets.

If the bus had passed the bus stop, it would reverse back and pick up any passengers. It's true, *Saya*. It was possible in those days because the buses weren't crowded. They could hang on to pick a passenger up if they saw them coming along the side-streets. And the assistant would carry the passenger's baggage. But that was then. Nowadays, the population of Rangoon is growing and there aren't enough buses. The buses are always crowded and they certainly don't wait for passengers like they used to in the old days. In my father's day, there was no need to rush.

My father got promotion. As a spare, he collected fares and gave out tickets. He worked on almost all the bus routes except Mingaladon and Htaukkyant. I don't think they had Renault or Hino buses in those days. My father told me that the buses then looked like the ones which are still running in Kemmendine. They were pre-war buses with refurbished bodywork. Some had short bonnets, some were long. In those days, the well-known bodyshops were 'Yathayon' and 'Bala'. You'd see their trademarks on almost every bus in those days apparently. Yathayon? Yes, that's what he said, Yathayon and Bala were bodyshops. Maybe they don't exist any more. I only know their names because that's what my father told me.

He married my mother while he was working as a bus driver. From what I can remember, she was selling fried rice near the bus terminal at the time and that was how he met her. They moved to North Okkalapa and I was born the same year. I was the oldest. When I was young, there were no shade trees in North Okkalapa and the houses were plonked down in the middle of fields under the blazing sun. Every family had to knock together a rickety bridge to their front doors because the ditches outside always flooded in the rainy season. The land the houses were built on used to be paddy field so every rainy season the water would come up to your knees.

When I was young I attended primary school in North Okkalapa. I went on to middle school but I dropped out once I'd failed seventh standard a couple of times. After that I went to work on the buses with my father. I couldn't go straight in as a spare. I asked the bosses for whatever job they were willing to give me and they let me begin as an assistant. After two years I became a full spare when one of the conductors working for the bus company was killed when he fell off the bus.

Did I pocket some of the fares? Once I got the job as a spare, sometimes I did. Sometimes I could earn extra money if I didn't give the passengers tickets. I'm sure you know what goes on. Sometimes, when the bus was crowded, I genuinely did forget to give the passenger a ticket. But sometimes I did it deliberately. Some passengers couldn't be bothered to ask for tickets because they were too tired or they just wanted to get home or the bus was crowded and once they'd paid their fare they were more interested in grabbing a free seat than getting a ticket.

I'll tell you something about passengers nowadays. They're not like they used to be in your day, *Saya*. In your day, if you saw an old person standing, or a pregnant woman, or a lady, or a monk or a nun, you would give up them your seat. Not any more. Nowadays, bus passengers don't give up their seats to anyone. Some kids will even push in and grab a free seat when there are old people still standing or mothers with children. If you do give up your seat people think you're soft in the head.

Bus conductors aren't what they used to be either. They aren't as disciplined. My father said that the phrases they use nowadays mean the opposite of what they used to. In the old days, if they wanted to tell passengers to hold on tight because the bus was about to start, they'd say '*Kholo!*' If they were telling you the bus was about to stop they'd say '*Hoh!*' My father told me these words come from the days of Indian rickshaw-pullers. Nowadays, bus conductors say '*Hoh*' when they're telling the driver the bus is full up and he should move off. That's the opposite of the old meaning.

How did I become a pickpocket? I'll tell you. I learned a lot about pickpockets once I started working on the buses because they often operate on them. I knew who they were, but unless you catch them redhanded, you can't do much about it. I used to warn the passengers if I knew there were some on board. I would say things like 'Pay attention and take care of your belongings' or 'Stand clear of the doors and take a seat inside the bus'. Pickpockets hang around at the door of the bus, you see, so they can escape easily. Some passengers didn't understand. They wanted to stand by the door of the bus. Some would even complain if I tried to get them to move inside. The truth was I was trying to warn them because there were pickpockets hanging around the door. But I couldn't tell them that openly. The one time I did, a gang of pickpockets slashed my thigh with an old razor blade. They hissed at me to mind my own business if I wanted to live to work another day. Later I discovered that they were from the gang run by the famous 'Gold Teeth' Maung Kyi. If I had known that, I'd have kept my mouth shut.

After that, I didn't dare tell passengers I'd spotted pickpockets. I just gave veiled warnings. Even then the pickpockets used to give me filthy looks.

So how exactly did I become a pickpocket myself? I'll tell you. My father died of diabetes while I was working as a spare. He'd worked on the buses since he was twenty right up until he was getting old, going on sixty. It was a stressful life for him. He was in the driving seat all day. He used to get very tired and then he'd drink every evening. In the summer, he'd be stuck in his seat all day under the boiling hot roof and up next to the engine. That was why he got diabetes. It's like horses when they have to pull carts all day long in hot weather. They die of constipation and kidney disease. My father got it too from having to drive all day in all weather.

I'd been working as a spare on the buses for just over a year when he died. After I got promoted, I used to go out more often and get drunk and meet friends. I'd to be exhausted every night after working all day so I enjoyed a drink. To start with, it was just the occasional social drink. Then I began to drink on my days off. Then it became a habit.

One day I was drinking on my own at a speak-easy near Pawet-seik-kone in North Okkalapa. I hadn't been to work that day because I'd got a cold. I had ordered a quarter of a bottle of country spirit when Gold Teeth Maung Kyi, who I'd crossed swords with that time before, walked into the shop with two of his men. When I saw them, I quickly knocked back the rest of my drink and made to leave. They spotted me drinking alone and sat down at a table a little way away and started whispering amongst themselves. I couldn't hear what they were saying but I guessed they must be talking about me because they kept looking over.

As I was fumbling for the money to pay, one of the men came up to me. I suddenly heard a thud and I looked down and saw a nine-inch knife quivering in the table in front of me. I looked up angrily and found Gold Teeth Maung Kyi was standing beside me smiling. It wasn't a mocking smile though. It seemed almost genuine, almost friendly. He saw I was about to pay and said 'Brother, why don't you stay and join us for another drink?'

With three of them and only one of me, I decided I'd really rather not. So I said 'Thank you, but no thanks. I've got some things I need to do at home'. But Gold Teeth Maung Kyi was insistent and it was difficult to refuse. His invitation seemed genuine. And I did rather fancy another drink.

As we drank, they told me what they did for a living and said they needed my help. I was a bit drunk but I said I didn't know what they were after but I couldn't help them anyway because I wasn't a pickpocket. They said that wasn't necessary. All I needed to do was pretend that I didn't know they were on the bus. They said there'd been slim pickings recently because the police had been mounting a campaign against pickpockets. That was why they needed my help. I kept refusing to go along with it, but they were so insistent and I was so drunk that eventually I agreed. So that, in short, is how I fell amongst thieves.

They nicknamed me Kyet Taw because I look lumbering and simple. You can hear that's how I speak too—slow and heavy. So, as you can see, I joined forces with the pickpockets when I was still working as a bus conductor. They made sure I got a good share of the takings. Whenever they'd struck lucky we all went out drinking and visited a brothel.

Later on the company guessed I was collaborating with the pickpockets and sacked me. After that, I became a full-time gang member. I've picked up a lot of the street slang they use. Nowadays kids use it too. Like 'pork' for 'money'. 'I'm out of pork', 'I've got a lot of pork'. Then there's 'hands' meaning watch, *'dayaw'* for *longyi*, they use 'slipper' for shoe, 'baggy' for jacket, 'squashy' for gold necklace, a 'spinning wheel' is a lighter, 'telescope' is glasses.

While we're on the subject of glasses . . . . When you're a pickpocket, you need to know the value of the stuff you're stealing. Once I stole a pair of RayBans. I had no idea that they were worth anything, I just thought they were ordinary sunglasses so I flogged them for only a hundred *kyats*. I thought I'd done well. That was until Gold Teeth Maung Kyi told me they were worth about four thousand *kyats*. What a sucker!

In the world of the pickpocket, there are two 'lines'. The 'upper line' are the pickpockets who work the buses and the circular train and so on. The 'lower line' are the pickpockets who go to football matches, stage shows, pagoda festivals and cinemas. Upper line pickpockets don't cross over and work on the lower line and vice versa. If someone crossed over, he would get beaten up. Each side sticks to their own turf. You can't work both lines. If you try to, you get it in the neck.

There are a number of styles of pickpocketing such as *'nyein-swe'* or 'quiet-picking', *'taik-swe'*, or 'bumping and picking', *'daik'* when you just grab whatever chance you get.

'Nyein-swe' means picking the pocket of someone who you're sitting next to, for example in the cinema or on a bus or a train. There are

different levels of *nyein-swe*. Stealing from a passenger on the circular train is the easiest. It's more difficult to *nyein-swe* on the ferry boats or something like that because on the ferry boat you need to be careful and you need to be brave and you need to be good at the job. You're stuck on board the whole night with the other passengers so if they catch you, there's no way to get away. That's why you need to have guts and you need to be careful.

One time a friend and I had gone to steal on the 'Bandaka' ferry to Bassein. Near where I was sleeping were a half-Chinese couple and their children. He was a businessman and he looked quite well-off. They had got a lot of money on them in a canvas bag and I decided that was going to be my target. But the Chinese man was holding on to it tight and never put it down

I kept an eye on the bag constantly but he didn't leave it alone for an instant. The ferry had gone through the Twante Canal and the man had eaten dinner and laid out his mats and pillows to go to sleep. He was a fat man, so I reckoned he would sleep soundly. I watched him. He fell asleep just before the ferry called at Ma-U-Bin, and so did his wife and family. He had hidden the bag of money under his pillow.

I decided it was still too early to make a move because he probably wouldn't be fast enough asleep yet. He was lying next to me, almost touching, and his wife was on the other side with the children between them. I was keen to get started because it would be perfect if I could steal the bag just before we got to Ma-U-Bin and then jump off when the ferry docked. But I didn't dare start just yet because I suspected he wasn't sound asleep.

I lay down next to him and nudged him with my foot as if I'd kicked him accidentally in my sleep. He woke up immediately. I was right. He clearly wasn't off yet. So I let him go back to sleep and pretended to be asleep myself. I planned to get started just before the ferry called at Wakema.

By the time we drew near Wakema, he was sound asleep. My fingers were itching to get going. I calculated that I could steal the bag, jump off at Wakema and catch another ferry back to Rangoon the same night so no-one would find me. I prodded the fat chinaman. He was snoring loudly and didn't wake up. Just to make sure, I kicked his bum hard with my knee. But he didn't move and carried on snoring. The ceiling lights on board the boat were nice and dim.

I slipped the money bag out from under his pillow. It was easy as pie to remove it, easier than picking up my own bag. It was going well. I had the bag in my hands just as the ferry docked at Wakema. The two of us slipped off the boat and returned to Rangoon on a private ferry boat. We found we had ten thousand *kyats*—not bad, eh? There were also some papers in the bag including a Foreigner's Registration Card for the chinaman and a National Identity Card for his wife. We didn't have any use for that kind of thing so we used to send them back through the post because losing things like that could cause problems for our victims. We had certain rules, and sending things like that back through the post was one of them.

So for *nyein-swe* you need to be brave and careful. For *taik-swe* you have to bump into the victim as you steal from them. It's particularly used for people who are waiting in line to buy tickets for stage shows or football matches or queueing for the cinema or pushing forward to get onto the bus, or when you're in the crowd at the Tabaung Shwedagon Pagoda festival.

The '*daik*' method involves taking advantage of circumstances to snatch belongings. For example you might grab a gold necklace from a girl who's sitting by the door on the bus, or pull a watch off someone's hand through the window of the train or snatch their glasses while they're looking out the window as the train is moving. It's easy to do this, particularly on the trains. If the train is moving, they can't do anything about it, can they?

With '*taik-swe*' and '*daik*', and particularly with '*taik-swe*' you need a partner to talk to the victim and distract his attention. For example, if you're walking along the road towards your target, your partner could bump into him and while his attention was diverted, you would steal from him. Alternatively, your partner could ask the victim for a light or ask the time.

It works when you're stealing from a queue as well. It's good to have a partner who can distract the victim's attention by talking to him, for example by pushing in and then starting an argument. While they're arguing, you can move in. That's why you need a partner who can talk when you are using '*taik*' and '*daik*'.

You don't have to have tools for the job, other than sharp eyes, although it helps if you let your nails grow a bit or perhaps carry a broken razor blade. Longer nails help you to get things from out of pockets like pens and so on. A razor blade is useful for ripping the inside pocket of a jacket or handbags. You can also sharpen the edge of a twenty-five or a fifty *pya* coin. The fifty *pya* coin is hard and you can get a grip on it. If you sharpen the edge it's easily strong enough to cut through the strap of a leather bag.

I've been in this game for about seven years. Sometimes I've been flush, sometimes I've been skint. A bit like the cheeks of a clarinet player. Sometimes puffed out, sometimes sucked in.

I've been in jail twice before for pickpocketing, this is my third time. I've also been married twice before and I'm on my third wife. Each time

I've been to jail, my wife's left me. I shouldn't think my present wife has stuck around. She hasn't visited me for over three weeks now. I wouldn't be surprised if she's found another bloke. In the underworld it's not just stolen goods which change hands, people do too. So what? That's life.

That's the story of my life then, abridged version. I could you the whole story, but it would be getting on for a novel. What am I going to do when I get out? I'd like to go straight this time round. But it'll depend on the circumstances at the time.

Don't worry, *Saya*. I won't pick your pocket when they let me out. You'll never be one of my victims, I give you my word. We pickpockets have our rules. Never steal from your friends or respectable people.

My name again? Kyet Taw. The Parakeet.

[July 1989]

ရွှေတိဂုံ ဘုရား။

CHAPTER II

BEHIND THE FESTIVAL LIGHTS

6

THWARTED AMBITION

I placed him somewhere between twenty-five and thirty. He had a well-scrubbed face with thick eyebrows, a square jaw and a prominent nose. He was wearing a grey T-shirt, a cotton longyi, a gold necklace and a Seiko watch. His clothes were as well-scrubbed as his face. He had long hair and sideburns curling across his cheeks. We met in a theatre dressing room.

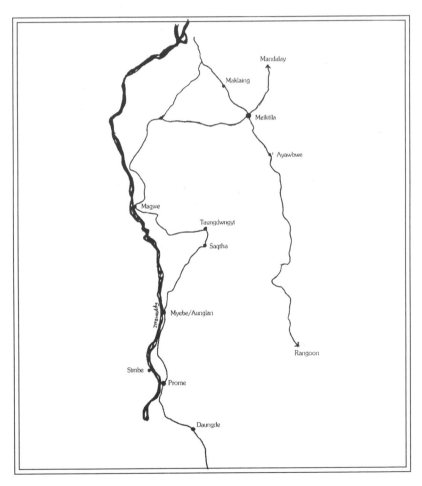

My name's Thaung Tan although I was originally called Thaung Shwe. I've got three brothers and sisters. My older brother is called Thaung Ngwe. I'm Thaung Shwe. My sisters are called Thaung May and Thaung Khin. My father's from Ma-hlaing township. He climbed toddy trees for a living. My Grandpa did the same. In those days, Grandpa used to climb other people's toddy trees and he would hand over a third of what he collected, and get to keep the other two thirds. Jaggery that is.

The climber buys his own tools and materials he needs to climb the trees and cook up the jaggery. You need earthenware pots for boiling up the juice to make it into jaggery, little pots for collecting the toddy, bigger pots that the little pots hang off, the bamboo and wood to make the two sizes of ladder—*yin-hswe*, the small one which is fixed permanently to the top of the tree and *yin-daung*, the long one you move around—as well as the firewood and charcoal for boiling down the juice. All the owner of the tree contributes is the tree itself. Basically they're hiring you to do the work. It's a bit like the way farmers down in Lower Burma rent the land from the owner and pay him back a share of the crop. No matter how much we collected, we had to pay the owner a third. We never used to try and cheat him though. There's no point as the owner knows how much jaggery he can expect in a year from his toddy plantation. Rather than waiting until the end of the year before settling up, we used to give him his share throughout the year, starting from when the tree was ripe for tapping and the sap starts to flow. We used to collect the sap and boil it up into jaggery every day. For two of those days, we kept the jaggery ourselves and on the third day we'd give it to the owner. In other words, out of a month's production, we'd get to keep twenty days' worth.

The toddy palms are ripe for tapping from about the month of Tabodwe onwards. Once the wind starts to blow through the trees. Throughout the tapping season we'd share the jaggery out—two shares for us, one for the owner. That was how they did it in my grandfather's time. It was how we paid back the owner for the right to climb the trees. The same system went on in my father's time too. Then later on we stopped having to pay the owner anything because the Government Land Committee took over. They said that the people who were actually working on the land could carry on working on it. Instead of paying a share to the owner of the trees, we paid a land tax to the government.

So we carried on climbing the trees and we were a bit better off than before. My brother Thaung Ngwe was able to go to school in town. He failed tenth standard but learned how to drive a tractor and got a job working at the tractor works in Meiktila. My father was getting on a bit and couldn't climb the trees as quickly as he used to so it was left up to me to help him out. But I never took enough care when I went up the trees so my father was only prepared to let me go up the young ones which weren't very tall yet.

My father used to go up all the trees including the very oldest but he told me not to because they were too tall for me. My elder sister Thaung May went off and married another toddy-farmer. My younger sister Thaung Khin was the only one left. She used to come out with us and gather up the pots while my father and I were up the trees. We'd bring the little pots down and just dump them on the ground at the foot of the tree and then go up another one. We had no time to empty them ourselves.

We'd take the long ladder from tree to tree. Climb up and undo the pots which had been put there the evening before. Put in place the empty pots which we carried tied to our waists. Climb back down again and drop the full pots at the foot of the tree. Thaung Khin would come and pick them up and take them back to the hut where she and my mother would boil up the juice into jaggery.

One day my father was feeling a bit rough and had a slight headache. That day he had a number of old trees to climb which had been growing for years and were very tall. I said I'd do it for him but he told me I couldn't. The trees were too tall and I was too careless. I was saying to him, look you're not well, let me do it. But he was having none of it and got ready to go up the tree. He pulled his *longyi* up and tucked it into his waist to make a pair of shorts. He popped some tobacco into his cheek, and strapped on his knife and the hook he hung the pots from.

I went off to collect firewood. I was cutting away the twigs to get the right size of wood. A little while later, when my father could have only climbed a couple of trees, I heard a scream from the toddy plantation. So did my mother and Thaung Khin. My mother turned pale and said to my sister 'Was that a scream I heard coming from our toddy trees? Do you think your father has dropped out of the tree?'

The two of them shrieked and went running off towards the trees. I dropped my knife and ran after them. My father had indeed dropped out of the tree. We say 'dropped out' when people fall out of toddy trees. We couldn't bear to look. He was already dead by the time we got there. He'd died on the spot. If you fall out of a thirty foot toddy palm, you can't really expect to survive, can you?

Once my father had been killed, it was up to me to collect all the toddy. I wasn't too chuffed. I'd never wanted to climb toddy trees for a living in the first place. I didn't want to go off and get a job like my brother either. My interests were in another direction. I wanted to go on the stage.

I'll tell you how I got into the theatre. Before my father died, when I was still little, I used to like singing. I'd learnt quite a few of the ballads from the *zat-pwes* and some of the comic songs which the clowns used to sing. Even before I was allowed to climb the trees, when I was still just picking up the pots, I used to sing as I did it.

I liked modern songs too. Not the modern pop songs you get nowadays. I'm talking about the songs from about twenty years ago that singers like Ko Mya Gyi, Ko Chit Swe, Ko Maung Maung Gyi, Ko Min Naung and 'Twante' Thein Tan used to sing. When I used to climb the toddy trees, I'd get up to the top and start singing up there. My mother said I'd got such a strong voice you could hear it through the whole plantation. In fact people often used to say to me that the girls collecting water at the well would say to one another 'That Ko Thaung Shwe sounds just like 'Twante' Thein Tan when he's up a toddy tree'. I don't know if they were joking. But I knew anyway that I'd got a pretty good voice.

One day, there was a pagoda festival near our village over at Pan-aing and 'Twante' Thein Tan came to perform. He was a damn good-looking actor, *Saya*, and he had a great voice too. I really liked him. The girls from the well were teasing me and saying that Ko Thaung Shwe was no name for a famous singer and I should change my name to 'Pan-aing' Thaung Tan and go off and join 'Twante' Thein Tan's theatre company. From then on they started calling me Ko Thaung Tan.

In those days 'Twante' Thein Tan was singing that song 'Htwe Nyo' about a country girl. I really liked it. I suppose I must be quite quick on the uptake, because if I hear a song two or three times, I can pick it up. I went to see 'Twante' Thein Tan almost every night while he was appearing at Pan-aing. It must have been about three or four miles from my village. In the afternoon I'd come down from the toddy tree, have a shower and get dressed, strap on my knife, and go off to the show with my friends. Not just one night. I was going every night.

My mother liked my singing a lot. She used to tell me about Aung Nyein, Aung Maung and 'Shwe Man' Tin Maung who she'd seen when she was a girl. She'd tell me which their best performances were. She liked it when I'd sing her the ballads. My father just used to tell me I was stage-struck.

He had a point. I had to see any show going. I especially liked modern plays. If there were Independence Day shows or pagoda festivals at any of the towns nearby, I was there like a shot. I went to the Ma-hlaing festival, the Pan-aing festival, puppet shows, anything. If I could, I'd catch the train. If there was no train, I'd go by bus. If there was no bus either, I'd walk there with a group of friends. I was that crazy about the theatre.

Trouble was, I wasn't just interested in going to see plays. I think I must have caught some sort of an acting bug. I was crazy about being on stage. I wanted to be a star.

One day, 'Shwe Man' Aung Ngwe's group turned up to perform in Meiktila at the Wishing Pagoda festival. It was an open air show, not inside a theatre. One of the actresses was called Nay Kyi San. I thought she was really something. She was about nineteen or twenty, about my age. A couple of years older maybe. She was beautiful, had a great voice and was a good actress. I thought she was the best. So I stayed all six days at the pagoda festival without going home and every night I'd go and watch 'Shwe Man' Aung Ngwe's group. By the end, I knew almost all the songs off by heart. When I got back home, my father yelled at me and told me off for acting more like a rich man's son than a toddy-farmer.

Well I hope that's given you some idea just how mad about the stage I was. It didn't matter how much my father yelled at me. As soon as I heard the orchestra strike up, I'd be right there at the front of the stage. All I wanted was to grow up to be an actor and a singer and tread the boards. No-one in my family had ever been in show business. I don't know where I caught the bug from. But one thing was for sure—I was badly infected.

My father was getting on then, and couldn't climb all the trees on his own, so it was down to me to help out since Thaung Ngwe had gone off to be a tractor driver. I couldn't go off and join a theatre troupe. If my father was sick, I had to climb the trees myself. And if I was sick, he'd have to cover for me. So between us, we had to do the whole plantation and there was no question of either of us being able to go away permanently.

Once Dad died, I took on the whole job myself. That meant I had even less spare time than before. In the old days, I'd been able to take time off and go and see a show if there was a pagoda festival nearby. If I wasn't around, my father could cope. I used to try and help him out by moving the ladder when I thought he was getting tired. But he even used to stop me doing that. He used to insist on taking the ladder from tree to tree and propping it up himself. So while my father was still alive and well, I got to see quite a few shows. Once he was killed though, I hardly saw any. But it still didn't cure my obsession.

About that time, my younger sister Thaung Khin got married. I was pretty pleased, because her new husband was a toddy-farmer's son like me, and their family had lots of children. So he came over and lived with us and climbed the trees together with me. We were friends anyway, so it all worked out pretty well.

The following year, when the Pan-aing pagoda festival came around, I went off to see it. I ate and slept there. The theatre troupe they'd booked was led by Sein Win Aung. They were from Pyawbwe. They were only a small group but the director was talented. People preferred his old-fashioned plays and operas to his more modern plays. Sein Win Aung wasn't very good at dancing in the double-acts. He didn't have much of a singing voice either. In the duets, he sounded alright. But his voice wasn't much use for modern plays. The ballads in modern plays are pitched quite high. There's a lot of weeping and wailing and beating of chests. He wasn't much good at all of that so he didn't come across well in the modern plays. His performances in the operas and the old plays were much better.

Operas aren't that difficult though. You've got the standard love scenes with the actress emerging from the lotus flower to do a dance. The actor and the actress do their love scenes and dance and sing duets together in the mock harp or on the stage prop piano. If you've got the money to spend on good props and lighting, it's easy to put on a good show.

I preferred plays myself. The plots were bang up to date. The main actor was good-looking and had a good voice. I found out he was from Taundwingyi. Someone said he'd joined the troupe because he was crazy about the theatre and ended up as the star performer. And I was over the moon because the main actress was my favourite, Nay Kyi San. She'd left 'Shwe Man' Aung Ngwe's company and joined Sein Win Aung's.

I decided I couldn't wait any longer. I joined that company. I suppose you're wondering how I could just join a theatre company without any experience or training. All I had was my obsession. Most other people who get into acting are used to being on stage because they've been dancing or acting in their school plays or their neighbourhood shows since they were young. In my case, my only previous experience was singing from the tops of the toddy trees.

I was so keen to join up that next day I went to see the head of the company, Sein Win Aung. He was the main actor. It wasn't easy to get to see him. The first day, I didn't manage it. They told me he was asleep, or praying, or playing poker. The second day I went, I managed to catch him just before he went off for a shower.

He looked me up and down and asked me what I could do. I told him I could sing a bit. He grinned and said 'Do you think that performing on stage is child's play?' I fled without answering. The wife of U Dat Sann, the clown, had been watching me from across the way. She must have felt sorry for me, because she called me over and said 'Come on kid. You're never going to get into show business without ever having been on stage. But if you're that desperate to get into the business, why don't you try out for a bit part in a modern play. See that man over there—that's Maung Garuna, the director. Let's go and ask him if you can try out.'

She took me over to where Maung Garuna was rehearsing with a group of actors including Nay Kyi San and said to him 'Saya, you said you needed an extra. What about this kid here who says he wants to join the company?' Maung Garuna asked me to wait outside while he finished the rehearsal. Then he came out and asked me if I was prepared to take on any part, and I told him I was. So I got a part as a servant in Nay Kyi San's house. Maung Garuna told me later that he'd only given me the part because he felt sorry for me. In fact, anybody could have done that part. All you had to do was say 'Yes Miss, certainly Miss' and carry a tea tray and put it down. Anyone could have done that.

I did exactly what the director told me. Of course, what I really wanted to be was the star. The money you got for a walk-on part was hardly anything. But Maung Garuna took a shine to me. He told me where they were going next, and asked me if I wanted to come along. I said I'd go wherever they went. So I just took off and joined the company without even going home first. I've no idea what my family thought.

I was about twenty at the time. At the next place we were performing, I asked Maung Garuna if he could give me a job as an understudy or something. I said that I didn't mind if I didn't get paid, so long as they gave me some food. So Maung Garuna gave me a voice test and I sang as loud as I could. He told me my voice wasn't too bad, but that I was singing much too loud. Nowadays with microphones, it simply wasn't necessary to belt the songs out. If you did, you'd break the loudspeakers. He asked me to try again, but to sing softer. I tried, but no matter how hard I tried, my voice was still too loud and although I could sing, I didn't really have a sense of rhythm. So after a few attempts, Maung Garuna said to me 'You're never going to make it with a voice like that, except perhaps as a singer behind the orchestra'.

I realised then that I was never going to be a great actor. And if I carried on doing walk-on parts, I wouldn't earn enough to survive on. So Maung Garuna suggested I work as a scene shifter, and operate the backdrops. I did that, and from time to time, if they needed me, I did a walk-on part as a policeman or a servant.

A scene-shifter has to know all the ropes. Once the *a-pyo-daw* dance is over, he needs to know which backdrop to pull down next. He's always got to know what the next scene is, and if it's opera he has to know which songs come before which scene-change. In a play he has to know the lines which come before the scene changes, which act comes after which, which backdrop he has to prepare. He has to know the whole thing off by heart, the whole programme. When the Four Ministers come on, he needs to know who says what last and where so that he's ready to drop the curtain when the orchestra starts up. Same goes for the duets. He needs to know how many verses, how many lines each singer is going to sing.

So there's a lot more to the scene-shifter's job than just pulling ropes up and down. You've got to understand quite a bit about plays, about direction, about what the director wants. I've been doing the job about eight years now. I did two years with Sein Win Aung's troupe before the show folded after playing the Paungde Sacred Tooth Pagoda festival. Business had been really bad that year. We had to stay on living in the theatre after the company had broken up. Some people went back to their home towns but some of the actors didn't even have enough money to get home and were stranded there, including me. I had no money to get home, but even if I had, I don't know if I'd have gone back. I hadn't been back in those two or three years. I hadn't seen my mother or my brothers and sisters. Even if I'd gone home, I wouldn't have had anything to do. There was no way I was going back to climbing toddy trees for a living.

Then, while I was washed up in Paungde, I got married. My wife's name was Ma Htay Win. She came from near Paungde. She had come with her mother to the festival to sell snacks. Fried gourd, fried banana, that kind of thing. I'd started eating at her stall on a regular basis, and gradually we'd got talking and got to know one another and if I was free during the day I'd go and help her out. I wouldn't do anything in particular, but while I was eating we'd chat or I'd help her fish the food out of the pan.

When the company broke up, I had no money coming in and I was living off what I'd managed to save. When I ran out, I'd go and pawn a shirt or a *longyi*. All I could afford to eat was half a *kyat* or a *kyat's* worth of rice which I'd take over to Ma Htay Win's stall and eat with a couple of her fried snacks. Her father had been a farmer but then he went and died and left her and her mother and a little brother who was about ten. They had to start selling fried snacks. We started going out together and got married. Instead of going back on the road with the theatre, I ended up staying with her family and helping out on the stall.

But you know how it is with us theatrical types. All we have to do is hear the orchestra strike up and we start getting itchy feet. The following year Aung Pan Sein's troupe turned up at the Paungde Sacred Tooth Pagoda festival. You may remember it, it was just a small troupe. I got to know the manager when I went to visit the show and managed to get a job as a stage-hand. It was pretty lucky because he just happened to mention that his scene-shifter was off sick and I asked him if I could fill in. Since they were pleased with me, I got the job permanently.

I worked with them for about two years, travelling round and coming back to Ma Htay Win in Paungde during the breaks in the schedule until we took off again. During that time, her mother died and her little brother went off and joined the army so she was left on her own in Paungde.

When you work in a travelling theatre you tend to just eat and sleep wherever you pitch up. But I didn't want to leave my wife home alone.

She wanted to come with me too, but on my income it was going to be difficult for the two of us to get by. She couldn't sing or dance either. But she wanted to come with me, so I decided to take her along and we were just going to have to see how we got on.

Luckily she got a job as dresser to Sein Hla Kyi, the wife of the manager, who was also an actress. A dresser looks after the costumes and makes sure that the actress has the right clothes ready for each scene. She tidies up the clothes which the actress has already worn. She earned about the same as a girl in the chorus line, so it wasn't too bad for us.

We spent about three years working in Aung Pan Sein's troupe and everything was going well. I hadn't made it as an actor of course, and had to make do with being a scene-shifter. But I wasn't too unhappy. So long as I could work close to the stage and hear the orchestra, I was satisfied.

One day we were travelling from Taungdwingyi to Mye-de (Aunglan) when the truck turned over. That year we were being kept incredibly busy and the actors and actresses barely had a day to rest. We'd set off as soon as the show was over and get to the next place by midday and then have to set everything up in a big hurry and fix the scenery up in time for the evening's performance. We barely had a chance to eat. That day we were rushing from Taungdwingyi to Mye-de as we had a dance engagement in Sinde. Near Saq-tha village, the truck turned over. Some of the performers were injured. Two people were killed. One was a chorus girl. The other was my wife.

The night after the accident, the promoter put pressure on us to perform because he'd paid us a deposit. So once we'd sent the bodies and the injured people to the hospital, we had to go on. The programme was completely topsy-turvy and we couldn't put the dancing girls on. The manager and the two stars had gone ahead in a car though, so they weren't hurt. We apologised to the audience. We explained that the truck had overturned and two people had been killed. But, as they say 'The show must go on'. So we apologised in advance for any mistakes. The audience were very sympathetic and gave us lots of encouragement. There was even a full house.

I've been in show business for eight years now. I came into it wanting to be a star. But that wasn't the way it turned out. Still, I'm happy being a stage-hand. I get to hear the orchestra and watch the dancing on stage. That keeps me happy enough.

I haven't re-married. But I'm going out with a girl. She's in show business too. She's a dancer in the chorus line in this troupe. She's like me. She ran off to join the theatre with stars in her eyes and big dreams about being a great actress. But she's ended up in the chorus line.

Have I been home? To see my mother? Once, I did. After my wife was killed, I was very depressed and I went back home to the village. But my mother had already died. My sister Thaung Khin is still there with her husband. They're still in the toddy business.

[January 1988]

7

THE TWELVE FESTIVAL TRADER

I met her about four years ago at the Shwesettaw pagoda festival. She told me to call her Ma Swe and she referred to herself as 'Swe' as she spoke. She was about forty with fair skin and deep-set eyes and had kept her looks. Although she was starting to put on weight you could see that she had once been a slim girl. When we met, her hair was unfastened and in disarray and her yellowy skin was puffy. Her clothes were shabby but neat and she had a Chinese hand-towel over her shoulders and an old airline bag.

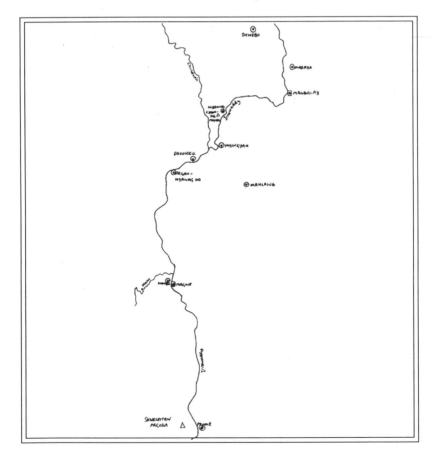

I read your stuff, you know, and your novel *Da-daun*. I saw the play they made of it. Have they made the film with Kyaw Hein yet? So you're asking me all this to get some raw material, are you? No problem. Fire away. I've been all over the country, and there's a million things I could tell you. If I could write myself, I'd be able to write loads of film scripts.

But the things I'd write about wouldn't be things that have happened to me, mind you. They would be things I've seen or heard or occasionally been party to. Oh? Don't you want to hear about things that have happened to other people? You're only interested in my story are you? I see.

Well, my story isn't really that interesting. It's just been one long struggle, first as a girl, then as a mother of five, and now as a widow. When I was a girl, I lived under the wing of my parents, and life was a struggle in those days. When I got married, life was a struggle there too. Now I'm a widow, and life's even harder. Still, that's not to say I'm not happy struggling. Even if I won the hundred thousand *kyat* lottery prize a couple of times, and could live a life of luxury, I wouldn't want it. I'm sure I'd be too bored.

I'm from a town in Upper Burma. My father was a surveyor, a Land Settlements Clerk, but by the time I was growing up, he was out of a job. I'm not too sure how it happened. But I'm sure that there was nothing criminal involved because my father was an honest man, and not at all interested in money.

He did have one fault, though, which was his addiction. What do I mean by that exactly? Let's see. Well, nowadays, you'd say he was hooked on dope. What I mean is, he was an opium addict. He told us that he became an addict before he met my mother. He was an opium-smoker at first, and I sometimes think that it must have been his Chinese blood which made him that way. And when you're a young, unmarried surveyor, it's a habit you can easily afford.

You'll remember, *Saya*, how in those days during the British period, opium dens were springing up all over the place like mushrooms. Some of them were licensed[1], but there were underground ones as well. My father said that to start off with, he was worried people would find out, so he used to go to the underground dens. They were more expensive. They didn't have a licence and so they couldn't compete with the official

---

[1] Under the colonial administration, opium was a state monopoly controlled by the Opium Act of 1910 and the 1938 Opium Rules. The authorities allotted licences to selected vendors for a fixed fee. At each shop, the resident Excise Officer oversaw sales and the disposal of the surplus each evening.

dens. But addicts who were concerned that people would find out about their habit used to go secretly to the unofficial dens, where the prices were much higher. The unofficial dens had to bribe the authorities, and they had to bribe the licensed dens as well, otherwise they'd get closed down. If the licensed opium dens were doing good business, they would let the unlicensed dens open because they knew they wouldn't lose customers. Even so, the unlicensed dens still had to pay them a share of their earnings.

Since my father was concerned about his reputation, he used to go to the illegal dens to smoke. Opium smokers are the aristocracy of addicts. It's the most expensive type of habit. They just inhale the vapours, so it's a real luxury. But after we were born, my father had to give it up and turn to opium-eating which they say is nowhere near as good. An opium eater takes a quid of opium—twenty-five *pyas* or half a *kyat's* worth—and puts it in his cheek. He doesn't swallow it in one, but chews it very gradually. The flavour isn't as good as if you smoke it, so they say, and the effects aren't as pleasant. But he had to eat opium rather than smoke it because we needed the money at home.

He couldn't work properly, because opium made him dopy. I've always found the behaviour of opium-eaters very interesting. Whenever my father wanted to eat some opium, he'd put a quid in his mouth and go silent, walk straight into his bedroom and lie down. To start off with he'd go to an opium den but later on he ate opium at home.

He wouldn't bother with a mattress or pillows, he'd just lie on a mat on the floor with a block of wood for a pillow and gaze into space. My mother used to tell him to get off the floor and get onto the bed or use a pillow but he took no notice. He told her a mat and a pillow were all he needed.

When the Land Superintendent, who in those days was English, noticed he couldn't put in a proper day's work, he got angry with him and my father was fired. My father was left without a job and we were left without food. I was, let me see, how old? Five? So my mother had to open up a shop in the house. Not a big one mind, just selling cigarettes and sweets and little bags of snacks. In a whole day, we wouldn't make more than two *kyats* profit. My mother's friends who were government officials took pity on our family and went to the Land Superintendent and got him to pay my father a pension. But my father sold off his pension rights and after he'd given us a little bit to put into the shop, he smoked the rest. Then, when he had no more money to smoke opium, he went back to eating it.

As we grew up, my father couldn't afford to eat opium regularly. Maybe that's why his health started to get worse. He lost a lot of weight. But although he wasn't eating opium regularly, he still managed a bit from time to time when his friends gave him some money.

When he got to the point where he could no longer get enough opium to eat, he joined the very lowest class of opium addicts. He would hang around opium dens and the other addicts and collect the rags they used to clean out their opium pipes. Then he'd boil them up to make tea. If you looked in his pockets, you'd find smelly dirty old opium rags instead of a handkerchief.

I remember how I learnt about it. I was washing his jacket one day and took out an old rag from each of his pockets. I threw them out because they were so disgusting. When my father found out he flew into a violent rage. I can't tell you how angry he was, yelling at me and beating me. He told me never to touch his jacket, he'd wash it himself. Although he was an opium addict and living off other people's rags, you'd never have guessed. He still kept himself looking smart. He'd wear a fawn woollen jacket, a starched white shirt with a stiff collar, and a smooth cotton Pakokku *longyi*. He only had the one jacket, but he never went out without it. He always slicked back his hair and wore a *gaung-baung*.

That was how he lived, drinking tea brewed from opium-rags. He couldn't kick the habit, no matter how hard he tried. So instead he became a 'twelve-festival worker'. As his name was U Ba Kay, he used to be called 'Twelve-Festival Ba Kay'.

The twelve pagoda festivals are like this, you see. In Upper Burma, there are always festivals going on. In the months of Tabaung and Tagu, it's the Shwesettaw; in Kason and Nayon you've got the Thiho-shin pagoda in Pakokku; then the Kyauk-yiq Pagoda festival in Waso and Wagaun; and then there's the Thihataw festival near Shwebo/Madaya and the Mya-malun in Magwe, the Shinpin-sekkate in Minbu, the Shwesandaw in Prome, Hniq-kyeiq-shiq-su in Myingyan, the Pan-aing Pagoda in Mahlaing, the festival in Meiktila and the Ananda and Shwezigon Pagoda festivals in Pagan/Nyaung-Oo and so on. Those are the big ones which are officially recognised in the gazette.

At all these festivals, people come to sell clothes, shoes, toys, drums, mats and all sorts of wares. The merchants follow the festivals around from month to month, which is why they're called 'twelve-festival workers', one for every month.

When my father stopped eating opium, he started to get restless at home and decided to go off and join the festivals. He didn't have any money to invest in a stall, but since he'd been a surveyor, he knew how to write application letters and so on, and understood how bureaucracy worked, things like how to go about hiring a stall and contacting the pagoda trustees and signing a stall rental agreement. He looked the part too, in his jacket and Pakokku *longyi* and with a *gaung-baung* on his head. He found himself a niche organising permits for the stall-holders and helping them with their form-filling and applications and contracts.

So when they were moving on to a new festival, they'd invite him to come with them, and they'd pay his food and expenses and give him some spending money in return for help with the paperwork.

My father didn't need a second invitation. Sometimes he wouldn't even bother to come and tell us himself. He'd just ask someone who'd be seeing us to let us know he was off to a festival, get up from the tea-shop, and leave. He could eat better at the festivals than he could at home. But I knew he didn't go to the festivals just for that. He went because he could eat the stuff he couldn't get at home. Opium was more important to him than food.

Sometimes he'd come back home with a bit of money saved up. Sometimes he'd come back with nothing except perhaps some clothes or toys or food for us. Meanwhile, we were left at home, living off the income from my mother's cigarette stall, which was just enough to get by on, topped up with what my father gave us.

While he was working the festivals, my father barely spent a night at home. At most, he must've stayed with us for all of a month each year, and not continuously, but in the gaps between festivals, moving on from one to another; Shwesettaw, then Thiho-shin then Kyauk-yiq then Shinpin-sekkate and on and on. He wouldn't stick with the same stall-holders, he would just pick up and go with whomever he happened to meet. For instance, I remember he went to Shwesettaw with a clothes-seller, but the next festival could've been with a shoe-seller and so on.

So that was the kind of twelve-festival worker my father was. He went followed the stall-holders around the gazetted pagoda festivals. He didn't have any capital. He couldn't afford to open a stall like me. All he did was fill in the forms and help people out selling things. You might not even have heard of people doing that sort of thing. There are so many types of people in the world, and so many different ways to earn a living. My father was just one more of them, trying to earn a living by following the festivals.

Anyway, one day he came back from a pagoda festival with malaria. He died soon afterwards. I'm sure the opium had something to do with it. By that time I was nineteen or twenty. Of course, I'd already had to drop out of school—I didn't even pass seventh standard. My mother's shop wasn't enough to keep us, so in the end we packed it in. After that my mother moved on to selling snacks in front of a liquor shop, nothing special, just curried chicken drumsticks and things.

I helped her out, selling peanuts and potato crisps. Little by little we started selling booze too. We set up a little speakeasy. We'd get hold of country spirit and sell it on. While we were selling liquor, I fell in love with one of the regular customers and got married. That's right, romance between the bar-maid and the boozer—a natural alliance. And boy, could he drink!! From dawn to dusk, he drank. Before he married me, he could only afford to drink in the evenings. Once we wed, he could drink all day long. Soon he didn't even wait for the sun to come up. You could say he was the sort of man who'd get out of bed and wash his face with alcohol. Our children started arriving. He still didn't cut down his drinking. He worked as a clerk for the anti-malaria campaign. He'd go out into the jungle to eradicate malaria and I know he'd carry on drinking out there. After a while, the drink started affecting his brain and he couldn't work any more. He took to his bed with liver disease. He'd be drinking one day and give up the next, only to start again. In the end, the doctor got angry with him and refused to help him any more. He'd sent him to hospital three times already. He scolded my husband, 'Don't come to me again! If you want to drink, drink, If you want to stop, stop. But I've already helped you so many times and I'm not going to help you any more'. The third time he sent him to hospital, he made my husband promise to give up drink. So he did, and promised that he would never touch another drop for the rest of his days. The doctor then sent him off to hospital for the third time, and this time he made a good recovery.

But you know what they say about trying to straighten a dog's tail. You straighten it out, but it only bounces back again. About a month or two after he got out, when his health had improved a little, he started drinking again, at the slightest excuse: because he was happy, because he was angry, because he was broke. After his fourth attack, he'd didn't dare go and see the doctor. So he died. Cirrhosis of the liver.

After he died, I didn't have a clue what to do. We had no savings at all, and were living from day to day, not knowing where the next meal was coming from. I went off and helped out in a dried goods shop down the market. I got two hundred *kyats* a month, plus chilies and onions and potatoes and dried fish and so forth to take home to the children, so altogether I was able to cover our expenses.

While I was working there, the stall-holder took the stall to Shwepandaw Pagoda festival and opened up in the market there, and invited me to come along. I don't know why—maybe it was a good beans and sesamum harvest—but we did excellent business. We kept selling out and having to go back to town for more. We couldn't keep up with demand. The stall-owner made so much money out of the festival that she decided to keep her shop in town open and open a second one which would do the rounds of the pagoda festivals.

Maybe it was something I caught from my father, but I really enjoyed selling at the festivals. You got to go to places where you hadn't been before, and pay your respects to the most revered pagodas. You earned merit and had a good time into the bargain. While I was travelling around, I could see plenty of ways to make a living myself.

I decided to set up my own business. One year, I arrived early at the Shwesettaw festival with the owner of the dried goods stall and her niece, so that we could get a good pitch for the shop. The festival hadn't been laid out yet, and we went along to the office of the pagoda trustees to apply. The other two asked me along because I knew how to read and write and I was good at negotiating. Luckily we got a good pitch and while we were there in the office, I met someone who had come to apply for space to set up a temporary guest house.

The guest houses at the Shwesettaw work like this. The festival goes on for a couple of months and pilgrims come from across the entire country. The market goes on for a long time, from the waxing moon of Tabaung until after the full moon of Tagu. There are never enough *zayat* shelters on the pagoda itself to house all the pilgrims, so people open up overnight guest houses: five *kyats* a night for a place to sleep.

The shelters have two, or maybe four rooms, and a thatched roof and bamboo matting walls. You sleep on bamboo mats. There's no need to build a bathroom because you can wash in the Mann creek. The trustees provide the toilets. All you've got to do is provide a place for the pilgrims to sleep. Generally they stay only one night, or two at the most. They spend the day-time going up to the pagoda, or exploring Hunters Hill, or wandering around the market or swimming in the creek, and they eat down at the stalls in the market.

That's how I got the idea to set up guesthouses at the Shwesettaw and other festivals. Think about the money that you can make; each pilgrim pays five *kyats* a night and you can fit a hundred into the shelter, so that's five hundred *kyats* a night, and the festival goes on for a month or so, so that works out at fifteen thousand *kyats* a month.

What do you need to get started? You have to pay the trustees to hire the site. You need bamboo but that's not a problem as it's easy to get it cheap in the area around the Shwesettaw. Thatch is cheap too and it doesn't cost much to hire people to weave bamboo walls. Altogether you need about four or five thousand *kyats* to start off with, which will leave you with ten thousand profit at the end of the festival. Taking miscellaneous expenses into account, you'll still have five or six thousand *kyats* profit—not bad for a month's work, eh?

I'd decided to set up in business running guesthouses at the festivals. But how could I afford to start up at a festival like the Shwesettaw, when you needed at least five thousand to get going? At least that. I had nothing like that much. So I thought to myself—Swe, even if you can't open up a guest house at a big festival, you can still get started at a small one.

The trouble is, at those sorts of festivals, no-one pays to stay in a guest-house. The peasants down from the jungle kip where they can. There are temporary cinema halls which show films all night long. Some of the peasants go to the cinemas and spend the night watching the films half the time and asleep the rest. So you can't make money out of guest houses at that sort of festival.

But on the other hand, I couldn't afford to open up at the big festivals like Shwesettaw and Mawdinsoun where people come from all over the country. What I needed were festivals which weren't big, but weren't completely rural either. At festivals like that, there's no need to build big huts. If they sleep twenty or thirty, that's enough. So if the hut's small, you don't need much capital, and the festivals themselves only last ten or fifteen days, so there's no need to make the huts particularly sturdy. You have to rent two or three stall spaces to set up a guest house. It doesn't have to be a good spot for having a shop, or in the middle of the market. It can be on the edge.

So I went to a small festival and had a go at setting up a guesthouse. I couldn't manage it with just my own money so I got together with a couple of friends. At the end of the festival I had over a thousand *kyats* in hand. When we split the profits, each of us had over four hundred. You've got to admit, that's not bad going for ten or fifteen days work.

So after a good start, I went on to more festivals, and gradually started to save up. I did have a problem at one of them. A couple of kids who were staying in my hut got drunk and got into a fight. I don't know how it started. They were actually friends from the same town. They came back to the guest house drunk and started brawling and this gave my shelter a bit of a bad name. The police arrived and carried out the usual investigations, but that was as far as it went. From then on, I made sure that all guests handed in their ID cards, and I introduced a 'No drinking' rule.

This is my fifth year at the Shwesettaw. The first couple of years, I did it jointly with my friends, but since then, I've managed to do it on my own with the money I've saved. My oldest son's eighteen or nineteen now, so he can help out a lot and the rest of the family pitch in too.

When the pagoda trustees send out the invitations, I move here with the entire family. As soon as the date for applications arrives, I buy up the wood and bamboo and store it on my pitch. As soon as they've handed out the pitches, I start to build. It doesn't take long, not more than two or three days. The earlier you can open, the better. Some stall-holders don't turn up until after the festival has started, by which time I've already finished building. They still have to get hold of their wood and bamboo. Until their roof and walls are finished, they have to stay in my shelter. That's why my first guests are usually other stall-holders. The pilgrims don't start arriving until after the festival has got going. We arrive early and stay until after the festival is over, which means being here about six or eight weeks.

People have to pay ten *kyats* a night to stay in my shelter. No, come on, that's not much. Yes, it was five *kyats* before, then it went up to seven and a half, and now its ten. But the price of the raw materials has gone up. So has the cost of a bus ticket to the pagoda. What can I do? I have to raise my prices too.

To begin with, I had four big rooms and everyone just lay together, but people didn't like this because of the lack of security—things used to disappear. Also people wouldn't get on and then they'd squabble, or they'd be kept awake by someone snoring. So now I've divided it up into ten rooms, each sleeping ten people. It's better that way because if you come with a group you can all share the same room.

Since I'm always travelling to the pagoda festivals, I rarely spend any time back in my house. At most, two or three months a year. After the Shwesettaw is over, there are a number of small festivals during Kason and after that in Nayon it's the Thiho-shin festival in Pakokku. During Wagaung, it's the Kyauk-yiq. I do get about a month off during Tawthalin. But after the end of Lent, it's almost non-stop all the way round to Wagaung again.

I now know everything there is to know about running these festival guest houses. If I could get a lot of money together, I'd like to open up a proper guest house in town. I'd like a spot in the middle of town, where there was plenty of custom. A spot near the bus station would be just perfect. Nowadays, people travel far more, don't they? And people are changing. In the old days, if Burmese people travelled, they'd stay with friends or relations. Nowadays, offering hospitality's become such a burden that people don't want to take advantage of their relatives or friends. If there's a guesthouse, they'll stay there instead, so long as its clean and comfortable and reputable.

I'm hoping that before I die, I'll be able to open up a guest house in town. Whether I manage to or not—well, that's up to fate.

[January 1989]

8

MAN AND MONKEY

He was about thirty-five; dark-skinned, stooping, skinny and long-limbed. He had a long narrow face with wide-set eyes and a big nose. He spoke quietly, and the words he used suggested he enjoyed music. He wore a old cotton longyi, *an old shirt and a pair of old rubber flip-flops. His hand permanently held a cheroot. I met him in a teashop in a town somewhere and as we talked, I learned a little about his life.*

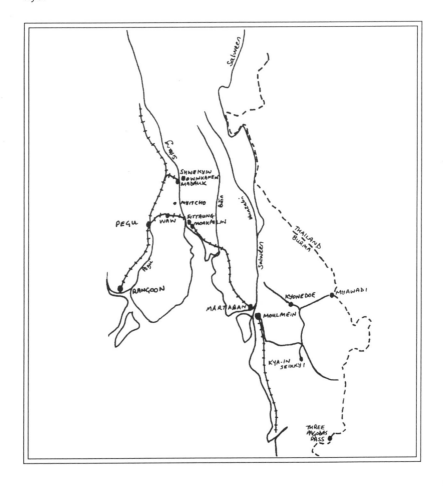

I was born in Sittaung. My parents grew betel. I'd helped them out ever since I was a kid. I'd water the plants, pick the leaves, train the plants through the trellis. The betel would be shipped out from our plantation to Rangoon or Pegu via Sittaung and Moakpalin. We couldn't afford to ship it ourselves. We had to sell it on to the brokers who'd ship it for us. Some people grow betel using borrowed money. Some have their own capital. But no matter how you do it, you can't afford to ship the stuff yourself. Instead, you have to rely on buyers to come with a hired railway truck and ship it out. Our plantation didn't produce enough for a whole truck. So the buyers would buy up everyone's production and combine it to make a truck-load which they'd then ship down to Rangoon and Pegu. You've got to have capital to do that. There was no way we could do it ourselves.

Then my father died. After that, we couldn't afford to carry on. I didn't really want to anyway. You see, for some reason, I'd always had a thing about going on the stage. Whenever theatre troupes came and performed near us, I'd go along for the show. My friends and I would go to Winkanein, Shwe-kyin and Madauk if there was a good show on. I'd even go as far as Waw and Myit-cho if it was a really good one. I must have seen an awful lot of shows in my time. When I was young, I saw Pantra Kyi Lin and Pantra Mya Thein. When I was older, we had Aung Thike (B Ed.), Mandalay Thein Zaw, 'Twante' Thein Tan and Pantra Tin Win, amongst others.

I liked singing and dancing. I knew almost all 'Twante' Thein Tan's songs off by heart. I couldn't dance much. I'd do it a bit at *Thingyan* and at pagoda festivals. But as I'm so tall and skinny, I don't look very good when I'm dancing so I tend not to do it much.

When my father died, we had to sell off the betel plantation and split the money between my father's brothers and sisters. Once it was sold, we had nowhere to live, so with the money we got, which wasn't much, we bought a little house near the Sittaung paper mill. My mother opened up a little grocery shop in the house, and sold betel, cheroots, oil, potatoes and onions to the workers at the mill. Business wasn't too bad.

While we were living there, I got a job in the paper mill. But I didn't last there very long. I was taken on on a daily wage, so when they made workers redundant, I was the first to go. Then my mother had to close down the store because her debtors didn't pay up. She moved back to the village to stay with her sister, and I moved down to Moulmein.

In those days, business was quite brisk in Moulmein. I had all sorts of jobs there. I queued for tickets at Martaban station. I was a porter at the long distance bus station in Martaban or over in the main market in Moulmein. I'd sleep in the bus station, in the manager's office.

I did this kind of thing for about ten years, turning my hand to whatever came my way. I had all sorts of experiences during that time. I visited Kyone-doe, Kya-in Seikkyi, Myawadi, Three Pagodas Pass. A few times I even crossed the border. You can guess why. I was smuggling of course. But I wasn't a proper black marketeer because I didn't have my own capital. I was working as a carrier for other people. As a carrier, you get to see all sorts. Arrests, stabbings, fights. You could write a whole book about it.

I've been living here in this town for a while now. Ten or fifteen years. When I first arrived, I was working as a porter in the market, and a carrier. Or I'd buy and sell. But I'd be buying and selling for other people, not with my own money. When customers came to the market I'd go and get them goods and sell them on for a slight profit.

But I don't want to go on too much about me, *Saya*. I'd rather tell you about White Paw. White Paw? He was my companion. My best friend. My meal ticket. White Paw was my monkey.

I'll begin with how we met. One day, I was on my way back from the river bank, where I'd been working as a porter, when I came across a group of children who were standing around a tree throwing sticks and stones. I was curious to see what was going on, so I stopped and looked up. There was this monkey in the tree. He'd climbed the tree because the children were throwing stones at him and trying to shoot him with their catapults. He was swinging from branch to branch trying to dodge the stones. He'd take cover behind a branch and then peek out from behind. He'd pick up the sticks and playfully throw them back at the kids. But he didn't seem to like the catapults. When they stopped shooting, he'd come down the tree a bit. But when he saw the children with catapults he'd climb straight back up. The children kept chucking rocks at him, calling him a cheeky little monkey so he hid up at the top of the tree where only a few could get him. One stone hit him quite hard and he lost his grip. I thought it must have hit him in the head and I was sure he would fall out of the tree. But he was too smart for that. Half way down, he grabbed hold of a branch and swung himself back up the tree.

When I asked how the monkey had got to town, someone said that he'd arrived on a sampan carrying firewood down the Salween river. No-one knew whether he'd boarded the sampan when it set off or if he'd jumped on later. But during the voyage, bits and pieces had started to disappear and the crew had started to quarrel and accuse one another of stealing. Sometimes *longyis* went missing, sometimes shirts, sometimes pots and pans. A bunch of bananas which someone had bought in case they got hungry went missing. A packet of nuts was stolen. No-one realised it was the monkey because he was hiding in amongst the firewood. So the crew were accusing one another of taking things, and when the shirts and the *longyis* turned up in the firewood, they accused each other of hiding them to smuggle onshore once the boat landed.

The problem was, not everything which disappeared was worth stealing. Sometimes it was just a cheroot butt, or a piece of cloth someone had offered to the *nats*, or a cigarette lighter or the tin of lime for betel or a pair of betel cutters. Things no-one would want to steal. Sometimes pots and pans were found in the toilet. So although the crew had started off thinking it must be someone on board, they decided it couldn't be. They concluded that it must be happening because they had offended a *nat*. So they made a lot of offerings and begged forgiveness. But even that didn't work. Things kept going missing.

One day, the captain lost his *longyi* and couldn't find it anywhere. The next day, one of the boatmen shouted out that he'd found it. The crew looked at where he was pointing to the top of the mast next to the national flag. Now there was no way you could climb up that mast. There was no ladder or anything. The flag was hoisted up there using guy ropes. Yet the *longyi* was fluttering from the top.

The crew decided that something was up. They reckoned that someone had put a curse on the boat. Maybe someone was jealous. So they searched high and low for the sign of the curse. That was how they found the monkey, who was hiding in the firewood. When they spotted him, they were more amused than angry, but they chased him and swore at him and one of them threatened to catch him, roast him and drink his blood. They threw bits of wood at him but they couldn't hit him and eventually he made a bid for the mast where no-one could get him. He swung around on the guy ropes about half-way up the mast, daring the men to come and get him. One man tried hanging on waiting for the monkey to climb down but he had to give up because his arms were killing him. Once the man had climbed down, the monkey scampered up to the top of the mast.

When the boat docked, they waited for the monkey to climb down. But he didn't come down. So some of them kept watch that night. But they fell asleep, and when they woke up the next morning, he had gone. Maybe he'd climbed down while they were fast asleep, or swung across to the bank on the guy ropes.

I discovered he'd been living on the bank of the river for about ten days. He'd been causing trouble stealing women's *longyis* and bananas from the houses nearby. That was why the children were throwing stones at him. Anyway, I watched him for a while, and then went home and forgot all about him.

One afternoon, about ten days later, I went up to Kyaikthanlan pagoda. At the time, I had no job and nothing to eat. I had nowhere to sleep either. So I was eating and sleeping wherever I could, and drinking from the water pots on the street. I was hungry and tired so I thought I would get a bunch of bananas and have a quick nap up at the pagoda.

Near the main hall of the pagoda, I spotted two young couples. I was too tired and hungry to bother about them. I went into the pagoda and got a bunch of bananas, thinking I would eat them and then catch forty winks.

I'd eaten about five bananas and I was getting drowsy when I was suddenly woken up by a noise. I opened my eyes and spotted a monkey creeping up on me ready to steal my bananas. I shouted at him and he backed off a little but didn't run away. He hung around waiting. I decided he must be hungry too, so I threw him a banana. He ate it, and edged a little closer.

I had a good look at him. He was an ordinary brown monkey, the kind I used to see when I lived in the village and went out into the jungle to collect bamboo and rattan. When I took a good look at him, I realised that he was the same monkey I had seen the children throwing rocks at the other day down on the riverbank. He had a scab on his temple and there was a white spot on one of his paws. I was quite sure it was the same one. As I watched him, he edged closer and closer, looking at me tentatively. I threw him another banana. He got a bit bolder. It was as if we were getting to know one another. So I chucked him another, and he ate it, and then another. With each banana, he become more friendly, and seemed to like me more and more.

It made my day, *Saya*. I didn't have a friend in the world, or a roof over my head and I had barely a penny to my name. So to make a new friend, even if he was an animal, made all the difference. I gave him the rest of the bunch of bananas. I don't know how hungry he was, or how many days he'd gone without food, but he ate every last one of them. That evening I went down the hill and bought another bunch of bananas, a plate of *mohinga*, a cup of tea and a cheroot for the evening.

As I climbed the steps back up to the pagoda, White Paw came bounding down from the roof of the pagoda to greet me. I suspected he'd been waiting for me, and I gave him a couple of bananas. That night I slept in a hut on the pagoda platform and he slept on one of the beams.

The next day, I went down into town and he followed me. I shouted at him to get lost, but he just hung back and then started following me again when I walked off. When I stopped, he stopped. When I carried on, he followed on behind me. Even though I tried to scare him off, it didn't work. He would just hang back a bit and then follow me. I decided he wasn't frightened because he thought we were friends now. When we reached the town, the dogs started to bark at him and the children were teasing him and so he stuck closer to me. I thought that he might get bitten by the dogs, so I let him climb onto my shoulder. He certainly liked that and sat there quietly. It made me realise that if you treat animals kindly they too will treat you kindly—and vice versa.

With White Paw perched on my shoulder, the children followed on behind me but they stopped throwing sticks and stones. Instead, they fed him bananas and peanuts. They'd buy him bananas and nuts and throw them and he'd catch them and eat them and it kept them all happy. In the end he couldn't eat any more so I picked them up and put them in my bag for supper. This was certainly a turn up for the books. I could walk through town with him on my shoulder and have all his meals bought and paid for. I did that for about four days. We didn't just get enough for him. There were enough extra bananas and peanuts left over for me too. And we both loved sweets, so if anyone threw him a packet, I'd eat some too.

Then I had an idea. I decided I would teach White Paw to dance like the famous dancer Po Sein. So I ordered some cloth to make him a *gaung-baung* hat and went looking for some material to make him a shirt and a *longyi*. Then I stitched him a shirt and a traditional-style wide *longyi* myself. It was quite easy. I just cut out a design and sewed it up with a needle.

In the evenings up on the pagoda, once there was hardly anyone around, I used to teach him how to dance the U Shwe Yoe dance. Or I taught him how to dance to a drum-beat, or a nursery rhyme by U Ka Lein, songs I must have heard my mother or my Aunty singing a thousand times. Then there was that comic song 'The Garuda Pounces on the Elephant' from the *a-nyeints*. I never knew the whole song, but I'd sing a few verses and beat time with a stick so that he could dance.

I don't know whether he had a natural talent for dancing or whether he was just good at copying humans but he soon picked it up. And then we went off down town to the markets to perform like Po Sein. All the children would come and watch. We were raking it in, you cannot believe how much we made. In a day, we could clear thirty or forty *kyats* easily. Everyone would give at least one *kyat*. We would also go and perform outside the schools when the children were arriving. Some would even give five or ten *kyats* each because they felt sorry for him. Sometimes I could even make a hundred *kyats* from just one performance.

When we'd finished a performance, the two of us would go back to the Kyaikthanlan Pagoda to spend the night. Then we got up the next morning and went downtown to go to work. It all worked out very well. Before then, I couldn't even afford a new *longyi* or a pair of shoes. But now, thanks to White Paw, I could afford new clothes.

In the morning we'd go down to the *mohinga* stall at the bottom of the hill. I'd have some *mohinga* and the girls in the shop who had got fond of White Paw would give him bananas and peanuts. I had to pay for my *mohinga* but White Paw got his breakfast for free. The girls would buy him fruit every morning for his breakfast. When I'd finished eating and White Paw jumped on my shoulder, we would set off and the girls would break off from cooking or washing the dishes and wave and call after him 'White Paw, now you make sure you come back and have breakfast with us tomorrow'. He would wave back from my shoulder. And if people blew him kisses, as they often did because they all thought he was so sweet, he'd blow them back. We must have worked together for eight or nine months like this. At *Thadingyut*, and at the pagoda festivals, we raked it in.

We lived together on the pagoda platform for about eight or nine months. Then one morning I woke up and couldn't find him. Usually he'd come and wake me up in the morning. This time he didn't and I slept late until about seven. I woke up and looked around for him, and called him, 'White Paw, time for breakfast, time for *mohinga*', but my voice just echoed around the empty pagoda. I spent an hour searching the hill and then went down to the *mohinga* stall. The girls asked me where White Paw was. I scoured town looking for him, but I couldn't find him.

Losing White Paw meant losing my closest friend. But it meant losing my meal ticket too. Without him, I started to run out of money. After I'd been looking for him for about two weeks, I started to run out of food and I still couldn't find him.

One morning, I went down to the *mohinga* stall and one of the girls asked me if I'd heard the news about White Paw. I said I hadn't. She told me that he'd been making a nuisance of himself down at the Lower Main Road. I asked what kind of a nuisance. She said that he'd been taking things from houses, and hiding them. He'd taken a woman's *longyi*, and shirts, pots and pans.

That wasn't too serious and people had been prepared to put up with it because they knew him. But one day he'd picked up a burning stick and started jumping from roof to roof. The children had been calling out to him to put it down, throw it down. But he wouldn't listen and just kept leaping around from roof to roof. Obviously they couldn't let him carry on like that so someone got a gun and shot him. That was how he died.

I was very upset. I couldn't work out why he'd suddenly gone wild like that. He'd gone back to his old tricks like on the sampan. I don't know what it was that did it to him. Maybe it was his jungle instincts coming back. Maybe it was just his monkey genes. Perhaps he'd got bored of living with people and dancing and decided to revert to being wild. I was choked with tears and I couldn't say a word to the girls. I suddenly realised that you couldn't make a monkey live like a man. Monkeys are monkeys, men are men. You can't mix the two for any length of time.

I thanked the girls and left. Monkey or not, I'd lost my closest friend. He was a good friend who'd taken care of me. The girls watched me leave, and stood there reflecting on the fate of White Paw.

[October 1990]

9

BACKSTAGE BOYFRIEND

I met her on a train on a branch line in upper Burma. She must have been about thirty-five. She was tall and slim, with shoulder length hair and delicate eyebrows. She had big eyes, a prominent nose and was of average colouring. She was wearing a shabby black one-set and old white sandals, earrings and a scarf tied around her waist. She carried a white sling bag with a narrow shoulder-strap. I noticed that the soles of her white shoes were dirty and that she smoked cigarettes, alternating them with cheroots. Her appearance, behaviour and manner all suggested that she was on the stage. From time to time she would refer to herself as 'Ohk Aw'.[1]

---

[1] *Koel* or cuckoo

You're right! I used to be an actress! I was in stage shows and danced in *a-nyeint*. I started off in *a-nyeint* and then got some occasional acting jobs with *zat-pwes*. But *zat-pwe* directors tend to look down on you if you started in *a-nyeint* so I didn't get much acting experience in the *zats* unless I got on with the directors. Mostly I was dancing in *a-nyeint*. I was originally called Ma Tin Mi but my stage name is Ohk Aw Tin. Once upon a time, everyone round here had heard of Ohk Aw Tin.

I was born in this township, in a village called Zee-byu-gone. There's no railway or road there but if you get off this train at Yan Aung station and go about eight miles into the country, you'll get to it. It's pretty remote, ten miles away from the nearest road.

My father used to grow sugar-cane. He had four or five acres. My mother's family were all sugar-cane growers too—there's never been any performers in our family. Well, except for one, perhaps. My uncle was a great fan of the stage—but he was a monk! He was the abbot of the monastery in our village. My mother's big brother. That's why I'm calling him U Gyi, not Ba Gyi. Aha!! I think I've confused you already. Round here, Ba Gyi is what you call your father's older brother, and Ba Dway for the younger brother. His big and little sisters are Ayee Gyi and Ayee Lay. Your mother's brothers are called U Gyi and U Lay. That way you know immediately whether someone's referring to an aunt or an uncle on your mother's side or your father's side, whether they're older or younger than your parents and so on. If I you told me about your 'Uncle's and 'Aunty's, like they do in Rangoon, I wouldn't know how they were related to you. But round here, you just have to know what they're called, and then you know how they're related. Oh—are you from Upper Burma too? Then I've been teaching my grandmother to suck eggs, haven't I?[2]

Anyway, where was I? Oh yes, my uncle the monk who liked show business. His monk's name was U Sobita. He'd been a monk since he was little. He went straight from being a novice to being a young monk. I don't know where along the way he picked up his passion for the stage. Although he couldn't take part himself because he had to obey the *Vinaya* Rules[3] he helped others. How did he do that? Well, for example, if there was a pagoda festival, he'd go and book an acting troupe. He used to say that he was worried that the younger generation would pick up the wrong message from some of the more modern shows instead of learn-

---

[2] In Burmese 'like telling a monk how to preach or teaching crocodile to swim'.

[3] There are several hundred *Vinaya* rules prescribed by Buddha which monks have to follow including ones which forbid them from enjoying musical performances.

ing about the *Jataka* tales the way Buddha told them. That was why he said he needed to book the show himself.

Whenever there was a festival in our village, whether it was for Independence Day or for the Twenty-Eight Buddhas Pagoda festival, he would go and book a troupe. If he couldn't go and hire them himself, he'd give one of his followers instructions about which actor from which troupe knew his texts, or which comedian could be relied on not to make risque jokes. He didn't watch the shows himself. He just made sure that the audience behaved itself. If everything was going smoothly, he would retire to the monastery where he could hear the band and the singers on the loudspeakers. That way, he could tell whether the acting and the performance were up to scratch. Apart from giving advice, he wouldn't get involved. He followed the *Vinaya* and observed the precepts and read the scriptures. The whole village respected him and regarded him as family. He did other welfare work for the village. For example, he organised the digging of a tube-well, and set up a primary school in the monastery, and put a *hti* on top of the pagoda.

At that time I was a young girl. I don't know why, but I was very much into singing and dancing. I'd been going to the shows of Shwe Man Kyaw Aung, Pantra Kyi Lin and Pantra Mya Thein since I was little. They'd come and perform at our pagoda festivals, and religious ceremonies like when a monastery was built, and at the Independence Day celebrations. Did I see any others? Yes. I saw Shwe Man Tin Maung and Sein Aung Min. We'd had famous *a-nyeint* stars like Maya Kyi, Independence Tin Tin and Hintha May. So all that exposure to acting at an early age must have had its effect and made me want to be a star too. I had a good voice—or at least that's what others told me. I could easily pick up a tune. I only had to hear a song a couple of times and I'd pick it up. It's a shame I couldn't master my school lessons as easily.

I still remember a Twenty-Eight Buddhas Pagoda festival one year when the sugar cane harvest hadn't been very successful. The village couldn't afford to hire a theatre troupe. Instead we had an *a-nyeint*. They performed for three nights in a row. That was when I heard that song by Maya Kyi. She was that Mon actress from somewhere like Theinzayaq. She was very pretty and charming so she was a big hit amongst the teenagers in our village. Since I was only a kid, I wasn't interested in how she looked. But I liked that song she sang. What was it called? Ah yes, I remember:

> 'Hey, my name is Gwet-taw
> Gwet-taw,
> What am I embarrassed for?
> I'm your little Mon girl
> Out in the forest'.

I discovered later, it wasn't her own song. In the old days it was sung by an actress called Sein Gwet Taw. I suppose I liked it so much because when I was very young, my parents used to call me Gwet Taw. It was only later on that I became Tin Mi.

So after I'd seen Maya Kyi singing that, I used to sing and dance when I was on my own, and pretend I was in an *a-nyeint*. I made myself a fan out of newspaper and put on the pointy-ended tunic I wore for my ear-piercing ceremony and wrapped myself in one of my mother's *longyis* and put on face powder. My mother always used to slap me when she caught me at it; probably because I was wasting her face powder and spoiling her new *longyi*.

I also liked that song 'Htwe Nyo' by Twante Thein Dan. I used to go out to harvest the sugar cane with my parents. There were lots of other children there and we used to dance together in the sugar cane field like we were in an *a-nyeint*. So I suppose that's where I first got interested in going on the stage.

One year we had a ceremony to put a *hti* on top of my uncle's monastery in the village. The price of sugar cane was so low that year that we couldn't even afford to hire an *a-nyeint*. So the monk told us we should put on an *a-yein* dance performance ourselves. Most of the dancers were just teenagers. I took part. We were dancing to an easy tune called 'Ja Aye'[4].

We sang the song three times and just danced to the music another three times. There were twelve dancers in three rows of four. I was in the front row with three other girls. There were four boys in the middle and at the back there were four more girls dressed up as old women. The girls in front danced like Ja Aye, as if they were making an offering to the monks, and the boys pretended they were wooing us. The 'old women' at the back walked forward together and slapped us 'Ja Ayes' at the front since they were meant to be our mothers. There were only four or five steps to the dance. We were all only young and we didn't think about what we were singing—we just concentrated on the steps.

It was my uncle the monk who first suggested we should dance to 'Ja Aye'. He said that he didn't know much about songs, but he'd heard this poem 'Ja Aye' and thought it could be turned into a dance. He mentioned this to Sein Ba Ee in the village who put the poem to music. Sein Ba Ee had visited our village once as part of an orchestra. He'd met a woman from the village and settled down with her. He put the song together and taught us the dance steps which weren't particularly difficult.

---

[4] A well-known circular nonsense song which is used to describe any unending chain of events.

We hired a local orchestra to accompany us. Our show was quite successful and we used to get invitations from other villages when they had festivals and ceremonies to go and perform. We'd perform for free but they'd pay our expenses and feed us and send us home with presents.

Since our dance performances were becoming quite well known, the monk bought us a small orchestra. Until then, when we had had a festival, it had been very complicated and expensive to hire a proper orchestra and move it from one village to another by bullock-cart. Our mini-orchestra didn't have the full range of instruments. There was a set of bronze gongs, although not a full set, some drums and a clarinet. Sein Ba Ee, who I mentioned earlier, took charge as leader and drummer in the orchestra.

I was about twelve at the time. We performed from time to time. Sein Ba Ee's orchestra became quite well-known in the area and used to be called 'the Zee-byu-gone band'.

When I was about thirteen, my father and mother died in quick succession leaving me and my brother. My uncle the monk looked after me and put me in a nunnery near his monastery. I was only young and I had no-one else to look after me apart from him.

I carried on dancing in the *a-yein* troupe every year. We had a number of set pieces: 'Ja Aye', 'Kone-ma-yi Dance', 'Kinnara[5] Dance', 'The Paddy-harvesters' Dance', 'Fun in the Sugar Cane Fields'. In that last one we used to dance as if we were harvesting sugar cane.

That was how I got more and more interested in going on the stage. Then one day, Sein Ba Ee said to me:

'Girlie, do you want to be the number two dancer in an *a-nyeint?*'

I said 'Of course!', although I was only joking because I didn't think he was serious.

'I'm serious', he said. 'A stage manager from the town, from a theatre troupe, has told me he's sick of having to manage a big show and he wants to set up on his own with an *a-nyeint* group. His wife is going to be the main dancer. He's asking me to lead the orchestra. He says all he needs is a number two dancer and he can get started. Are you interested?'

'I'm interested', I said, 'Of course I am. You must know that. But I don't think my uncle will let me do it.' He said he would go and ask the monk.

So come harvest-time, Sein Ba Ee took me away with him. I was fifteen or sixteen. At first, my uncle didn't want to let me go. But he

---

[5] A mythical bird.

realised that he would have to. If I stayed on in the monastery, it would cause lots of problems, what with him being a monk. I didn't want to stay with him any more either. It's not right for a girl to be living in a monastery. I couldn't even look after him when he was sick because although we were related by blood, he was a monk and I was a woman. All I could do was make his meals and prepare his medicine. It wasn't even necessary for me to do that because there were plenty of others in the monastery who could do it, and monks and novices. I was superfluous to requirements. And I was very conscious that I was eating alms food which had been offered to the monastery.

So really I just wanted to get out of there as soon as possible. Our parents had left us their sugar-cane fields. My brother said he would buy out my share. I left for town to join the *a-nyeint* of Myo Chit May Than Than.

Where did I learn to dance? Well . . . I didn't really learn from anywhere. I've been watching dancers and copying them ever since I was young. As soon as I'd learnt how to run, I was watching the dancers and watching their individual styles. Ma Ya Kyi, for example, was very good at making her *longyi* trail behind her gracefully. Sein Gwet Taw was very graceful in the way she moved her hands and feet. Aung Ma Kyi had a good singing voice. Anything she sang sounded good. Hla Ohn May was very beautiful. I used to pay attention and then copy them in front of the mirror. That was how I learned how to dance.

Myo Chit May Than Than, who was the main dancer in the *a-nyeint* that Sein Ba Ee took me to, taught me a little bit. But she was more interested in playing *kyin*. So was her husband. You know what *kyin* is, don't you? It's a Chinese gambling game with cards about the size of dominoes. The cards are made of paper rather than wood. I don't know how to play. The two of them used to play all the time and it affected the show. Sometimes she was still playing *kyin* when I came off-stage. It meant that she had to rush around to get changed and so she didn't dance at all well.

We used to perform thirty or forty times a year, but the engagements started to get less frequent. The touring season is usually between October and March or April, especially during the *kathina* robe-offering festivals in November and the pagoda festivals in December and January.

While I was performing as the number two dancer, Myo Chit May Than Than said to me: 'I'm getting too old for this. I want you to be the lead dancer. If you can put half the money into the business, I'll start handing over the main role to you and you can eventually take over the lead completely'.

She knew I'd inherited some money from my parents' cane fields. Since Sein Ba Ee egged me on, I eventually agreed. I handed over my savings, three thousand *kyats*. And as soon as they got the money, they lost it in a card-game. I never made it to be lead dancer. Not only that, but the company folded soon after.

Sein Ba Ee went back to the village. I couldn't. My uncle had died of a stroke by then. My brother had moved away. There was no-one left there for me. So I stayed on with the two of them. They told me to stay with them and not to go back to my village as they would start up another *a-nyeint*. So I did. I had no full-time job of course. But I used to help out with the housework and the cooking. They spent most of their time down at the gambling-den. From what I heard, they had a permanent losing streak.

They were always telling me it was going to be OK. They told me they'd set up the *a-nyeint* again and that I'd be the star dancer. They did manage to get me a couple of parts dancing with another orchestra.

I was stuck with them for about two years, hardly dancing at all. During that time, the husband used to rape me. His wife said that it was quite natural that since we were partners, I should be his mistress. She said that she wasn't jealous and that she was happy to share him. I suspected that this might not be the first time for her.

I spent about a year as his mistress, but they never got round to setting up the *a-nyeint* again.

I was about twenty. I had left home wanting to be an *a-nyeint* dancer and instead I'd ended up losing all my money and being set up as another man's mistress. And despite what she'd said about being prepared to share her husband, Myo Chit May was getting more and more jealous and unpleasant towards me. Eventually I decided I couldn't stand it any more. I wasn't making it as an *a-nyeint* dancer and I wasn't in a position to find myself a good husband. I wasn't much better off than an ordinary servant.

So one day when a theatre troupe came to town, I took off and left with them. I didn't get the star part of course. I was just one of the dancers who used to come on and accompany the main actor. I was about twenty. I had been a year in that company when I met a theatre agent in one of the towns we went to. He acted as an agent because he was interested in the theatre. But this was just a side-line to his main job, which was owner of a motor workshop. He was one of the big cheeses in the town and he'd been the one who booked us. When he saw our show, he took a fancy to me and told the director of the troupe that he wanted to set up an *a-nyeint* with me as the star. The director always did whatever this man said, so he handed me over to him.

The businessman was my benefactor. He was about my father's age. He'd always wanted to own his own *a-nyeint* because he was a big fan of the stage. He made me the main dancer and after we'd done a few performances, I made quite a name for myself in the township as Ohk Aw Tin. He was wealthy, so not only were the comedians good but we could afford a complete set of instruments for the orchestra. It was a Burmese orchestra, but we had a piano band as well, including a violin, a xylophone, a clarinet, a banjo, a jazz drum-set and a cornet.

It certainly was a stroke of good luck for me. And in those days, most a-nyeint dancers, even the ones from Rangoon, didn't have their own songs. Only the ones from Mandalay did. And me. My song-writer was also the clarinettist in the band. Saya Htar. He was very good. He knew how my voice sounded so he could write me songs that suited my voice, mostly in the key of A. My trade-mark song was called 'The one who's waiting for me'. It was a big hit in town.

When I say in the key of A, let me explain a little. Most songs written for the a-nyeint are like that. They usually have five parts: an intro, three main verses and a final verse a bit like a chorus. The introduction generally has no particularly rhythm and the orchestra doesn't play a tune, just chords as backing music. The first verse has a medium tempo and is quite staccato. In the final chorus, the tempo quickens and the comedians join in too.

My song, 'The one who's waiting for me' was like that. The introduction went like this:

'Oh, my darling,
I see you every night in my dreams
I'm dancing for you
If you find me
Will you marry me?'

Towards the end I start to sing:

'Backstage boyfriend, you're the one for me
Will you come along with me?
Backstage boyfriend, don't say another word
Come closer and I'll show you
How much I love you.
If we get along, then I'll marry you'.

And then the chorus comes in:

'Let me know when you'll come to me
I know you will
You won't need to persuade me
If you want me, I'll come'.

81

It's a song in A. So it's quite easy to sing. And it sounds good too and is easy to dance to because it has quick staccato wording and the drum beats a rhythm along to it. I never used to get tired dancing to it. I made my name with that song, thanks to *Saya* Htar. If a writer knows the style of the dancer, he can write her a good song and get the rhythm right.

Our drummer was Ko Thein Maung. He was about twenty-five. He was skinny and very arrogant. We fell out as soon as he started in the band. The first night I went on stage, he deliberately played extra notes which he hadn't played in rehearsal so that I kept losing my step. I looked across at him but even though he knew I was looking at him, he pretended not to notice and carried on playing all these bum notes. After the show was over, I was ashamed of my performance and I was furious with him. I felt he had done it all on purpose to teach me some kind of a lesson. I went to complain to the manager and burst into tears.

'That guy's always like that. Sometimes he's just crazy', he said. 'Even I can't do anything about him. Don't take any notice. I'll talk to him about it'.

But I felt that I didn't want to dance with that drummer playing. He was scary.

The following night I was so angry with him I came on after the comedians and just danced any steps I felt like and totally ignored whatever rhythm he was trying to beat out. I danced well and deliberately ignored him and scowled. For a good *a-nyeint* dance, there should be a genuine understanding between the drummer and the dancer. The better the rhythm they build up, the better the dance. But I just let him bang away and ignored him and only looked at the leader of the orchestra. He indicated to me that I should look over to Ko Thein Maung. So I did glance over, and saw that he was smiling at me. I listened for the drum beats and realised that the rhythm was a good one. And with a good rhythm, I could dance a good dance. He was supporting my dance with his drum beat. I remembered the manager's words. 'Sometimes he's just crazy'. And I thought, 'Well maybe he was crazy last night and now he's not tonight'. He was giving me a great drum-beat for my own song. And the more I pouted, the better he played for me. From time to time I'd glance over at him and I'd see him looking at my dance steps and drumming along with them. I realised that he was as good a drummer as the others had claimed. I respected him for that.

After the show, the leader of the orchestra said, 'What a fine drum performance we had tonight from you, Thein Maung—you sounded really inspired!' Ko Thein Maung just smiled and glanced over at me.

Ko Thein Maung used to drink a lot, although he didn't let it affect his performance. He said it improved his drumming, and relaxed him.

I spent quite a while with that *a-nyeint*. In fact, I ended up marrying Ko Thein Maung. Maybe that surprises you? It's not that unusual. In our business, marriages between drummers and dancers, or between dancers and comedians, are quite common. They have to be close when they're performing and so they tend to develop an understanding and a respect for one another. And often the drummer or the comedian has to support the dancer when there's a break in the dancing or when they need a different beat. The dancer needs their support.

Ko Thein Maung fell in love with me, but the problem was, I wasn't in love with him. I respected him. But he was like a big brother to me. While we were together and I was dancing for him I even had another boyfriend although it wasn't serious. He was in love with me. I was quite fond of him. But that was it.

How did I meet him? His town held a party because the football team had won. We were the entertainment. I was singing my song 'The one who's waiting for me' and dancing. I got to the middle verse:

'I'll see you in the audience, if you're there
Maybe you're not serious
Maybe not my darling
But you're always in my dreams . . .'

I heard someone in the middle of the audience shouting out 'Here he is! Here he is!' I was used to that. I thought it was the usual, just kids fooling around. I learned later that it wasn't just fooling around. I found out that one of the boys in the football team was in love with me and his friends were teasing him about it. His name was Aung Aung and he was a final year high school student. He was the son of the owner of a textile mill. He couldn't have been more than eighteen or nineteen. I was about thirty at the time—I'm thirty-five now.

Aung Aung was a big fan of mine, apparently, and had been to see me wherever we performed. U Hnget Yoe, the comedian, and his wife told me they'd found this out when they were down the market. That night, since Aung Aung was the captain of the football team, he came on stage and gave me a hundred *kyats* on behalf of the team. He seemed a bit drunk and I could smell alcohol on his breath.

After he gave me the hundred *kyats* he held on tight to my hands and gazed into my eyes until I felt embarrassed. His friends were yelling out, 'Bravo Aung Aung, go for it!' The audience was clapping. But he didn't get fresh with me. He just whispered to me 'I'll see you again' and then climbed down off the stage.

We did another night at that town, and I did my own song again on request. This was a special show arranged by Aung Aung's family rather

83

than one booked by the town authorities. Aung Aung was back-stage. I saw him after I'd done my song, singing about my 'back-stage boyfriend'. U Hnget Yoe, the comedian was teasing me, 'Hey Ohk Aw Tin, where's your boyfriend?'

'He's out there in the audience, Uncle' I retorted, as I always did. But U Hnget Yoe replied 'No he isn't, Ohk Aw Tin. You know that song you sing. The one about your backstage boyfriend. Well, your boyfriend's backstage waiting for you.'

Ko Thein Maung smiled. He was used to this kind of thing, being married to an actress.

When the show was over and I came off-stage, Aung Aung was waiting for me. 'Where are you playing next?' he asked.

I told him. Then he said 'Please will you accept this gift?' I looked at it and discovered he'd given me a gold brooch with my name, 'Ohk Aw Tin', engraved on it. I said I couldn't take it but he insisted. He told me he was giving it to me because he loved me. Then he left.

After that, he used to come and see me wherever we played. Ko Thein Maung knew about it. The whole company knew about it. Every time we met, he used to tell me that he loved me. I would tell him that it simply wasn't possible. I didn't tell him I was already married. We actresses all have to pretend we're unmarried if we're going to stay popular. That's why I lied.

He even started coming to my house. My town wasn't too far from his and he used to drive over in his jeep. Eventually I had to tell him I was already married. After that he stopped coming.

What else could I do? After all, I was married. There are so many of these young boys who are in love with actresses. If you reciprocate their feelings, people just accuse you of leading them on and taking advantage of them. That's why I had to tell him to his face. I felt really bad about it. I was very fond of him. But it was an impossible situation, really.

Am I still performing? Not any more. It's been a few years now. And it's not a business you can make much money in. We don't have the instruments. And nowadays people don't book *a-nyeints* so much. If they do, they don't book you for the whole night. You need about as much money to set up an *a-nyeint* as you do for the average-sized *zat*. You've got to put on the opera and the stereo show and then one of those famous Indian dances from a film. Or you need to have Moe Moe Myint Aung, the actress, wearing fancy Indian dress. Modern shows have lots and lots of backdrops. And a standard orchestra isn't enough—you need keyboards and so on. Even the big *a-nyeints* are going out of business. I heard that one lost so much they had to pawn the keyboards in order to get the money to get back home.

Ko Thein Maung's had a stroke. He was always drinking too much. Now he can't get out of bed.

What do I do now instead? All sorts of things. I suppose you could call me a trader. I buy and sell rice, iron, sugar cane, even luck. Iron? That means scrap iron that gets smuggled out of the oil-fields. Luck? That's lottery tickets.

Well, I've really enjoyed our conversation. We're almost at the station. If I was to write this story, I'd want to write about the things which I feel really deeply about. This last couple of hours, we've only just scratched the surface.

[June 1988]

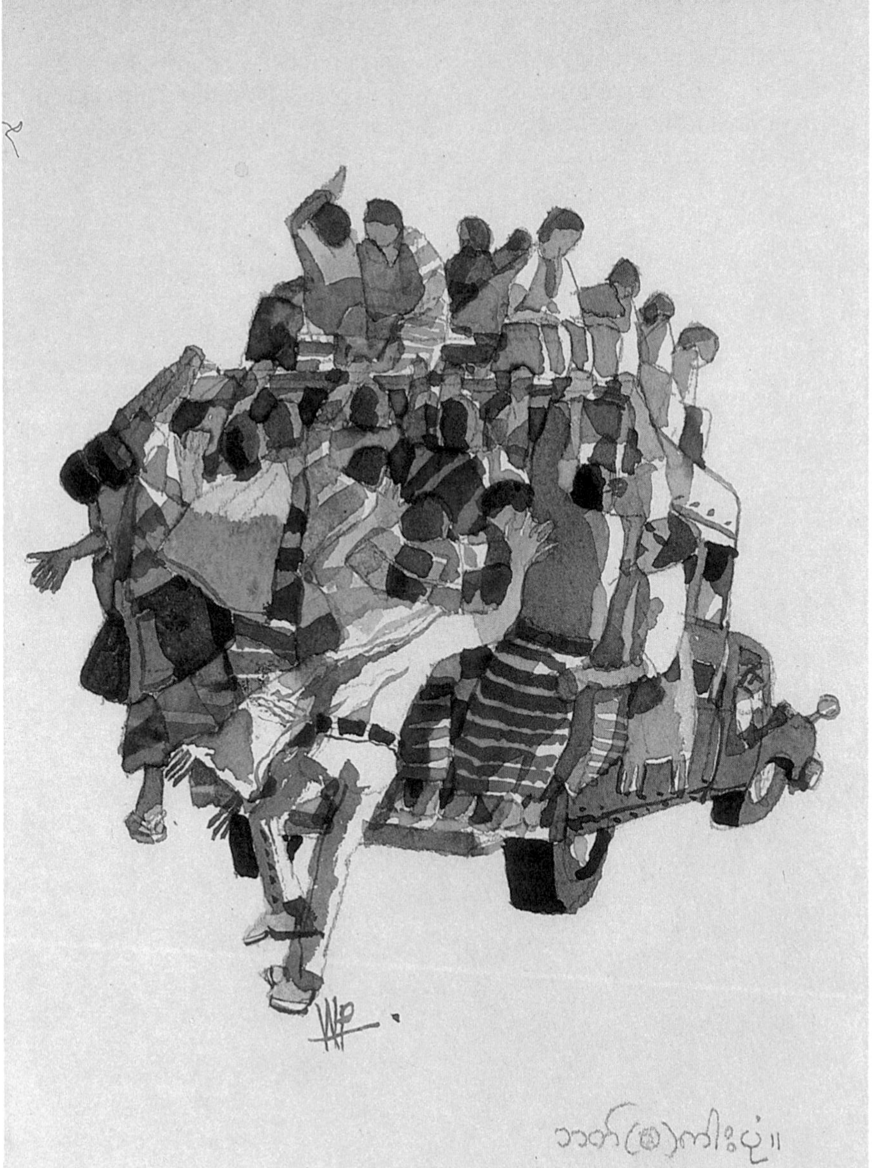
ဘတ်(စ)ကားပုံ။

CHAPTER III
HIGH HOPES

10

THET PYIN THE SPARE

I encountered him on the back of a truck on the road between Gangaw and Pakokku. He wore a cheap sports shirt and a faded longyi. His reddish hair poked out at all angles from under a dirty old golf cap which sported the 'Honda' logo. He was tanned, with a trace of a moustache. I put him at between twenty-five and thirty.

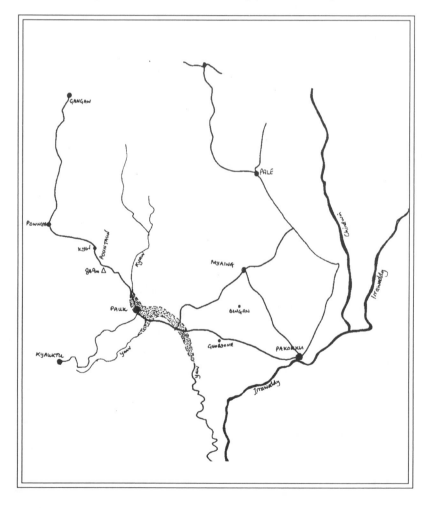

My name's Thet Pyin. I've never been nowhere, if y'know whaddamean. OK, I've seen the Irrawaddy river at Pakokku but I've never been across. I've always been doing the Gangaw to Pakokku run. But I haven't always been a spare. I started off at fifteen as an assistant spare. Did that for five years. Assistant spare? What does he do? He does what the spare tells him to. The spare takes the money and checks for passengers by the side of the road. He decides the rate for a part-journey. He decides what stuff can and can't go on the bus. For example, if the bus's already loaded down, and the stuff's only low-value, he won't load it. He won't get much money for it, and he could fit in another two or three passengers instead. Sometimes you'll get restricted goods being put on board, so if he's suspicious, he'll check them, see whether it's rice, sesamum, sticky rice, drums of oil, whatever. He's got to decide what to load up with bearing in mind there'll be problems if the car is stopped and searched. The driver—that's U Ba Han—he can't check these things out himself, so he tells the spare to check it first.

As spare's assistant, my job was to make room for the load, top up the water if the car was over-heating, top up the diesel or the engine oil. If it didn't start, I'd have to get down and crank the engine. If we were stopped on a slope, I'd have to jump off and stick a stone under the wheel—although that's not much of a problem round here. It's a bigger problem on Poun-taun and Poun-nya hills, you've got to put the chocks under. Especially when you're climbing, and that bit going up Poun-taun near the nat shrine. We were usually loaded to the brim with the government rice sacks. When you stop at the shrine, you start to roll backwards. That's when I really had to jump off quickly and stick the chocks underneath or we'd probably go over the edge.

Well, that's my five years as a spare's assistant for you. I was on the Gangaw-Pakokku run the whole time. I know all the streams, all the bends, and all the hills on this route. During the monsoon, we can't do the run because we can't be sure of getting across the Yaw stream when the current is strong. In just the forty miles between Pauk and Pakokku, there's about forty creeks to cross. So there's no way we can run the bus at times like that.

When the bus was running, the owner gave us our meals and five *kyats* a day. And a little bit more from 'outside'. When I say outside, what I meant was our truck carried government rice bags, so the owner only got government pay, but he got all the diesel and engine oil he needed. He'd hire us for the day. The driver, he got twenty *kyats*, the spare got ten and I got five. He paid for all our food. But on top of that you pick up passengers on the road, and share out the extra fares. What the owner doesn't see . . . . So if we could get more passengers on board, we'd get more 'outside' money. The driver got the biggest share, then the spare, then me with the smallest. Even so, it's better than nothing. I got at least ten or fifteen *kyats* extra 'outside money' a day, so I was on twenty or twenty-five altogether. Did we steal the government rice bags? Naah, very few people did. Well, what's the point? We got our wages from the owner. We got outside money from the passengers we picked up along the way. So that was about twenty or twenty-five *kyats* a day for me, more for the others. We didn't need to steal government property. Why take the risk? We made a decent living what with our daily wages and the extra from 'outside'. If we hadn't been able to count on the outside money, that would be a different matter. When someone's starving to death well, maybe they might consider it. What is it they say? 'You can only keep the commandments if your belly is full'.

After five years working as a spare's assistant, I met a girl in a village called Kyin which is a rest-stop between Poun-taun and Poun-nya. Daun Yin was her name. It's a pretty name, isn't it? Well, I thought it was anyway—even if it is a bit rustic—and I thought she was too. Maybe with your city eyes you wouldn't agree. She was fair-skinned and skinny, with these thick eyebrows, and just a hint of a moustache. Yes, I thought you'd be shocked. You could just see it, if you looked carefully. She was lovely. Really, I mean it. Maybe you've never seen a girl with a little moustache.

So I fell for Miss Moustachio. She was from a village called A-kyi-pan-ma-lun on the Pauk to Kyauk-tu road. I don't suppose you've heard of it. There's two villages, A-kyi-pan-ma-lun and A-nya-pan-ma-lun. She worked in the restaurant in Kyin, washing dishes, waiting tables. We'd leave Pakokku in the morning and stop off there for our evening meal. That was how she and I fell in love. It probably didn't look like that from outside.We started off just teasing. I used to say, 'I'd really like a moustache like yours', and she'd cuss me, and say 'Ach, you bloody man, you make me sick'. She never called me by my real name, she always called me 'you bloody man'. I never used to eat with the driver and the spare and the other passengers. I used to wait to eat with Daun Yin, because she'd give me loads of food, particularly if it had been a bad day for business. If there were several curries that day, she'd give me two or three behind the owner's back. She'd always come and slam the plates down with her 'Ach, you bloody man', but her eyes would be smiling and she said it in a friendly way.

I was so in love with her, more than anything. I thought I'd marry her once I got to be a spare. She used to say to me that if I did want to marry her, I had to become a spare. Well, in the end, I never did. Marry her that is. The next time we stopped in Kyin, she'd gone.

It was the last trip we did before the rains. She'd usually ask me to get her things in Pakokku—hair clips, make-up, handkerchiefs. This time she hadn't, but I knew she really liked those *hin-ngouk* flowers and she'd said to me, 'Ach, you bloody man, the *hin-ngouk* will be out on top of Poun-taun, pick me some and we'll have a salad'.

I'd bought her some presents anyway, and when we got to Poun-taun, I'd picked her some *hin-ngouk* flowers. They taste really good when they're mixed together with hot water and ground-nut flour, bean flour, sesamum, MSG and fried onions. I loved the way Daun Yin used to do them. So I filled a whole *longyi* full of flowers. Ko Thein Aung, the spare, was laughing at me: 'Hey kid, picking flowers for your girlfriend?'

It was after eight by the time we'd climbed Poun-taun and arrived in Kyin. Daun Yin was nowhere to be seen. They told me she'd run off about a month ago with a soldier from a battalion stationed at Gangaw. The battalion had been transferred to Chauk, or Yenangyaung or somewhere, and Daun Yin had gone with him.

That girl. She broke my heart. I don't know how to describe how I felt. You writers, what would you say? Devastated? I was devastated. That night was the first time I had ever got drunk. Once I was a bit tipsy, I unwrapped the flowers, and flung them away. Ko Thein Aung warned me, 'Hey kid, don't drink too much! We've still got to climb Poun-nya'. I hadn't drunk that much, just a couple of glasses of country spirit, but my head was spinning and I felt sick. I climbed onto a rice sack, pulled up a blanket and fell asleep.

Oh, remember when I said earlier that I was an assistant spare for five years? Well I forgot to tell you, that wasn't five years on the trot. I stopped working for almost a year. 'Resting'.

We left Kyin at about nine at night. I was deep in a drunken sleep. We started to climb up to the top of Poun-nya at about midnight. The wind was whistling like nobody's business. Once we'd got to the top, the alcohol had started to wear off, and I climbed in between the roof and the rice sacks. My mind was on nothing but Daun Yin. I could hear her voice, saying 'Ach, you bloody man, you make me sick' and see her bright eyes, her golden skin, her little moustache. 'What a life! What a worthless bloody life!', I thought. I'm nothing but a truck spare, and not even a *pukka* spare at that. In the trucking world, if you're not even a spare, you really are a nobody.

So I was sitting on the rice sack thinking this when we reached the top of Poun-nya. The lorry was gasping up the last stretch. I looked back across the Irrawaddy to where the lights of Chauk and Yenangyaung twinkled on the opposite bank. I've never even been there, I thought, and somewhere out there is my Daun Yin. I felt so empty. Just then I heard Ko Thein Aung shouting something but I couldn't make out what exactly through my drunken stupor. Then the passengers started to scream and I realised that we were slipping backwards. He'd had been yelling at me to go and stick the chocks under. I leapt off the truck, pulling a rice sack after me which pinned me to the ground. You should have heard the screams as the truck headed towards the edge.

Luckily, it hit a stone a few feet from the edge and stopped. But most of the passengers were hurt and the truck caught fire. As for me, I got two broken ribs and six months in hospital. I admit, it was my fault. I was so lost in thought about Daun Yin, I didn't notice we were climbing Poun-nya, and never heard Ko Thein Aung yelling at me to stick the chocks under.

That put the owner out of business, and when I came out of hospital, I was out of a job. I went back to my village and hung around until my father got me a job with U Hpo Taik, a friend of his who had a Hino truck. I had to do about seven months helping out the spare before I became a *pukka* spare. I've been a spare now for ten years, always on this route.

What did I do when I came out of hospital? Well, I hadn't got a job, so I went back to my father's house, which is in a village called Bin-gan in Myaing district, I doubt you'll know it. The area has lots of forges. They make knives, scissors, cartwheel spokes, betel cutters. My father's a blacksmith, making cartwheels. So when I went home, I helped out in the forge, but my injury from the accident meant I couldn't do much, 'cos smithying needs lots of strength. You have to stand next to the furnace all day, tempering the iron bars they use for hammering out the spokes. They can weigh eight, ten, twelve pounds, and the hammers themselves weigh ten or twelve pounds. I found I'd get short of breath after only a short while. That's why I had to go back to being a spare.

Actually, my blacksmith father isn't my real father. He's the third father I've had. You're probably thinking that means my mother's been married three times. Well you'd be wrong. If you want me to explain, I'd better tell you the whole story. My mother and father went underground to fight in the jungle. In those days it was the Red Flag Communists[1]. I was born in jungle off the road between Pa-le and Gangaw. Not long after I was born, government troops attacked the camp and my parents took me off into the jungle with their battalion to escape. We didn't have to go far to escape the government soldiers, so they took me with them. But children can get hungry and out of sorts and start to cry. So the government soldiers could often track you and ambush you. That's why sometimes, when they had to leg it, they left the children behind with the villagers.

I was left behind like that in a small village you won't have heard of, Let-pan-khin-aye, off the Gangaw road. Actually it's two villages next door to one another, Let-pan and Khin-aye but we run the two names together. Soon after I was born, the government troops attacked the village and my parents fled and left me behind with a man called U Sein. He was a carpenter. Not the sort that builds houses though. He used to make hoe-shafts and carts. One time he went into the jungle to collect wood for the shafts and bumped into my parents. They gave me to him. I never even knew the name of my real father.

I stayed with U Sein for about two years. One year he went to the Shwe-myin-tin pagoda festival in Myaing to sell his hoe and cart shafts at the market. After the festival was over, he spent the night gambling and lost all his profit. Since he was broke, on the last hand of cards, he put me up as a stake. He lost. He had to hand me over to U Htun Gyi, a blacksmith from Bin-gan. So that's how he became my third father. After that, I stayed put. Since he brought me up, I think of him as my father. Although I must have seen my first father, I wouldn't know him if I saw him again. I vaguely remember U Sein, my second father. He had a top-knot, but I don't remember anything else about him. So now do you understand what I mean by 'my third father'?

I stayed with him until I was fifteen. I passed fourth standard and then I went to work in a forge at Pakokku. From there I got a job as an assistant spare. I did that for five years, then ten years as a spare, which makes me thirty.

My wife? She's from Gyo-byone, it's a village on the Pakokku to Pauk road. You might've heard of it, since it's famous for its toddy. After I split up with Daun Yin, I wanted nothing more to do with women. I thought they were nothing but trouble. I really loved her, y'know. When she jilted me, it really hurt.

Anyway, while I was going back and forth on this road, I met Mya Shin. She sells toddy at the bus stop in Gyo-byone. Her father's a toddy collector, so she sells toddy in season, and picks tobacco at the harvest.

---

[1] The Red Flag Communists, led by Thakin Soe, were expelled from the main Communist Party of Burma (or 'White Flags') in 1946 after accusing the other leaders of taking too moderate a line. In the late 1940s, they had strongholds in the delta (Ma-U-Bin, Pyapon, Hanthawaddy), where Thakin Soe had originally gone 'underground', in Arakan, and between Pakokku and Minbu, and in the Upper Chindwin. They were one of the most militant of Burma's insurgent groups, executing villagers for allegedly collaborating with the Army and instituting forced collectivisation. Their heavy-handedness won them more intellectual than rural support. Thus they were never a major force to be reckoned with, always competing for supporters with a number of other insurgent groups. By 1970, when Thakin Soe was captured, they were reduced to approximately 200 men scattered amongst their former strongholds.

Seasonal work. I can't say I really love her. We sort of ended up together by accident.

It was the day she rode to Gangaw in our truck to buy butter beans. We smooched a bit, and on the way back, when we got to Gyo-byone, she said she didn't dare go home any more so she came on with me to Pakokku. So that's how it happened. No great romance eh? One smooch and we end up eloping.

The world's a strange place, isn't it? Daun Yin and I, we really loved one another. I loved her little moustache. I often wonder what it would have been like if we'd got married. I would have taken such great care of her. I'd have brought her *hin-ngouq* flowers to make salad everytime I came to Kyin. But it wasn't to be.

Instead, with Mya Shin . . . well, it's not that I never think about her, but it's just that she's not that interested in me either. All it took with her was a trip to Gangaw and by the time we got back, we were married in all but name. Well, of course I love her now—she's my wife, after all. I suppose I started to love her once we got married. We've got a couple of children now, and I'm a *pukka* spare.

So, that's all there is to tell. Born to a couple of insurgents, abandoned to the care of a carpenter, and lost to a blacksmith in a card game. Well, I suppose you could say that's a bit unusual. Of course, I only learnt about this later from U Htun Gyi. To be honest, I think the strangest thing about my life is my marriage. There I was, in love with Daun Yin. Even though the two of us wanted to, we never got married. Then I meet Mya Shin on the top of a truck, I fancy her a bit and the next thing I know, we're married. Fate can be so strange. Mya Shin and I had never thought about one another, but because it was written in our stars, we ended up together.

My ambition? To become a driver, and from there move up to being an owner. Just owning one truck would be enough for me. I'd like to have gone from being an assistant spare to being an owner. And Mya Shin would rather be an owner's wife than a toddy seller. She says she's never travelled in the front seat of a car. She's always saying to me that if I was an owner, she could ride in the front seat of our own car, and go and show off to the girls from her village. So that's what I'm working towards. I'm still young. It could still happen.

[November 1987]

11

MISS PALEFACE

I met her in a town in one of the states of the Union. She must have been just over twenty-five at the time though her fresh, fair skin, slim figure suggested she was younger. She had a girl's body but her face was serious like that of an older woman. Her eyes were bright and her lips drew a straight line under her sharp nose. She spoke quietly and deliberately. At her age she should have been smiling and laughing, teasing her girlfriends and singing. But she didn't look as though this was the case. Her face was stern and never cracked a smile. Her eyes were serious and she spoke softly, never laughing or exclaiming out loud. She seemed to be in deep thought. Her name was Hpyu Hpyu but she said her friends used to call her Paleface.

I met her in surroundings which seemed entirely at odds with her appearance. She would not have been out of place in a grand hall draped with curtains. Instead, I met her in the hot dusty surroundings of a sawmill. All around, the workers were carrying planks, operating the saws, shouting and swearing at one another. I was astonished to see such a delicate looking girl working amongst all these rough men. When she turned up on her bicycle with a Kachin shoulder bag slung over her back, I felt uneasy. It seemed to me that she had no place here, and that this work should be left to men.

Are you surprised to see someone like me running the business, *Saya*? Well someone's got to do it and there's no-one else at home who could. I've got no brothers to take it on now that my father's not here. Our family is entirely girls and since I'm the oldest daughter and my sisters are all still at school, it's up to me.

My mother can't take it on because she's not been well and she needs to stay home and do the cooking. Even if she wasn't sick, I don't think she'd be cut out for this kind of work. Somehow I don't see her out here with the workers in the heat and the dirt and the noise. To tell you the truth, I don't think this is the sort of work women should be expected to do. You have to clamber over the logs and you're surrounded all day by men. Ideally it should be left to the men.

But you asked me why I'm doing it. It'll take a while to explain. I've been running this timber business. Well to be more accurate, this sawmill. Timber business sounds a bit grand. After all, all you need for a sawmill is a couple of circular saws and the facilities to cut up a few logs at a time. Anyway, I've been running this sawmill for about the last eight years, since I was sixteen or seventeen. You're surprised? Well don't be. I didn't get the job because of any relevant expertise, it just turned out this way. You could say it was God's will. That's right, I'm a Christian, Baptist. So were both my parents. My father was the manager of a government sawmill before he met my mother.

My father was transferred here and arrived a single man. He met my mother here—she was born here—and they got married. Then he was accused of stealing logs and got the sack and was sent to jail. My mother says he had nothing to do with it, it was his staff who were stealing the logs. But she might just be saying that out of loyalty to my father. All I know is what she's told me.

I think I was about seven when my father went to jail. It was quite a serious case of stealing government property and he was given four or five years. When he got out of jail, I was already a teenager. I might have even been in ninth standard.

Something strange happened to him when he went into jail. Before then, he'd been a cheerful man. He'd always treated me like a grown-up. If there was something I didn't understand, he'd explain it to me carefully. I used to like reading and he would tell me which books I should read and we would discuss them. I was a little bookworm and before I was ten I'd polished off your translations of 'War and Peace' and so on. I didn't understand Tolstoy's message, but I enjoyed the story. Natasha in the story was about my age wasn't she? That was one reason why I enjoyed the book. If I didn't understand what was going on, my father would explain it to me. It was him that told me about it in the first place.

My father was really my first teacher. He taught me how to read. He broadened my horizons. But when he came out of jail, he'd stopped reading books and started drinking. He'd been a cheerful smiling man but now he just sat around looking blank and miserable as if he hated life. He broke off contact with his old friends and stopped going out. As soon as he got up in the morning, he'd have a drink and then start arguing with the rest of the family. I think prison had turned him into a bitter twisted man, *Saya*. To him, everything was wrong, people, the world. He had been an eternal optimist but now he was a total pessimist. I wondered how he could have changed so completely. Could I ask you something? Is it possible that a change in environment and surroundings can change someone's character so that it is diametrically opposed to what it was? I realise it's a big question. Philosophers and scientists still haven't got an answer to the relationship between man and his environment, have they? But I'm asking because of what happened to my father. He'd been such a calm, composed, gentle man. I might be a little biased because he was my father, but I'd always thought him the most sensible, brave and strong man I had ever met in my life. In fact I always used to look on him as the model for the type of man I'd want to marry.

I hardly recognised him when he was released. He had become confused, cowardly, weak-willed. He couldn't cope any more. Before, he'd been prepared to sacrifice everything for the good of his wife and family. Now he was selfish. Previously he'd been able to survive whatever life threw up at him. Now he was a coward. That was why he started to drink and bully the family. I can't understand why he changed so totally. That's why I was asking you that question about man and his environment. If you don't want to answer it, don't worry. But certainly my opinion of my father changed as completely as he'd changed himself.

While this was happening, our family's fortunes started to fare badly. The sawmill business which my mother had set up using money given to her by her parents started to go downhill. We had problems with the workers, the logs started to disappear, the machines were breaking down. Whatever could go wrong, did go wrong. There was no-one to take charge. My mother couldn't do it. She asked one of her younger brothers to help out but he just took the money and walked out. My father started drinking the moment he rolled out of bed and didn't give a damn about his family. He wandered off whenever he felt like it. Once he went off to Mandalay and didn't come back for a couple of months. He went to Taunggyi for over a month. He stopped bothering about his appearance. As they say nowadays he'd turned into a bum.

There was no-one left to look after us or who we could rely on to take charge of the sawmill. I was taking my tenth standard exam at the time. Luckily I passed it first time round and got three distinctions. I could have gone to university with marks like that but we didn't have the money to send me there. Unless we could get the sawmill rolling again, we couldn't afford it. I was desperate to go, particularly when I knew all the other students were going. I was certainly bright enough, and I was ambitious. I wanted to be a doctor or a lady engineer, or a scientist or even a literary critic. I'd read about Madame Curie the scientist when I was little. She was poor but she'd got where she wanted to by working hard. I took encouragement from that. You probably think I was silly, don't you? But in those days, I'd read books and daydream like that.

So I was begging my mother to let me go to university. But she said she couldn't afford it. I was furious with both my parents and went into a massive sulk for three or four days. I stopped eating and shut myself in my bedroom and cried my heart out. I decided life wasn't even worth living if I couldn't go to university.

One day when the university term was about to begin, my father said he was going to Taunggyi again, but he didn't come home. Not after one month. Not after two. Not after three months. My mother and the rest of the family started to get worried and went searching in the towns where he usually went, like Mandalay, Taunggyi and Lashio. But there was no trace of him. His friends said they didn't know where he was. He seemed to have vanished off the face of the earth. To this day, we still don't know if he's alive or dead. My mother went crazy after waiting all that time for him to come back.

Think about it, Saya. My father had gone away, no-one knew where, and simply vanished off the face of the earth. My mother was suffering from clinical depression. I had four sisters younger than me. If I didn't assume responsibility for the family, who would?

That's when I tried to get the sawmill back into business again. I got in touch with the workers and the machine-operators. They used to look down on me for being a woman. Some of them even tried to tease me and touch me up. But I don't tolerate any of that and I lose my temper quickly. If any of them try it on too much, they get a slap from me.

Look at how I live now, Saya. This sawmill is about three miles from town. I have to come and go by bike. I have a quick breakfast of fried rice at 5.30 and then cycle over here to let the workers in. I have to manage them, tell them which logs to use for which jobs, what size of planks to cut and so on. Then I measure the output and calculate the tonnage. We take a short break for lunch and then carry on until half past four. Then I cycle home. That's what I do every day, in all seasons, riding my bike to work and back, except when there aren't any logs to process.

How did I learn to run a sawmill? Experience, Saya, that's all. I've always been quick on the uptake. I learn something once and it sticks with me. Like riding a bike. Other people take about a week to learn. I mastered it in three or four days. Other people need to read something four or five times to learn it by heart. I can manage with just reading it twice. I'm the same with songs. I can sing them after I've only heard them a couple of times.

When I started off working here, I didn't know how to calculate tonnage. A tonne of sawn timber is 7200 running feet. But you need first to work out how many running feet there are in a tonne of various sizes of timber like six by six, five by five and so on. I bought a ready reckoner which gives the figures. If I didn't understand, I'd ask the workers who did. That's how I learnt to calculate tonnage. And the rest of it isn't difficult. It's easy enough to run a sawmill provided your workers know the rules and you make sure they stick to them.

How do I feel about doing this now? I'm enjoying it. I reckon I've turned the business round. But I'm not enjoying it simply because I'm making money. It's because I've been successful in getting to grips with the work. When I started, there were all those people who said that I would run the mill into the ground, that I wouldn't have a clue. I've been able to show them that I can do it and make a success of it.

I've been running the sawmill going on eight years. My sisters have all got an education. My mother and my youngest sister are still at home, she's doing tenth standard. The rest of them are at university.

Do I ever think about what? Marriage? I haven't done so far, and I'm not sure that I ever will. When I look at what happened to my father, it leads me to take a pretty dim view of men. If my father, whom I always had the highest possible opinion of, whom I thought was a model father, if he could change so much, what hope is there for the rest of them? You don't need to be a man to be brave and determined. Some women are smart enough to be like that, and so are some men. Some aren't. Maybe I'll get married if I meet a man I admire enough. But unless I meet him soon, I'll stay a spinster.

Love is like a flower, it blooms only in season, doesn't it? Out of season, you don't see any flowers, do you?

[November 1989]

12

THIS LAND, THIS EARTH

His name was Khin Maung Aye. He was tall, brown-skinned and sturdy with thick hair that curled down his neck but was tousled and unoiled, rather than slicked down. He had wide-set eyes and white sparkling teeth. His face was good-humoured and he had a constant grin. From time to time he hummed a bar or two of a song by Khaing Htoo. I met him 1,200 feet under the ground in a silver mine near Namtu-Bawdwin. He was dressed in full miner's gear with a carbide lamp strapped to his forehead. He carried a pick. A trolley for the rocks sat nearby. At 1,200 feet under, I was having difficulty breathing but Khin Maung Aye was speaking normally, as if he was breathing fresh air. He could even manage a song.

You might be surprised to hear I'm originally from Seik-hpyu. I'm sure you'll know it, on the west bank of the Irrawaddy where the Yaw creek empties out. My family weren't workers—they were just paddy farmers. Actually, even paddy-farmers is too fancy a name for them. They were only cultivators. There isn't any good paddy land around Seik-hpyu. There aren't even the sort of upland fields where you could grow peanuts, corn or sesamum. All we had was the land which the river left behind in the dry season, the silt islands in the Yaw creek, where you could grow onions, garlic, tomatoes, mouli, cauliflower. Mostly we just grew onions and garlic.

During my grandparents time, we had a few fields over in Seik-hkun. But my father pawned the land and lost it, and we had to go over to farming onions and tomatoes on the land left in the Yaw stream once the water level dropped. We did that until I was about ten years old. When onions fetched a high price in those days, we could get by. They sent me off to school in Seik-hpyu. I did about seven years in school. During the school term, my father used to send me to live with his younger sister in Seik-hpyu. She was a midwife. He couldn't afford to give her any rent for me, so he just used to send her a sack of onions or some oil or some rice, and even that not regularly. But more often than not, he sent something back with me as a present, when school re-opened. Since my aunt's husband was a pharmacist, a 'compounder', and he used to make a bit extra by giving people injections, their family lived quite comfortably anyway. Also, I used to help out with the housework, doing the cooking and fetching water, and accompanying my aunt if she had to go and attend births in nearby villages. Nothing too strenuous.

After I'd failed the eighth standard exam a couple of times, I dropped out of school. I went back to the village to help my father with the cultivating. But that year there was unseasonably heavy rain and the Yaw stream filled up, flooding our plots, so that we lost our whole crop, and didn't even get enough back for next year's seed.

That year things were very tough for us. Next year's seed belonged to the people whom we borrowed the fertiliser from. If a cultivator's crop fails one year, it's impossible for him to recover the next. Even if he's successful regularly, he still has to pay back his debts and buy his next year's seed—it's like paying off your debts from your last existence. If the crop fails just one year, you're stuck. You can't afford to pay back your debts and you can't borrow for the next year's crop. My father was left without a livelihood. What's more, the stream changed course and we were left without our usual plots of silt. All that was left was the dry banks which made cultivation much more difficult. It needed more fertiliser. The spits on the other bank had already been taken over by people so we had nowhere left to farm. My father lost heart and gave up. He decided to move to Seik-hpyu in the hope of finding a job. Once my father decided to jack in cultivating we had nothing to do. I hadn't even passed eighth standard. I must have been about fifteen or sixteen. My father said he was going off to look for work and headed off to Chauk and Lan-ywa. There was oil in Chauk and there was an old oil-field in Lan-ywa so he thought he might be able to get a job in those places. He was wrong, though. There was very little oil left in Lan-ywa, and it was difficult to get a job in Chauk unless you came from round there. There wasn't even enough work for the locals.

My father came back from Chauk and Lan-ywa even more miserable. He looked absolutely exhausted. At the time, since I was the oldest boy, I was selling water around the neighbourhood. It was only a small neighbourhood though, and there was no way doing that could earn us enough to stay fed and clothed. Most of the people there collected their own water anyway. The only houses who bought from me were the ones where the local officials lived. My mother had to go out to work as well, washing clothes for one of those houses. She brought home about a hundred *kyats* a month. Even though we worked hard, it wasn't enough for our family. There were seven of us in all. We lived in a shack in my aunt's compound so accommodation wasn't the problem but food and drink was. We felt we could only stay there for a short time, otherwise we'd be a burden.

Although my father couldn't find a permanent job in Chauk or Lan-ywa, he used to bring home a little bit of money from time to time. He said he earned it from labouring down at the jetty in Chauk. But it wasn't a regular income.

We'd been living like this in Seik-hpyu for about a year, when one day my father was arrested and went to jail. We found out it was because he'd been mixed up with a gang who were stealing steel pipes from the oil fields. After that, all the household had to rely on was the money my mother and I earned. One of my younger sisters who used to go and take food to my father in jail in Magwe got married to one of the prison warders she met there. It may sound strange, but much as I loved my little sister, I was delighted when she got married, more pleased than most brothers would be to discover their sisters had got themselves a man. It meant that now I had one less mouth to feed. My little sister stayed in touch, and when my mother went to Magwe, my sister would send back clothes and food for the children back at home.

I was still having trouble earning enough for us all to keep body and soul together. I wondered if I should do what my father had done and break the law to earn some money. I knew a lot of people who did it. It would have been the easy way out. But I didn't want to end up like that.

It wasn't because these things belonged to the government or anything. I just didn't want to get caught. I didn't want to get a criminal record. And you can't do that kind of thing for the whole of your life. So I steered clear of all that.

At about that time, I bumped into a friend who said he'd got some contacts in Namtu-Bawdwin and he was off to look for a job up there. Did I want to come along and keep him company? He'd never been up there before and he didn't want to go on his own because he wasn't sure what kind of people he'd find. I checked with my mother and set off with him for Namtu.

I hadn't travelled much. The furthest I'd been up till then was Magwe. Places like Rangoon and Mandalay were just names to me. I had no idea where they were even. All I had was a shoulder bag with two changes of clothing and a hundred *kyats*. We went from Chauk to Mandalay and then on through Lashio to Namtu. In Mandalay we had to spend the night sleeping in the station because we didn't know anyone there. A hotel was well out of our league.

Once we got to Namtu, we didn't walk straight into a job, of course. We had to stay for a while with my friend's uncle. It was a good two or three months, and we soon ran out of money. Although we were staying for free in this man's quarters, we had to buy our own food. The entire room was only about ten foot by twelve. Luckily he wasn't married. The three of us would sleep in there, huddled round a stove if the weather was cold. We hadn't brought any blankets with us, so I had to buy a Chinese quilt. Food consisted of Shan sticky rice, *peh-byouk* boiled beans and *mohnyin* pickled mustard leaves. Generally we just ate our rice with pickle, chili and salt. Up in Shan States you can't always get the beans and pulses to make *peh-byouk*, so they eat *peh-pouk* made out of fermented soya beans. Once in a while, we could afford it. Whatever else you want to say about it, there's more food up here than down where I'd come from.

There was a library in Bawdwin which the workers had opened, and I used to go there a lot, because I enjoyed books. I would help them out in the library if there was something that needed doing, and by doing that I got friendly with the men in charge who used to give me food and then got me a job there, lending out the books. The workers were on shifts. When they were on the night shift, they'd come back up in the morning and sleep. When they were on the day shift, they'd be too tired to come and help out in the library. So when they found me and discovered I was interested in books, they put me in charge. My friend had got a job in the mine by then. He got it through his uncle.

I worked in the library for about six months, until the mine needed new workers and some of the miners went and spoke on my behalf. The boss took pity on me and gave me a job working on the surface.

Surface workers don't get to go down the mines, because they aren't properly trained yet. Usually they have to move the earth around, and pile up the earth that is left over once the ore has been extracted. In fact, that kind of work should really be done by machines, but this mine doesn't have many cranes and bulldozers and the machinery we do have is always breaking down, so we have to use manpower instead to carry the earth around.

The slag that is left once the metal has been extracted has to be put on a heap on a designated part of the hill-side. Once, while we were using a bulldozer to move the earth, it started to roll down the hill and went into the ravine, and we lost both the driver and the bulldozer. I was on the bulldozer that day, and when I started to feel it sliding out of control, I jumped out. If I hadn't, I'd have gone into the ravine with it.

Surface workers got about thirteen *kyats* a day, which wasn't bad pay for those days, especially since there was nothing to spend it on round there. Apart from food, I didn't have anything to spend my wages on. There was no cinema, and nowhere else to go, so once work was over, all you could do was go for a walk, or depending on the season, go and watch football. Or, in my case, you could go and work as a volunteer in the library.

I worked above ground for about two years, until a job came free and they promoted me to miner. A miner got about sixteen *kyats* a day on average. You can see what it's like down here. When I first went underground, I was quite scared. We went down by elevator. This mine has sixteen levels, and the lowest one is about 1,400 feet below ground. It's a strange feeling when you first start working this far beneath the surface. You can't get enough air to breathe and the air down here isn't clean at all. Sometimes the smell of earth and metal and oil gets quite unpleasant. I got used to it after a while. When you first go down, you can't see very well in the dark and you trip over in the mud. You have to wear a lamp on your head so that you can mine and carry the ore around. The mattock and the pick-axe tied to your waist weigh you down. You have to move the rocks you've dynamited and mined and load them onto the trolley and push it back to the elevator.

Have we had any big cave-ins? So far we haven't. Sometimes the walls fall in and block the way but it's not actually a landslide collapsing, so you can clear it away.

I've only been home once since I started working here. My father had been let out. He was a broken man, and told me that all he wanted to do was leave the town and go back to working in the fields. His troubles had all started once he left the countryside for the town. But it was difficult to see what he could do if he went back to the countryside, since he had no land, and no bullocks or anything. So I told him I would save up and buy him a plot of land. I've been saving up for a while. I've told myself I won't go back until I can afford to buy him a plot. I should be able to manage it in one or two years time—so long as the price of land doesn't go up. Do I have a girlfriend? Yes, I do. She's the daughter of one of the other miners. She sells vegetables in the morning market. But we can't get married at the moment. Most miners are young men, and live by themselves. It's exhausting work, so it's only really suitable for young men. Once a miner gets to be over thirty, he can't take the strain. Few miners want to go down the mines once they're married. Mostly they work on the surface, or get another job somewhere else. I've wondered whether I should carry on working in the mine once I get married. But for the time-being I've got to carry on to save up for a plot of land for my parents. Then I'll have to save up to get married. I've already saved enough for a gold chain.

I enjoy reading. Sometimes I think to myself that if I could write, I'd write my life-story. It would be all about how my grandfather owned his own land, and was a farmer, and how my father slid from being a cultivator, to a casual labourer, and got into black market steel pipes. Then there's me, a working miner. It would be a tale of working life in Burma, a story about the lives of the farmers who become workers. But since I'm not a writer, I can't put it down on paper. The point of the story would be to show how the system of land ownership turned my father and his family into landless peasants and forced them to be workers. But no matter where we ended up, or what our lives turn into, we are still kept alive by Mother Earth. That would be the theme. You can see how I've arrived at it. In my father and my grandfather's time, they used to till the earth to keep themselves alive. Nowadays, I descend into the earth and dig it to earn a living. So no matter what you do, whether you're a farmer or a worker, Mother Earth feeds you. I often think to myself that that is the sort of book I would write if I knew how.

Although I can't write books, I've had a go at writing poetry. Here's a poem I've written about the mine. It's not written down on paper. I wrote it here on the wall of the mine with a piece of chalk. I'll read it to you by the light of my carbide lamp. You'd better just listen, because you won't be able to read it.

[December 1988]

13

WHAT NEXT?

He was just over five foot six with wide shoulders and a broad chest. His thick black hair curled around the nape of his neck. His forehead was neither too wide nor too narrow and his eyes were wide-set with thick eyebrows. He had masculine good looks with a square jaw and a moustache. He told me he was twenty-five. On first appearances, you would have said he looked like the film star Htay Win. I met him twice. The first time was on board a prawn fishing boat owned by a co-operative which was on the way from Kawthaung to Mergui. He was an assistant Captain. He was wearing a denim jacket and jeans and was never without a 555 cigarette. Round his neck, a gold necklace. On his wrist, the latest Seiko Quartz watch. The second time, we were in a dirty teashop on the outskirts of Mergui. He was no longer the stylish young man of yesteryear. He looked rather shabby and was wearing a faded T-shirt and Elephant-Star brand flip flops. 555 cigarettes were beyond his means now. Instead his hand held the butt-end of an extinguished cheroot. His hair was dull and lifeless. I was shocked by the transformation which had taken place in less than eighteen months.

I was hoping it was you *Saya*. I saw someone walking past while I was in the teashop, and I thought that it looked like you. Then someone else said your name and I was sure. That was why I called after you. I wasn't sure if I ought to, because I thought that you mightn't recognise me or you might think that I was trying something on. After all, I look a bit different to the way I did when we last met. So I was worrying that if I shouted out to you you might get the wrong end of the stick.

Anyway, *Saya*, I've got a lot of things on my mind that I want to tell you about. I want to tell you the story of my life. Last time, when we were on the trawler, you only got half the story. I didn't have the chance to tell you as much as I wanted because I was on duty. If you remember, it was really windy at the time and there was a heavy sea. Besides, since then, my life's been turned around. So there's loads more I want to tell you.

That's why I called out after you. That's why I took the risk. I'm so pleased you can sit down here with me and have a cup of tea and hear what I've got to say.

Are you surprised to see how I've changed, *Saya*? But I should think someone like you would understand that that's the way it goes. Life's forever changing. Life's like a bird really, up and down, up and down. You can't keeping going up forever can you? Sometimes you have to dive.

Not that I'm that bothered. Look at me. I'm just a country bumpkin really. Look where I've got to already. I reckon I'm still ahead. I was from a small town. I didn't even make it through high school. My father was just a cleaner at a British cemetery. Not even a watchman. Just a cleaner. The watchman at the cemetery had his own house. The gardeners too. Not my Dad though, he was just one of the two cleaners. Sweeping up the rubbish.

Before that Dad was a farmer. Not with his own land mind you. He used to hire himself out to other farmers. Then when there was all the insurgency in the countryside, he took whatever job he could get. Like, there's salt-pans round Pa-nga. They make salt there from the sea water. They use the sun to evaporate off the water. But they can only do it in the dry season, not in the monsoon. And there's insurgents round there too. So Dad went and got a job at the rubber plantations instead. He was collecting latex from the trees. You know, a rubber-tapper.

Then the rubber plantations got nationalised by the government. Dad got the sack. The rubber plantations were owned by a company, and the company employed the workers. When the government took over, the workers got the sack. Except the government didn't take over directly, because the plantation was controlled jointly by the owner and the co-operative. Look, to be honest, I'm not too sure what I'm talking about. I was only two or three at the time anyway. I don't know much about it all, except what Mum and Dad told me. But I do know Dad lost his job. That's when he started work at the cemetery in Thanbyuzayat. As a cleaner. One of his friends was already there working as a cleaner. He'd told the boss that he couldn't manage on his own, and he managed to get Dad a job helping him. We had to move into the town when he got the job.

Before that we'd been living out in the countryside. We had to find a place in town, once Dad got the cleaning job. There was a building which had two flats and Dad and us got to stay in one of them. He worked ten years in the cemetery as a cleaner. I grew up there. In the evenings, we'd go around with Dad and help him sweep up the leaves and light bonfires. We'd sweep up the cheroot stubs and the rubbish which the visitors had left behind. The gardeners would look after the flowers. It wasn't frightening, not like a Burmese boneyard. The cemetery was full of flowers, crosses, mausoleums. They don't use it any more for burying people. It's a war cemetery. It's full of British soldiers who were killed in the war.

When Dad died, I was fourteen. We lost his salary, but we still got a pension. A cleaner's pension wasn't much though, not enough for us to live on. And we had to move out of the cemetery. We moved into one of the squatters' huts nearby. My mum started flogging fried snacks round the neighbourhood for a living. She'd buy them from a wholesaler, for a hundred items a time. Sale or return. She'd make a profit of five or ten *pyas* a piece. She would be making ten or fifteen *kyats* profit a day.

I had to drop out of school in eighth standard. We couldn't afford for me to go on, the books and stuff. My mother had to put food before learning. And I had to drop out so my little brothers and sisters could continue. My Mum couldn't afford to pay for all of us. I was about fifteen or sixteen at the time.

One day I met this fisherman from over in Zee-byu-thaung. He took me back there and showed me the cooperative. The fishing industry was picking up so I got a job quite easily, going out to sea and helping with the nets. When the rainy season was over, the south-westerly winds would die down and the north-easterlies would pick up and then we could go out to sea. We used to stay out for ten or fifteen days. Sometimes we'd be back sooner, within three or four days. It would depend how quickly we caught the fish. The more we caught, the quicker we'd get back to shore.

Usually we went out in *doan* boats. We'd take all our ice and food with us. When we got out to sea, we'd drop the nets and then haul them back in when they were full of fish. It's an exhausting job. You're working in the wind and the full glare of the sun, sometimes all day long. Putting the nets out, hauling them in and sticking the fish in the ice chest. Sometimes we fished at night too. Once we'd caught all we could carry, we'd turn for home. I did that for about five years.

Later on, black boats started running round there. You know what I mean by black boats don't you? Illegal motor boats which they use for smuggling. One time I got a job with one going to Penang. I went during the monsoon. There was a strong wind and torrential rain. But that was why we went. During the monsoon, the smugglers have no problem with the Navy patrols because they only go out when the weather's good. In the dry season though, the smugglers' boats might get picked up by a Navy patrol boat. Then you'd get arrested and charged and the cargo would be confiscated. It's quite difficult to get away. A boat that was with us tried it once, and the patrol boat shot at them and holed the boat and it sank. Another time we were caught in a storm just west of Mergui and spent several days adrift at sea. A couple of sailors died.

It's dangerous work, making the trips to Penang. There's so much stress what with worrying about the Navy patrol boats and the storms and the *Pashu* Malay pirates. They don't just steal your boat. They chop your head off and throw your body into the sea.

For the black-marketeers who were putting in the money, it's a good business. Just one trip can make you a big profit. Some Burmese, if they don't have the money themselves, they'll go to a rich trader in Penang or Thailand and ask for a motor boat. Then they'll split the profits. If a smuggler tries to pull a fast one and doesn't hand over the share of the profits and the boat, the investors send foreign assassins after him to knock him off. One boat I went on, the Burmese man had tried to steal the boat and the cargo. They had him killed.

So smuggling goods from Penang to Burma is all well and good for the businessmen but there isn't as much in it for us workers as you might think. I did alright. I got to travel and earned enough to keep me going. But it was dangerous work.

I did about three or four trips before giving up and returning to town. I'd earned enough to get some money to my mother for her to invest. It wasn't much. From three or four trips, I earned about four or five thousand *kyats*. But it was enough for her to open a grocery stall near the market. I used to help out from time to time.

Meanwhile I bumped into a gem-dealer who took me off to Khamti near the Indian border, to do some digging. I worked in some of the gem tracts like Bogadaw which are quite well-known. But I didn't make as much as I'd thought I would. Particularly if you consider how exhausting the work was. The one good thing was that the owner of the mine gave us our food for free. But it was hardly worth it just for that.

In the end, all I got for my trouble was malaria. I spent about a year in Khamti, digging for gems on and off, and going down with malaria. I couldn't send my mother any money home, and I didn't get to see her during all that time. All I had was the odd letter telling me that she was still alright.

So after that, I gave up and went off to Tamu and from there to Morre and Prinaga, doing some smuggling. I had no money of my own, so I was hiring myself out. I was a carrier. For example, we used to smuggle bikes in from Bangladesh. We'd ride them down the side-roads in the jungle so as to avoid the customs posts on the way to Tamu. In Tamu, we'd drop the bicycle off with the merchant in Tahan market and he'd pay us the going rate for carrying it. Then we'd set off again. When smuggling bicycles was profitable we'd do that. Otherwise we'd bring in Indian *longyis* or make-up, or betel ingredients or bits of machinery.

During that time, someone told me sandalwood was a good business to be in so I went out into the jungle to look for some. But I couldn't find any and anyway it was exhausting in the jungle and there was too much malaria. So I went back to being a carrier.

I earned just about enough to live on. Certainly I never made much money out of it. I did it for about a year between Morre and Tamu before I gave up and went back home. I'd managed to save about two or three thousand *kyats*. Once I got home, I kept getting malaria so I couldn't get a proper job. I spent most of the money I'd saved on medicine.

I wasn't too happy that I'd had to spend all my savings. My mother was getting old and she wasn't too well either, she had some sort of women's troubles. My little sister was quite clever and had got a place at college in Moulmein. I wanted to make sure she could stay in college. She was the first one in our family ever to get through high school. She wanted to stay on and so did my mother and all our relatives. But none of us could afford to give her more than moral support.

So I went back to the co-operative at Zee-byu-thaung where I'd worked before and got myself a job on the prawn boat which went from Mergui to Kawthaung. The government would buy up prawns which were over four inches long from the co-operative in Kawthaung and the Zee-byu-thaung cooperative would export them through Mergui. Anything less than four inches the government would reject because it's not export quality.

The co-operative had its own boats and it would also hire them from outside if they didn't have enough. I started off on board one of the co-operative's boats. I was crewing, dealing with the ropes and putting down the gangplank and so on. Just usual crew-member's duties. I did that for about four or five years. Then they promoted me to assistant captain but I hadn't got the certificate for it. I was only working on a provisional basis. I started to learn about the wind and the currents and how to navigate. I already knew a lot about the wind and the currents between

Kawthaung and Mergui because I'd been doing that route for so many years. So I knew where the islands and the rocks and the reefs were already although I didn't know how to find them on the map. I wanted to make it to Ship's Captain. But I needed to get the certificate and pass the exams. I reckoned that once I passed the exams, I could marry my girlfriend. She lives in Mergui. She's a waitress in a coffee shop. I met her in the shop and she used to ask me to get her things from Kawthaung and that's how we got to know one another.

But things have a way of not working out don't they? I had it all planned out. I'd pass the exams and get my certificate and then I'd be able to get married. An assistant captain only earns five hundred *kyats* a month. A qualified captain earns double that. But you've got to pass those exams. So I was trying to get there.

But all my dreams went down the drain. I still don't know what happened for sure. About six months after I met you that first time, they closed down the prawn fisheries co-operative. The trawlers stopped work and I lost my job as assistant captain. They gave me a redundancy payoff, three months salary. Hardly enough to be going on with is it? That's how I've ended up stranded here. The money's long gone.

I've heard they're looking for sailors in Kuwait. So I've come into Mergui to register at the labour office. It'd be great if I could get the job. I'm not afraid of hard work. I'm not bothered if the job's long hours. I'll do anything, providing it's a good job. I'm not worried. After all, they say all labour is dignified. So I'll do whatever I can get.

Still, I don't know whether I'll get this Kuwait job. If I don't—well, we'll see. That's life isn't it? If I don't get it, who knows where I'll end up next?

[March 1989]

14

A SNAPSHOT ON SAGAING HILLS

I used to run into him whenever I visited the Sagaing hills, first at Padamya Pagoda, then Lwan Pagoda, then at Ponnyashin Pagoda and the Thirty Caves. Sometimes I'd bump into him at a scenic viewpoint in the woods. Generally I met him at Padamya, although he moved on later to other pagodas nearby. His name was Maung Kyaw Win. I put him at around thirty. Since we were walking on the Sagaing Hills, I never saw him in shoes. On his head he wore an old 'Yamaha' cap. His clothes were quite scruffy, an old shirt and a shabby Shwebo-Seik-hkun longyi, *which had faded until the checks were no longer visible and you could only see the colour. He had a camera slung around his neck, and a shoulder bag for his flash gun.*

If a visitor caught his eye, he would come hurrying over, humming and when he reached the pilgrims he would ask them 'Would you like your picture taken, brother? We can develop it on-the-spot. You'll have a colour souvenir of your trip within five minutes'. In particular, he'd hang around the couples, following close behind them, and begging them to have their picture taken. They would submit. Sometimes he would ask a group of girls. They needed no persuasion. Singly, in pairs, threesomes, or in a group, they would all pose for the camera. When he met me, his entreaties were in vain, but he seemed happy enough just to tell me his life story. You could call it 'The Tale of an Odinary Photographer'.

I haven't been doing this photography thing for very long. It can't be more than five or six years. You couldn't really call me a professional photographer, I'm more like someone who just takes photographs. Proper photographers have to acquire certain skills, don't they? They need to know how to set the camera, how to check the exposure meter, how to develop film and print it. Even focussing the camera and setting the aperture requires experience. After all, photography is an art form like you were saying. But you'd know more about that than me. When you're taking pictures of the scenery, you mustn't spoil the natural beauty of the scene. You've got to expose it properly, get the picture in the viewfinder, check the composition. That's the sort of thing only a real photographer knows how to do. I don't understand any of that. I just point and shoot.

How did I become a photographer? It came about by accident really. To tell you the truth, I've had very little experience with cameras. I didn't even see one until I was quite old. When I first saw one, I was scared of it. I was living in a monastery at the time, and they took me to a photographer's studio and the man had a tripod camera and he went underneath this big black hood and fired off the camera with a flash—I was terrified.

I was scared when I saw the camera because I was wondering what was going to come out of it. I thought maybe it was going to shoot bullets at me like a gun. Although I knew that this thing was responsible for taking photographs, I had no idea how it worked. So when I saw this man fiddling about under the big black hood behind the camera, I was thinking, 'Uh-oh, what's he up to?' I was scared, just a peasant boy fresh from the jungle. It wasn't just that I'd never seen a camera before. Where I was born we never even saw tripods or anything.

Where was I born? . . . . Not far from here, it's a village called Wachet. You can get to it by following this ridge for about four or five miles towards Mingun.

My father 'caught swallows' for a living. Well, what we call swallows round here, because of the way they're shaped, you people in Rangoon would call sampans. Like in the song. You know the one I mean? So my father was a swallow ferryman, between Mandalay Mayan-gyan jetty and Mingun. But I don't come from a long line of ferrymen. His father, my grandfather, was a farmer. He grew sesamum and groundnuts on land between here and Monywa, and sometimes he climbed trees to collect toddy. But when he couldn't afford to be a Southerner any more, he became a Northerner. You look confused *Saya*! You see, a Southerner farms his own land—a Northerner can't afford his own land and rents himself out as a labourer. Like a rice paddy coolie.

During the war, my grandfather came and hid out in the Sagaing Hills. Because of the disturbances, the countryside round him was full of bandits, so he fled here. But when he got here, he had no work, because a farmer can only work when he's got fields and here in the Sagaing Hills he had no land. So he caught himself a swallow and started to row a sampan. But what kind of a sampan-rower does a farmer make? A farmer is only used to steering bullocks and ploughing fields. He can't hold an oar. He turned the boat over once, said he was lucky not to drown. After the war, my grandfather carried on rowing and didn't go back to the land. He made a living as a sampan-rower over in Mingun. My father followed in his footsteps, and so did I. First I went to school in the monastery in Wa-chet village. I learnt the prayers, and the blessings, and the stories of Buddha's inner and outer victories. After that I left the monastery and went out and worked as a sampan-rower.

Why didn't I carry on at school? Well, my father went out in his swallow when he was drunk and turned the boat over and drowned. After that, I had no choice. When my father drowned, he left behind a wife and children. I was the oldest, I must have been about twelve, so I had to get a job and look after my family. But what could I do? Nothing. I had no skills, so all I could do was take over his sampan.

You don't have to be big or strong to row a sampan. Getting the rhythm right is the most important thing. Dipping the oars into the water and pulling them out again, in-out, in-out, is only tiring for people who don't know how to row. If you know what you're doing, it's not tiring at all. You just have to know the way to go, because if you don't, you'll be worn out. You need to know about the currents, and you need to understand a bit about the winds too. If you haven't sussed out the currents, you can row with all your might and never get anywhere. And sometimes if the wind's not in the right direction, you can row and row and all you'll get is tired. I often used to go out in the boat with my father before he died, so I already knew a bit about it.

When my father died, we still had the swallow. I used it to ferry people between Mayan-gyan jetty and Mingun. It wasn't too bad—I could just about keep our family fed and clothed on what I earned. But that was in the old days of course. Nowadays it wouldn't be the case. In those days though, our income equalled our expenses. So we managed like this, until one day I turned the boat over and nearly drowned.

At the time I wasn't carrying any passengers, just me. There was a strong wind blowing off Sagaing Hills, and the ferrymen who were on the Mayan-gyan side couldn't cross back, so they had to sleep the night on that side. All except for me. I set off back on my own because I didn't want to stay. No sooner had I got forty or fifty yards away from the shore, the wind got up. At first nothing happened, but as I kept on rowing and rowing, the waves started to get bigger and bigger. I hadn't been scared to start off with, but the bigger the waves got, the more frightened I was.

So I tried to turn round and go back to Mayan-gyan jetty, but I couldn't turn the boat around, no matter how hard I tried. The sampan was going round and round in circles and I couldn't make it go forward or backward. Then the boat started shipping water and there was too much coming in for me to be able to bail it out. So I held onto the sides of the sampan, knowing that it was going to go under. There was nothing I could do about it. Finally the boat went under and I had to start swimming. I was lucky the wind near me wasn't that strong. The storm or cyclone-thing didn't last much longer and passed by where I was.

I don't know how long I had to swim for. I was conscious enough to see that the water were getting calmer, and the wind was dropping off. A couple of fishing boats and sampans came out to rescue me. I haven't gone back to rowing since then. Anyway, we couldn't afford to buy a new boat.

After that, I went to Sagaing and got a job. Not a salaried job of course. I had to wash the dishes in a restaurant near Moe-Zar market. I was paid three *kyats* a day, plus food. I suppose you would called me a wage-slave. Since my food was paid for, I could send some of the three *kyats* home. I couldn't send it all, but after I'd taken out some money for cigarettes and stuff, I could send home about two *kyats*.

Near my restaurant there was a photographer's studio. When we weren't busy, I used to go over there for a chat and pass the time with a boy I knew who worked there. Sometimes while I was sitting around they asked me to move the furniture and the lighting cables they used for taking photos. I would do it quickly and I didn't complain. They could see I was a good worker.

On fast days, when the restaurant was closed, I would go over and hang out at the photographer's and give them a hand with whatever they wanted doing. Sometimes, if the assistant photographer was going on an outside shoot in the Sagaing Hills or somewhere, I would accompany him, and help him by carrying the camera and the flash gun and the lights. When he took a break, I would run errands for him like getting him cigarettes and betel. Because of that, he took a liking to me.

Around that time, the restaurant closed down. Not because it wasn't making money, mind you. The owner was doing very well, so well in fact that he could give up running a restaurant, which is hard work, buy a lorry and go into the transport business. It came at the right time for me, because the photographer felt sorry for me and asked me to work in his shop.

For about a year I followed the cameraman around on outdoor shoots. When we stayed in the studio, I would hold the lights or arrange the tables and chairs. After that I was given the chance to handle the camera—up until then, I'd never been allowed to. I'd only been able to carry the tripod, and the bag with the lights. I still wasn't allowed to handle the small cameras, but I could look through the big one they used in the studio and see whether it was lined up or not. If the aperture was out of line, I was allowed to move the camera, and after that, the photographer would come and stand behind it and adjust the lighting, and then take the picture. I wasn't allowed to do that yet. All I could do was move the camera into position.

After a year of this, I was sent out on an outdoor shoot, but even then, I wasn't allowed out on my own. They sent me out with the assistant photographer. We used to go to the Sagaing Hills, or the Ava Bridge, or the Kaung-hmu-daw Pagoda, because these places have lots of people at the weekends and on full-moon days. Some come to keep the sabbath, some come to see the pagodas. We did particularly well out of couples there on dates. We used to take loads of pictures of them. And if there were groups of girls or students out on a daytrip, we could get through four or five rolls of film. After that, the owner gave me the chance to handle the camera.

In the days before colour came along, we were only taking black and white, and didn't take many pictures, maybe one roll a day, or two at the most. But when we started taking colour, we were sometimes getting through four or five rolls a day. And then when we got instant developing we opened up a branch of the studio on the hill and took even more pictures.

I'm married now. My wife sells flowers on way up to Ponnyashin Pagoda. That's right, I met her here. Her aunt came to Sagaing to join a nunnery. Her father's dead, but her mother, the nun's younger sister, is still alive. They all came to live in the nunnery and then she started selling flowers at the pagoda. We met while she was selling flowers and I was taking pictures, and now we're married. We've got two children, both girls. They're at middle school. We all live in the nunnery. Just like in the song. When the Burmese people get into difficulties and have nowhere to live, they can live in the monastery. That's what's happened to us.

Business isn't so bad nowadays. What with my wife selling flowers and me taking photos, I've even been able to buy my own Nikon. I'll be able to buy my own developing equipment one day.

Would I go and live in town? No, not even if I get rich. I'll still want to live in the shadow of the Sagaing Hills, because this was where I grew up. If I could open my own shop, I'd do it here on the hill. I wouldn't have a life without the Hills. I grew up here, I married here, I became successful here, my parents died here, all here in the shadow of the Hills.

That's why I could never separate my life from the Hills, *Saya*. And if I do better than I am doing now, I'll open my shop here. I won't move anywhere else. I've already decided to die here.

I want to live and die meritoriously, within the sound of the tinkling of pagoda bells and the ringing of the gongs. Even if I get rich, I'll still stay here living in peace. If I don't, I'll stay here anyway. Isn't it best life in this world if you live honestly and die happily within the sound of pagoda bells, *Saya*?

[October 1989]

119

15

MOONSHINE AND MIDWIFERY

Nam Lone Hkam told me her life story one cold December night as we sat drinking Shan liquor in Namhkam. She was about thirty years old and like many Shan women in the area she was good-looking and fair-skinned. She was wearing a white Panda sweater and a green Shan longyi with yellow stripes. The tassels of the red woollen sweater draped around her neck bounced around on her chest as she spoke. She was slim and of medium height but the high-heeled shoes she wore made her look taller and more imposing. She spoke with a delightfully strong Shan accent.

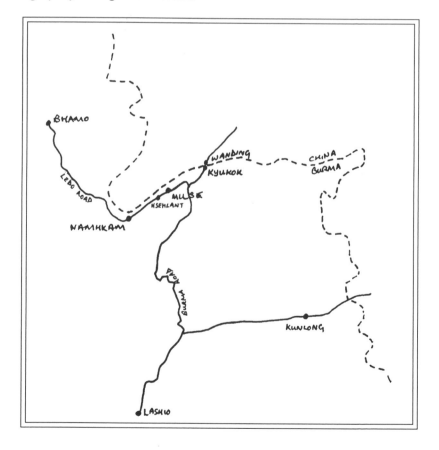

I was born in Hseh-lant. I'm sure you've heard of it, you might even have been there. It's where Saw Mun Hla, the Shan princess who married a Burmese king, was born. Everyone says the girls from Hseh-lant are good-looking but I wouldn't know. I've not travelled that much or seen girls elsewhere, so I've got nothing to compare us with. Maybe we are good-looking in our village. Who's to say? We all look quite similar. It's only people from outside who could say if we're better-looking than other women. *Saya*, you've been all over the place. Do you think it's true?

I started selling Shan moonshine when I was still quite young. You've been to Hseh-lant market, haven't you? On market days I used to sell liquor there. On days when there was no market I'd sell it under the wood-oil tree at the edge of the village. Since it gets cold here in the winter, we did good business all day long.

As soon as it got light we'd catch the farmers on their way to the fields. They'd warm themselves up with a glass of hooch. I'm sure you've had some before. We'd serve it with strong bitter tea and pickled mustard-leaf for nibbles. Some would stop by for just one glass, some would take two or three. Winter in Hseh-lant is terribly cold, so tea alone isn't enough to warm you up in the morning—you need something stronger.

We weren't the only hooch stall in the village. Some people had stalls in their houses, others had good sites on the road. There were three or four more stalls under the tree near us. For some reason though, we used to sell more than the rest. I never was too sure why. It couldn't have been because our hooch was better than the rest. It was the same as everyone else's. As for us being more polite and friendly to the customers and looking after them better—it couldn't have been that either. In fact I'd even go so far as to say that we were less welcoming to our customers than the other stalls. It couldn't have been that we tended to chat more to our customers than the other stall-holders either. We never exchanged more words with them than we had to and the looks we'd give them said no more than 'Drink here if you want, it's all the same to us'.

The only thing I can think of was that people came to our stall because I was a single girl. In our village, the girls would get married very early but here I was, over twenty and still single. Plenty of boys would come and chat me up but I always turned them down. Some of them even tried to force me to run away with them but I always carried a knife and if they tried anything on I'd pull the knife on them. So most of them didn't dare to mess with me. They knew what I'd do if they did.

My father was dead by then, but my mother was still alive. I'm an only child. My father died young from malaria. He caught it while he was out farming in the jungle. My mother and I were left to fend for ourselves. After my father died, she started to sell hooch. When I was about twelve years old, she had a stroke and had to stay in bed. I had to take over the running of the stall and work to support the two of us. All my friends who were the same age as me were getting married. Personally I couldn't understand why. I didn't trust men. In fact, not just men, I didn't trust anyone. I was quite happy just living with my mother. I didn't want to go out with anyone. At the *Thadingyut* and *Tazaungmon* festivals and the parties for the new harvest, my girlfriends used to take part in traditional dancing. At the pagoda festivals, they'd all dance *a-yein* dances except for me. I just couldn't get into it like they could. There was something about it which irritated me and I found it all faintly humiliating.

I sold liquor for about eight years, until I got to about twenty. One day, a rural Health Assistant came to our village. His name was Sai Leit. I reckoned him about twenty-five. He was based in Namhkam and used to visit our village to inspect the market and the streets and make sure they were clean. He'd check the liquor stalls too. If the cups were dirty or if there were clouds of flies, he would tell us to clean up. Some people would get fined by the village officials. He also used to come and treat the people in the village, particularly the pregnant women and the people with malaria. There's so much malaria in our village.

One time there was a case with a woman in the village who was pregnant or something, and he came and visited two or three times in a month. One of those times he came to inspect my stall. He picked up a glass and said it was dirty. I wasn't having that. I snatched the glass out of his hand, filled it up with liquor and plonked it down in front of one of the people waiting to be served. The customer knocked back the glass, got up and left. He might scare other people, but he didn't scare me. Why should he? Anyway, I only had these glasses and these plates and I was damned if I was going to buy any more. If people found my stall dirty, no-one was forcing them to drink there.

One day I couldn't set out my stall because I had a bad attack of malaria and had to stay home in bed with the blankets pulled up over me. I dosed myself with a mixture of hooch and boiled and ground up Indian nightshade berries. My father always used to take the same mixture when he had malaria, and then go to bed. In one or two days the fever would clear up. So I followed his example.

While I was tucked up in bed I heard the sound of footsteps at the doorway and looked up. It was Dr Sai Leit. How did he know where we lived? How did he find our house? I couldn't believe it. We were out in the middle of nowhere, in a plantation of bananas and mango trees, in a little hut which we'd built ourselves.

When he turned up, I was racked with a high fever. My lips were parched. My eyes felt like they were on fire and when I closed them I could see shooting colours. Earlier on I had been groaning but as soon as he arrived I stopped short and stared at him. My mother was sitting by my bed weeping. He walked in and felt my hand and then took his stethoscope out of his medicine bag. When he was out on tour in the districts, he always brought a medicine bag with his equipment and syringes and so on. I had never seen a stethoscope before and had no idea what it was used for so when he fitted it to his ears and sat down beside me, I leapt up out of bed, propelled by a mixture of terror, suspicion and panic. 'What are you going to do to me?' I screamed. My mother yelled at him in Shan 'Go away! Get out! Leave us alone!' Neither of us trusted doctors or hospitals. We detested them in fact, and with good reason. When I was younger, my father had had an attack of malaria and lost consciousness. We went running to the doctor for help. Except really he was no doctor, he was just a quack. But how were we to know that? He examined my father and shook his head and said that he would surely die. So my mother begged and pleaded with him to do what he could to save him. That meant we had to put this quack up for over a month and feed him. We sold off our field to pay for the cost of the treatment, and eventually had to sell our house in the village—we hadn't always lived in the banana plantation, you see. But it was all a big waste of time and money, because my father died and just as he was about to die, this quack doctor took off and left. He had eaten us out of house and home. I can't begin to calculate how much it had cost us. We had had to sell our house and move to the banana plantation. So that's why we hated doctors.

Dr Sai Leit had no idea about all of this of course. He simply called in a couple of women from the quarter to calm me down, and examined me with the stethoscope and took my pulse. He said that I had a very severe case of malaria. That night he spoke to one of his friends who was influential in the village and got permission for the two of them to sleep in our hut and watch over me.

Luckily I got better and after about a week he went back to Namhkam and we didn't see him again. I heard that he'd been transferred to Lashio District Hospital and was attending more training. I carried on selling hooch. There was nothing else we could do, since we didn't have the money to do any other business.

One day, I accompanied a friend to Namhkam hospital. The matron asked me if I wanted to work there. I said I did, so she gave me a job working in the nurses' hostel. It wasn't much of a job, just cooking and cleaning and doing the nurses' laundry. But if I had an attack of malaria, the nurses and doctors would take care of me and give me medicine. To show my gratitude, I said I would come and clean their homes too. But they just laughed and said that in hospital, they treated the patients for free. There was no need to pay anything. All I needed to do was carry on with my job in the hostel. So I used to do everything I could to help the nurses there.

To cut a long story short, since I was a good worker and I made their white uniforms sparkle and cooked them good meals, the matron and the other nurses were fond of me. One day the matron called me in to her room to meet one of the doctors. He looked me over carefully and said that they wanted to send me on a course for midwives in Lashio. I wasn't too sure what a midwife was, but I said that if the matron and the doctor wanted me to go, I would. So I did. I attended the course in Lashio and the doctors and nurses taught me about midwifery. It all came as news to me. In our village, when a woman gave birth there were never any doctors around, just the traditional birth attendant who would often cut the cord with whatever knife came to hand. Sometimes if she couldn't get the baby out, she would press on the stomach, or if the baby's head was round the wrong way, she would try and turn it round. But the success rate wasn't good and a lot of women died in childbirth. I realised once I'd finished my course that I could probably have saved their lives with the skills I had learnt.

Once I had qualified, I went to work in a village in the mountains some distance from Namhkam. The village had never had a midwife before and when I first arrived, I think they were scared I was a murderer or a witch. But little by little I won their trust.

One day, some people came to see me from a nearby village. They said there was a pregnant Palaung woman who'd been screaming for days because of the pains in her stomach. But they said she wasn't due yet. The villagers had been making offerings to the *nats* and praying, but the woman's pain wouldn't go away. I set off to the village, but unfortunately it was the rainy season and the mountain streams were in full spate. When it's been raining that hard, it takes four or five days for the water levels to drop. I knew that if we waited that long, the woman would die.

I followed the villagers, and when we got to the stream, sure enough, we found that we couldn't cross. The current was very strong. But it would have been pointless to sit it out and wait for the water to drop. So I told them to chop down a tree and we would float across. They all looked at me in amazement and asked me if I really wanted to do it like that. I said of course I did, if they dared do it, why shouldn't I? So they quickly felled a tree and chopped away the branches and I got across on it. Luckily no-one was washed away but I did get quite bruised.

When we got to the village, the woman was already in a bad way but I did what I could and in the end she safely gave birth to twins. In all my life, I've never been so happy as I was when I realised I had saved not just one life but three. It was enough to make me forget how exhausted I was. It wasn't until I looked down at myself that I remembered all the bruises I had got from banging against the rocks and the trees. I went off to bed. They told me later that while I was asleep, a man called Sai Leit had been to see me. He had been in a nearby village treating malaria cases, and when he heard I was there, he'd come over to see me. But when he'd seen me fast asleep, he told them not to wake me, and left. They told me he'd come to say goodbye because he was being transferred.

My mother died during the two years I spent in that village. Sai Leit didn't come back again. I wanted a chance to thank him for opening my eyes, so I kept an ear open for news of him. Some people said he'd left his job, and others said he'd been transferred down to Southern Shan State or across to Kunlong. Either way, I didn't see him again.

Until he came back to live in Namhkam, that was. And we fell in love and got married. The story of a midwife and a Health Assistant. We both work in Namhkam, but at the moment he's off in the jungle so I can't introduce you.

I remember the way he turned up again in my life. I had gone back to my old village on leave and I was staying with a friend. One day I was just about to go out when he suddenly appeared in person at the door. I just stood there staring. Wondering if it could be him. He walked straight in and greeted me. I was so shocked I even took a step backwards. I didn't believe it was him until he said hello.

'I heard you came to see me before, when you were about to be transferred'.

'That's right, I came to say goodbye, but you were fast asleep, and they told me you'd been up all night with a delivery, so I didn't want to wake you'.

We walked along, deep in conversation, until we found ourselves at the banana grove where I'd once lived. Apart from the buzz of the cicadas, everything was quiet. Then our feet took us further until we reached the wood-oil tree at the edge of the village. When we got to it, he looked around and said, 'This was where I first laid eyes on you. You were selling hooch. I even bought a glass myself. I had no idea that the hooch merchant would grow up to be a midwife'.

'It only happened because of you' I said. 'It's getting dark, let's go back to the house and I'll make you some Shan liquor'.

So that's my story. And the story of how I met my husband.

[June 1990]

16

MI WIN WA

*I met her at Ye-seq-taun rubber plantation near Thanbyuzayat. She
was twenty-two, quite tall, slim, with a once bright yellow hat perched
jauntily on her head. Lustrous thick black hair curled out from underneath. She wore a grubby sports shirt, a green school longyi and
Elephant Star sandals. A Thai bicycle was propped up against a rubber tree nearby, with a plastic basket tied to the front which contained a lunchbox and a towel. She put down the almost full zinc
bucket of latex which she had already tapped.*

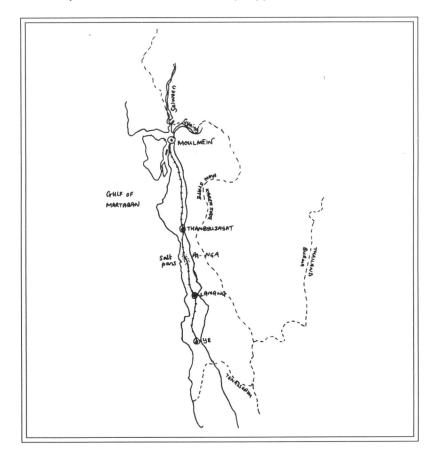

My name's Mi Win Wa—Miss Buttercup. That's right, it's a Mon name, you can tell, can't you, because it has 'Mi' in front, like we have 'Nai' for boy's names—Nai Pan Myint. In Burmese, you'd say Ko Pan Myint. My name would be Ma Win Wa. But of course you must know all that, *Saya*. I don't read much myself, just the odd cartoon book. There's no book shop or rental shop in our village. We can only rent books if we go to Thanbyuzayat or somewhere. So . . . you want to write a story about me, *Saya*? It won't be very interesting— what is there to say?

Yes, my father's Mon. So's my mother. I was born in a village. My father used to be a paddy farmer and had a little plantation, pineapples, bananas, that kind of thing. Ummm . . . no, no, it wasn't our own plantation. They weren't our paddy fields either, we were tenant farmers, cropping farmers, it wasn't regular work, maybe one year my father'd grow paddy, the next year pineapples. Oh yes, and sometimes we'd go down to the sea and harvest the salt.

My mother wasn't much help to him, because she had all us children. Seven, would you believe? I'm the oldest. So she spent her whole time cooking and looking after us, which meant my father was the only bread-winner.

My father used to be able to grow enough to support us. Prices in those days weren't as high as they are today, and we were still only little. We didn't eat much. We were still kids, so it didn't matter what we wore. My brothers would even wear my father's old vests.

In those days, I was going to the middle school in our village. I attended until eighth standard, but I had to leave after that, because I failed the class twice, I'm afraid. It wasn't my fault I failed. If I'd been able to attend regularly like the others, I could have passed easily. But I couldn't go regularly, and we couldn't afford to buy the books and things either.

My father disappeared the year I reached seventh standard.'Disappeared' is the only word for it. Ah, you're looking a bit confused there, *Saya*. You see we're not sure if he died or simply disappeared. He still hasn't come home to this day, and it must be eight or nine years now, because I was only fourteen at the time.

So, anyway, he disappeared. Before that, he was just a simple farmer. He didn't even drink country spirit or anything. He'd work the whole day long with just a quid of tobacco in his cheek, growing paddy in season and boiling down salt in the quiet time of year. And even once he got home at night, he wouldn't stop. He'd be cutting bamboo into strips and weaving it into trays and baskets. But as we grew bigger, and children came one after another, it wasn't enough to feed us, so he had to go and look for 'other work'. 'Other work' means smuggling. You know about smuggling don't you *Saya*? 'Carrier' work, it's called.

You know, people that carry goods—black market stuff of course. To start off with, he didn't earn much, just bringing stuff from Ye and Lamaing. You don't need your own money to do it, you can carry it for other people. Those people they're always arresting on the Ye train, they're carrying other people's stuff. But doing that doesn't get you much, hardly enough to live on.

One day my father had come back from Lamaing and was talking to my mother. To start with, she was shaking her head and saying she wouldn't stand for it. But after a while she relented. Of course I knew what it was he was saying. My father was telling her he should go with one of the smuggler's boats to Singapore or Penang. You know about them don't you, *Saya*? Well, it didn't take long for them to discuss it, and then my father left. After a week he hadn't come back. After two weeks, he hadn't come back. He said at the time that he'd only be going for ten days. But when after two, and then three weeks, he still hadn't returned, my mother started to get anxious and she'd pray every day in front of our altar. After a month of that, my father suddenly showed up.

Well!! You should have seen him! He'd set off empty-handed and now he returned loaded down with presents, and two or three thousand *kyats*. He returned looking like a new man. A new sports shirt, a watch, a Malaysian *longyi*. For my mother he'd bought batik and material for blouses. She was delighted. This was a bit better than growing paddy!! You grow rice for a year and what do you get? Even though you call them your own fields, you've still got to pay money to the real owner. You can work a whole year and only end up with three or four thousand. And here was my father, earning that in a month and more besides. And what a change in him too—he looked quite the well-dressed man about town!

My mother still didn't want him to do this sort of work though. 'It's so dangerous', she said. 'It's dangerous because you're outside the law, and the sea is full of pirates. And then there's the weather—I'm scared you'll get caught in a storm'. She said she'd rather he didn't do it again. She wanted him to stay home and work the paddy fields.

But my father said he wanted to go just one more time. He said that this time he'd get enough money to buy a pair of buffalo or oxen. The first time he went, he came back in December. When he set off, it was May. He told us that this would be the last time, that he'd bring us back blouses and skirts and watches, and trousers for the boys. He said he'd go to Penang this time.

He left in May, and a month later he hadn't come back. Then two months. When he left, he said he'd only be gone a month. Now it's been years and he's still not come back. We don't know if he was caught in a storm and drowned, if he was attacked by pirates . . . . We haven't heard a word. He's been gone eight or nine years now. For the first two or three years, my mother still thought he might come back, but after that, she gave up hope, and when he'd been gone four years, she held an alms-offering ceremony for him.

After my father left, we didn't have much money. I missed more and more days of school and couldn't buy the books. That's why I failed the national exams at eighth standard. I resat them the following year, and failed again. After that, I left.

With my father gone, we were having trouble making ends meet. My mother would go and pick pineapples or durians, depending on the season, and leave me at home to do the cooking and look after the children. One day she called me and told me 'I'm going to Lamaing to do a bit of business. Stay here and take care of the children'.

I asked her 'Are you going to be a carrier?'

'I'll do whatever I have to. Maybe I'll be a carrier and use the money to buy some stuff to sell'.

'Don't go Mummy', I said. 'Daddy went off to do that and never came back. Are you going to do the same?'

'If I don't, how are we going to eat?'

'Mummy, there must be something else you can do apart from that', I said. 'Don't you remember, you were the one who told Daddy in the first place not to go and work on the smuggling boat. Now you're doing it too'.

My mother hesitated a bit when I said this, because she knew it was true. The first time Daddy had gone, she had tried to stop him. And the second time too, when he said he was going to Penang.

'Look, you're not old enough to understand. I might have said that once. But if you want to have regular meals, you've got to do what you can. I've got no choice. You're not old enough yet to go out and earn'.

'I could go out and get a job!'

My mother looked at me in disbelief. She seemed astonished by what I'd just said.'What would you do?'

I told her what I was thinking of. Not long ago, an old woman from Thanbyuzayat market had been in our village looking for servant girls. She said you could go and live in a rich man's house in Rangoon, and do the housework. It was good work, she said, and you'd get clothes and food and one hundred and fifty *kyats* a month. One of my friends from the village had gone, and the other day I'd got a letter from her. She had invited me to come to Rangoon if I wanted to work as a housemaid. I explained this to my mother. She refused flat out.

'Good Lord, you are not to do that! I didn't bring you up so you could go and work as a housemaid. And I've heard about girls who go to Rangoon to work as servants. Before long they're pressured by the owner into sex or some crafty woman will sell them off into prostitution. I've heard about that sort of thing since I was young, and there's no way I'm going to let a teenage daughter of mine do that kind of thing. Anyway, one hundred and fifty *kyats* isn't going to go very far in this day and age'. I agreed with her, but I said that I felt sorry for her. She never been anywhere in her life, she'd only been to Moulmein once. And I worried about her. She wasn't that old, and she still looked good, with a good figure and face. If you stood the two of us together, you might have thought we were sisters. I explained why I was worried, and she grinned and shook her head: 'You little nit, don't worry about me! Worry about yourself!'

So anyway, she set off for Lamaing, and it turned out all right, just as she'd predicted. The first time she came back, she brought back a heap of gold necklaces and when she went the second time, she brought back more and soon we were decked out with jewellery.

But I felt there was something not quite right about it. I was full of foreboding. I was just a child, I know, and all I wanted was to have enough to wear and enough to eat. But I worried that my mother was going to get arrested.

My fears came true. After about four or five trips, my mother changed. She started to wear make-up and dress fashionably. You wouldn't have believed that she was once a farmer's wife. She stopped wearing batik and started smoking. My mother had never used to even chew betel, let alone smoke. I didn't like what I saw. And she was starting to be careless with money.

The days she came back from her trips, we didn't cook at home. She'd bring back some ready-made noodles from town, and if that wasn't enough we'd go to the Chinese restaurant at the end of town and have roast duck or pork. The children were delighted to be able to eat as much as they wanted. But I couldn't enjoy myself, because I was starting to have doubts about her.

Sometimes, when my mother went to Lamaing, she'd tell me she had some business to do in Thanbyuzayat and disappear off there. I'd look at her suspiciously but she'd insist she'd got business to attend to, and I couldn't go with her. I said nothing. But then I heard that she was going out with a man in Thanbyuzayat market and that you could often see them there. My suspicions were confirmed.

One day, my mother was all dressed up. 'I'm off to Thanbyuzayat', she said. I let her leave and then a little while later caught a bus up to Thanbyuzayat. When I got there, I went to the stall of a friend who I often visited. I sat talking to her and kept a look out for my mother. I looked once or twice around the whole market but I couldn't find her. I thought to myself that what I'd heard couldn't be true. I went to get the bus home. My mother had probably already left for home, I thought, so I'd better get going. It was already three o'clock in the afternoon. Near the bus station, I spotted a man leaving a tea-shop with a woman. I knew straight away that it was my mother. There was no doubt about that.The two of them were holding hands. The man was much younger than her, not more than twenty-five. Much younger. He was wearing jeans and a denim shirt. They were laughing and talking but they didn't see me. I looked for a place to escape and ran and hid under a tree near the bus station.

At that moment, my mother looked across to where I was and caught sight of me. She was startled and looked astonished. Then she looked furious. She turned to the man and said something to him, I don't know what. At that moment, the bus decided to leave and I climbed on and left the two of them standing at the bus station.

My mother got home about an hour after me in the next bus. As soon as she got home, we flew into an argument. I accused her, screaming and crying, rebuking her.

My mother said nothing in response to my accusations. She simply said, 'I had to work as a carrier because I didn't want my young daughter going into service. It's because of you that I'm doing this. If I was single, there wouldn't be any problems. You should thank me instead of acting like this'.

I scolded her and went off to bed. When I'd calmed down a bit, I started to think to myself. There was some truth in what she'd said. I'd offered to go to Rangoon and work as a maid but she'd said she didn't want her teenage daughter to do that kind of lowly work. So she'd gone to work as a carrier, and it was while she was working that she'd become like this.

Although I was angry that she'd gone and done this, I couldn't blame her. How could I blame anyone, Saya? Once I was calm and had had a chance to think, I realised what was to blame for bringing this chaos into our home. Smuggling. My father had lost his life on the sea while he was doing this business. My mother's reputation was in ruins for doing it. It had brought us money, sure, and made things easy, but it had destroyed our lives.

Although I'm called Mi Win Wa, it's the wrong name for the day of the week I was born. I'm actually Saturday's child: proud, stubborn. I don't know if it's a good thing or not but I don't change my mind easily. And by now I felt sure that this smuggling business had ruined our lives. I decided that no matter what my mother wanted to do, I could never do it. I still haven't changed my mind.

I'll be tired. I'll be poor. But I'll do honest work. That's why I came to work in this rubber plantation. Every day, I have to tap three hundred and fifty trees. I'm saving my money. Why? Because once I've saved up, I'm going to take the eighth standard exam again. I'm going to pass tenth standard too. After that I'll go to college somewhere, maybe Technical College, maybe in Moulmein.

Lots of my friends are smuggling. They look good for a while, but it's not long before they fade. But I've got just as many friends who are trying hard and succeeding at doing an honest job. Some of them have gone to medical school, some of them are working as rubber-tappers like me and working hard to pass their exams.

Who says a rubber-tapper can't become a school-teacher one day? Who says one can't become a doctor? Or a lawyer? All you need is the strength to overcome the obstacles. I'm just trying to gather my strength.

[July 1988]

PART IV
STEADY AS YOU GO

17

THE MOON AND THE FLOWER

He must have been about ten. Maybe even younger. Fair-skinned, with a sweet face and lovely eyes. His hair curled unslicked around his forehead and the nape of his neck. He was wearing a hand-me-down jacket from across the border in Bangladesh and a shabby green school longyi. I met him on a bullock-cart on the road which runs from Tat-wet bus shelter, on the Magwe-Taundwingyi road, to Wa-gyi-aing village.

My name is Kyaw Kyaw. I'm in fourth standard at primary school. Mummy and I are on our way back from Thityagauk market. She buys vegetables from the farmers who grow them in the Yinn creek. She gets onions, chili, tomatoes, cauliflower. Then she sells them at the five day market in Thityagauk. The day before market, we catch one of the buses which goes there from our village. When we get there, we dump the vegetable baskets in front of a stall. Some of the stall-holders live in Thityagauk so they don't turn up until market day morning and some of the stalls are empty the night before the market and we can sleep on them.

Scared? Why should I be? There are other market traders around. Some of them come from our village, some come from nearby. On the night before the market the place is full of people sleeping on the stalls. Mummy doesn't get much sleep because she's always busy trying to freshen up the vegetables with water and then tying the mint and the coriander into bundles.

Some of the traders spend the whole night chatting. If it's very cold, they'll huddle round the fire. Once Mummy's finished doing her work, she comes and curls up with me on the bench. We sleep on top of a plastic sheet and wrapped up in a blanket.

We have to get up early in the morning before the stall-owners arrive. We move off and find a space somewhere in the market where we empty out the baskets and start selling. Sometimes we sell out immediately, but sometimes it takes us until the market closes up. After it closes, Mummy goes off to buy things like clips and hair-grips, baby clothes and bras and second-hand clothes from Bangladesh from a wholesaler in the town. She buys them on sale or return, not cash. Then she sells it for a bit more than the wholesaler's price and keeps the profit.

The market packs up in the late morning and then we do our shopping in town and then go back to the village by bus. So that's how we always spend market day and the evening before. We go off to Thityagauk by bus and then back the next day.

My mother's name? Ma May Thu. It's a pretty name isn't it? I think she is too. You must have noticed her waiting with the other passengers when the car broke down at the junction near the Tat-wet shelter. She was the tall fair one in the red sweater. She was wearing a scarf on her head because she worries about dust getting in her hair. Uncle, you should see Mummy's hair. It comes all the way down to the back of her knees. She's only thirty-four. She must have been about twenty when she had me. People say she was as pretty then as she is now.

Actually, we're not from this village. We come from a town on the Rangoon-Mandalay railway. Mummy's father was a nightwatchman at a rice mill in the town. Mummy hated her father. She always felt sorry for

135

Grandma. My grandfather came from a rich and respectable family. When his parents died, their business failed and my grandfather dropped out of school and started drinking. He had to get a job as a nightwatchman.

He started off a rich man's son but he soon became an alcoholic. He treated Grandma very badly. He wasted his salary drinking and gave nothing to her. Mummy had to drop out of school at about eighth standard and go and take sewing classes. She took up tailoring using a rented sewing machine. We couldn't afford one of our own.

In that town, there was this businesswoman who owned about five treadle sewing machines. She employed my mother to make up bras and she'd take them and sell them. Mummy and Grandma had to make do on the small amount of money Mummy's tailoring was bringing in. They couldn't expect anything from Grandpa. He drank all his wages. That's why Mummy hates drink. Later on, the drink sent Grandpa to an early death. I never even met him because all this happened before my mother had me.

When Grandpa died, Mummy and Grandma couldn't stay on in the servants' quarters at the rice mill. Up till then, they'd had a free room of course. Mummy used to be sewing all day and even at night she'd have to work because clients would turn up with jobs for her to do like sewing on *kyay-thee-dan* cloth buttons.

You know, it always makes me sad to think about the way Mummy had to live, Uncle. She worked all day long at her workbench, stitching up bra after bra. Then at night she had to carry on working sewing on those cloth buttons by the light of a 'frog-lamp'. Do you know what I mean by a frog-lamp? It's a kerosene lamp with a long handle. The tinkers round here make them. We use them to catch edible frogs on a rainy night. That's why they're called that.

Mummy and Grandma didn't know where to go when Grandpa died. They wondered if they should move back to Wa-gyi-aing, where my Grandma came from, or whether they should stay in town where Mummy was born. My Grandpa had been from one of richest families in town when he met Grandma. But he'd ended up broke and working there as a nightwatchman.

Since Mummy hadn't finished high school, she had to live off her sewing. This was barely enough for her and Grandma to survive on. And once Grandpa died, they couldn't stay on at the mill. That was when she became the mistress of the son of the rice mill owner. She's never told me herself. But Grandma has explained to me what happened. 'At that time', she said, 'we were told we had to vacate the room. But then we were allowed to stay on because the owner's son felt sorry for us. He used to pay regular visits to our room and sometimes your mother would cook him dinner and he would spend the night'.

Whenever I ask Mummy about my father, her eyes fill with tears and she tells me that he's dead. I haven't asked her that many times. Once or twice maybe. One time, when I was in second standard at primary school, my friends were teasing me. There was a pagoda festival in town and a bullock race near the Independence monument just outside of town. My friends all went there with their fathers, but I had to go on my own.

I really, really, wished I could have gone with my father too, Uncle. Just like the others. At the race, I met one of my friends, Po Aung. His father was a clerk at the Trade Corporation. Po Aung was wearing brand-new shorts and white canvas shoes. I was just wearing my everyday green school *longyi*. And he had a watch. Not a real one though, just plastic.

When I bumped into him, he said to me, 'Poor you, not having a father. Look what my Dad bought me—a watch'. He showed it to me. Then he wandered off holding his father's hand. You can probably guess how I felt Uncle. I wanted a watch like that too. I went to the watch shop and asked how much it cost. Six *kyats*. I only had one *kyat*. The shop-keeper told me 'If you want that watch, sonny, you'd better ask your Daddy for five more *kyats*'.

That made it even worse. I went back home and asked my mother for some money. She was sewing on cloth buttons. She looked in her pocket and told me she'd only got two *kyats* but she'd get me a watch one day. That was when I asked her about my father. 'Mummy, why can't I go to the bullock race with my Daddy like my friends?'. 'Your father is dead, don't ask me about him', she replied and started to cry.

I wished I hadn't asked her and I've never done it again. But Grandma's told me all about him. He was the son of a rich man, but he went off and married the daughter of a rice mill owner in another town.

In fact, I actually saw him once, even though Mummy has tried to pretend he isn't around any more. I was selling cigarettes at the bus-stop near the market at the time. Mummy wasn't feeling very well. I probably had four packets of Duya cigarettes, which was our quota from the government shop. Mummy must have told me to go off and sell them at the bus-stop. I'd sell them individually or sometimes a whole packet at once. That day, I was selling cigarettes near the petrol station by the market. A Japanese pick-up car pulled out of the petrol station and the driver called me over. He was about thirty. In the seat next to him there was a young boy about a year or two younger than me with curly hair, wearing a denim jacket and jeans.

He asked me for some cigarettes. I found myself staring at him. For some reason I felt my heart skip a beat. He stared at my face too as he took the packet.

'How much is a packet?'

'Six *kyats*.'

I looked at him closely as he looked in his pocket for the money. I thought I had seen him somewhere before. Maybe I'd seen him in a dream. Then he took out a twenty-five *kyat* note.

'What's your name?'

'Kyaw Kyaw'.

'Do you go to school, Kyaw Kyaw?'

'Yes'.

'So why aren't you there today?'

'Mummy's sick, so I'm selling cigarettes.'

'Who's your mother'

'She's called Ma May Thu'.

'You're May Thu's son?!'

He gave me the twenty-five *kyat* note. I said I didn't have any change. So he said:

'How many cigarettes have you got left?'

'I've only got one new packet left. I've already opened the other one'.

'OK then, give me the new packet and take this twenty-five *kyat* note, seeing as you don't have change'.

I was so happy and grateful to that man. I thought he must be one of Mummy's friends. He waved to me and then drove away. The car drove off out of town down the Rangoon-Mandalay road. Since I'd never seen him in our town before, I reckoned he must be from somewhere else.

When I got home, I told Mummy what had happened and how I'd got the twenty-five *kyat* note. I told her how he'd said 'You're May Thu's son!' She looked shocked at first and then sad and her eyes misted over.

'Here, you must be hungry. I've already had my dinner, but I've left you some fried catfish. If that's not enough, go and get some salad for fifty *pyas* from Daw Ohn Tin's shop', she said, and returned to her buttons.

Mummy used to sing songs when she was sewing on cloth buttons. She had a great voice, and I'm not just saying that because she's my mother. Her favourite song was Mar Mar Aye's 'Trying to Forget the Past': 'I can't blame anyone, I was blinded by love . . . .' She was singing when I got home, but she stopped dead when I gave her the twenty-five *kyat* note.

Really, Mummy doesn't look like a poor woman. She has sparkling eyes, fair skin and pink smooth hands. I have decided that when I grow up I'm going to look after her so that she doesn't have to work any more.

At that time, Mummy and I weren't living in the rice mill compound any more because by then it had been sold off. We'd moved out to a room near the railway station for the families of the railway workers. Since one of the families wasn't very big, we rented a lean-to in their quarters for fifty *kyats* a month. Grandma had already died by then. She died while we were still living in the rice mill.

All we had to live on was my mother's cloth buttons. We were struggling to make ends meet because girls don't like wearing that type of button any more. The landlord used to look down his nose at us as if we were always behind with the rent. He spread lies about our situation behind our backs. When word got back to Mummy she was very unhappy. She'd never had to borrow and she'd always paid the rent regularly on the first day of each month.

One day Mummy came home from the market with a woman who she said was an old class-mate she'd run across in town. The woman wore very stylish clothes, a big watch and had short wavy hair. She said that she was doing business trading between Moulmein and our town. She asked Mummy if she wanted to come in on it. To judge by Mummy's look, she certainly did. Soon after that they went off together to Moulmein.

When she came back, she was loaded down with things including shirts and jeans for me. I was very happy. She was very happy too because she'd made quite a big profit out of her first trip. She said she'd just about doubled her money, although I don't know how much she put in to start off with. After a few trips, we were able to start saving. It put a new lease of life into Mummy.

I was happy because I was able to wear smart clothes and so could she. She was still under thirty and very pretty and I liked it if she wore pretty clothes. I had always felt embarrassed by her old shabby ones.

She went about four or five times to Moulmein with her friend who I called Aunty San. Then one time, shortly after she'd got back, this man turned up at our house. He was tall, about two or three years older than Mummy and light-skinned. He told me he was a ticket-collector. He used to come and see us since our flat was near the station. Mummy said he had checked their tickets and helped them on the train.

When men called on Mummy, I used to feel angry, jealous, miserable. So I didn't talk to this man much. Although he had a flashy uniform, I didn't go too close to look. I used to keep my distance. I didn't like him being with my mother.

Whenever the ticket collector came round he used to bring me presents. He'd bring me toys, or sweets, or clothes. He was always very nice to me. When he was on duty, he used to take Mummy off saying they were going to do some trading, and leave me in the house on my own.

Since he was a nice man and always brought me presents, I gradually got to like him. When he wasn't on duty, he used to get off at our station and come round for a meal and then catch the next train. Because of him, I decided I wanted to be a ticket collector. I wanted to wear a smart uniform. Aunty San didn't come round much to the house much any more. Later on we heard that she'd got married in Moulmein and I never saw her again.

Mummy did about fifteen trips to Moulmein in a year, first with Aunty San and then with the ticket collector when he was on duty. But after about a year, she stopped going. She always looked miserable and she stopped singing as she worked. She just stayed in bed, curled up. She sometimes didn't even bother cooking and we just ate from a shop. One time I didn't do something she asked me to, and she shouted at me 'This is all your fault. This would never have happened if I hadn't had you. If one of us were dead, we'd be much better off'.

She'd never spoken like that before. I was horrified. And I was angry too. So I yelled back at her 'Yes, sure, if I died, then you'd be able to live with your ticket collector wouldn't you?'.

Then she burst into tears and told me 'That's enough! Don't ever mention him again'. Since then she's never mentioned again any of that 'If only you or I were dead' stuff.

She was so angry with me that she didn't eat. She just stayed in bed. I was angry too. But I gradually calmed down and went over to look at her as she lay asleep. Her face was round and peaceful like the moon. Her hair curled around her forehead and her eyebrows were thick and glossy, her big eyes were closed. Her cheeks were stained with tears.

She stopped going out much. I guessed she'd probably heard what people were saying about her. I'm sure she must have. Even I did. My friends told me I had no father. Whenever they saw me they used to shout '2-Down, 4-Down'. You know, like the numbers of the trains. The ticket collector used to work on the 2-Down. The town we lived in was a small one and we lived near the railway so you could always hear the noise of the trains blowing their horns. Sometimes Mummy used to say, 'I hate the sound of trains'. That was all. No explanation.

Later on we moved out of the flat to a place on the outskirts of town because Mummy wasn't happy there. But she wasn't happy in the new place either, and said that the people looked down their noses at her there too. She could also see that I hated it when all the other kids told me I had no father.

So in the end she decided to move to Wa-gyi-aing, where her mother had come from. She told me we'd got relatives there and that the Yinn creek was a sight for sore eyes. She told me how the creek was full of gardens with onions and fresh vegetables. And she explained how the village was very peaceful because the mountains got in the way of the sound of the trains. When Mummy started telling me how she dreamt about Yinn Creek, I found myself dreaming about it too.

But we didn't move straight back from the town to Wa-gyi-aing. First we moved three or four times to villages on the eastern side of the Pegu

140

Yoma. To start off with I enjoyed being in a new place. But after a while my mother said she'd had enough of people looking down on us and gossiping so we moved on from village to village until eventually we arrived in Wa-gyi-aing where we rented a little house.

In the old days, when Mummy was miserable she used to curl up in bed or take it out on me. But since she's got back to Wa-gyi-aing she's stopped scolding me and and seems much happier. She's not bothered any more if people look down their noses at her or whisper behind her back. She tells me, 'So long as people don't look down on you, I'll be happy. Just make sure you study hard in school, because I want to give you a good education. You're all I've got. The only reason I'm still alive is because I've got to look after you'.

She's told me she's sacrificed her life for me. I'm not too sure what 'sacrificed' means. But I know that she has certainly done everything she can to make sure I get an education, and she doesn't spare a thought for herself. It's true. She's always done everything she can for me, and never considered herself. I look at her and feel very sorry for her. Sometimes, just to tease her, I ask her 'Mummy, if you get married, will you still love me?' and she tells me off, saying 'What rubbish you talk!'

Sometimes, when she gets cross, she says to me 'Kyaw Kyaw, you're my little flower that I've grown up from a seed, and sheltered from the sun. So don't abandon me if some girl comes along and picks you'.

But she doesn't often talk like that. Only if she's really angry with me. Then she tells me that she's hated every man in her life. She hated her drunken father. She hated my father, the man she tells me is dead. She says men have just used her. And she tells me I'd better not turn out like that too.

So nowadays I go with Mummy to Thityagauk market. We buy underwear and kids' clothes and sell them back in the village. I always go with her because I don't like to let her go on her own. She's still young and I have to keep an eye on her. She says I'm her little flower that she's always taken care of. I say she's the moon. I'm not happy unless she is shining peacefully. If she's miserable, if she curls up in bed, I feel sad too.

What more can I tell you about me? There's nothing more to say, Uncle. My mother's story is my story. If I've told you everything about her, that's all you need to know about me too.

[February 1988]

18

HOME SWEET HOME

I ran across him in a broken down railway carriage in a siding on the Mandalay-Myitkyina line. He was tall, dark and skinny and spoke with an Upper Burma accent. He must have been over forty. He was wearing a dirty old vest, a faded longyi and an old pair of flip-flops. He chewed betel as we spoke, occasionally spitting out the juice. His teeth were badly stained.

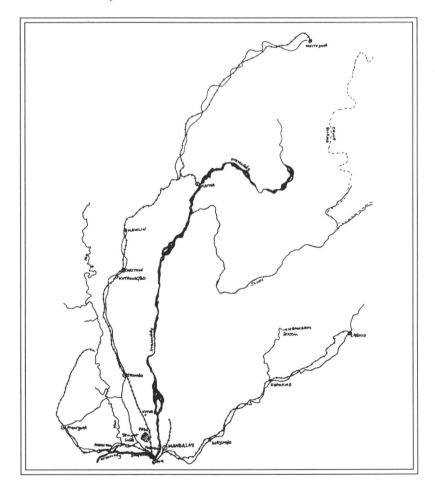

I was born in Padu-Ketka. Do you know Padu-Ketka, *Saya*? They're villages on the line between Shwebo and Sagaing. When I was a kid, I lived in a monastery. I never went to school or anything. My childhood was one long string of attacks by insurgents. Our village was often destroyed or burnt down. My father was a peasant farmer. He owned a plot of land near the village. Later on he went off to join the White Flag Communists[1]. I saw a fight between the government soldiers and the White Flags right in our village. At the time I was a kid and didn't know what was going on. I just sat there and watched. I couldn't have avoided seeing it, seeing as the fight was going on in the middle of the village outside our house. The insurgents went to the station first and then came into the village. The government soldiers pulled back into the village and the two sides fought there. People were using the big paddy silos and the tamarind trees as cover. People were cursing and shooting. You'd hear someone yelling out 'Hey, you, have you had your dinner yet? Ready to fire?' Then you'd hear someone else yell out, 'Yeah, I've eaten. Fire!!', and there'd be a volley of shots. We kids crouched at the base of a tamarind tree and watched the gunfight like it was a cock-fight. From time to time an insurgent would come across and take up position behind the tree. He'd tell us 'Buzz off, kids, or you'll all get shot'. But we took no notice. We were there for the show.

The White Flag Communists would capture our village for four or five days before the government soldiers took it back. This must have happened five or six times altogether. Eventually, my father joined the White Flags and we never saw him again after that. We heard later on that he had been killed over near Myinmu.

After he died, I had to work his fields myself. I must have been about thirteen, although I looked a lot older, more like fifteen or sixteen because I was already quite tall. Since I had to work in the fields I couldn't go to school, so all I've got is the learning I picked up in the monastery.

Around our village they used to grow all sorts of beans and pulses and corn. We grew groundnuts on our patch. Since I was an only child, it was enough for me and my mother. In fact it was more than enough and

---

[1] The main body of the Communist Party of Burma (CPB), the White Flags went underground in March 1948 when U Nu declared the party illegal. After an initial period of immediate post-independence success in which they captured a number of towns, in late 1950 they retreated to the countryside where they worked on setting up a rural base. In the early 1950s there were four main CPB divisions, each with an estimated thousand men; in Myingyan, Shan State, Yamethin-Pyinmana-Toungoo (their original stronghold), and in Monywa-Shwebo-Mandalay. They attracted support from peasants to whom they redistributed land.

143

we could live quite comfortably. The problem was that when there was fighting, we couldn't look after our land properly. There were a lot of ruffians and bandits and cattle rustlers around. One time a gang of bandits attacked the whole village and stole all our savings. But it wasn't too bad, because the next year we had a good harvest and we managed to put a bit away.

We had bad luck after that though. If it wasn't one thing it was another. First of all, we couldn't farm the fields properly because of the disturbances. Then, as soon as the situation had calmed down a bit and the bandits were under control, we had an unbelievable drought which destroyed all of the crops that year. It didn't just kill the crops. There was no cattle fodder or straw, or leftovers from the beans and the sesamum. We had to feed the cattle on branches from the banyans and the rain-trees. To start off with, they refused to eat it but later on they had no choice because there was no straw or grass. It wasn't just food that was in short supply. There was no water either. The nearby lake had always been full from one rainy season to the next. But even that all dried up. So as well as no food for the cattle, there was no water, and no food for the people either. You had to walk five miles for a couple of buckets of muddy yellow water.

That year, the village was burnt down in a firefight between the insurgents and the army. Once that had happened, we didn't have anywhere to live either. We left the village and went and built a hut on our land. Cows and buffalo died of starvation and thirst that year. It wasn't just the animals—some people got sick and died too, although they probably really died of hunger. Because of the drought there was no rice harvest all along the Mu river and around Shwebo. The fields were all dried up. Everywhere people were dying of thirst in the terrible heat, particularly the old and the young and people who were silly. The temperature must have been over a hundred and ten and these people couldn't stand it, so they'd bathe in what ever water they had and then get heatstroke and a fever and die.

My mother and I had no food or drink. Since the whole area was affected, there was no-one we could go to for help. You just had to do what you could for yourself. We lived off boiled yams and maize seed. Some people ate 'three-ply'. 'Three-ply' is what we used to call corn kernels, maize seed and cow-pea seed cooked up together. The corn kernels make it a bit more edible than just the other two on their own. Some people boiled up maize. The really lucky ones could afford to eat maize seed and rice. The rest of us just had to eat what we could find.

That year was pretty miserable, what with nowhere to live and nothing to eat. I came to realise what starvation really meant. We had no house and no food and lived in a palm leaf shack on our fields. But there was only the two of us and compared to others, I suppose I'd have to admit we weren't so badly off.

That year, since there was no work in our district and nothing to eat, a lot of people went off to Shan State to pick tea. Every year people would leave the village during the hot season, in the month of Tagu, when there was no work to do, and go off to Namhsam in the Shan States and hire themselves out to pick tea. I didn't used to go with them because we had enough to do at home. If we grew enough peanuts, then my mother and I had enough to live on. Also, I used to hire out our bullock cart. That gave us enough to go round easily. But that year, as I was saying, the village was burnt down, there was a drought, the animals were dying of hunger and we had no savings left. So I had to go up to Shan States for the tea harvest.

During Tagu the first *shwe-hpi* 'golden tips' tea shoots are ready for picking. Two truck loads of workers went up from our village, including me and my mother. We gave our shack to some other people. There were lots of trucks of people from other villages. Altogether our district probably sent up ten or fifteen truckloads, maybe six or seven hundred people altogether.

I really enjoyed the trip up. Perhaps it was the chance to see some different countryside. Compared to where we lived, Shan State is very different indeed. It was interesting to see the jungle and the mountains. The weather was good too. The people were simple and honest. From our village we travelled to Mandalay and from there to Kyaukme and from Kyaukme to Namhsam. From Namhsam we set off for the tea plantations. The tea is planted on the mountain-sides, and the slopes are very steep. You have be careful where you put your feet.

The plantation owner had built us a big dormitory outside the town. As soon as it was light, we would get up and have breakfast—sticky Shan rice, pickled mustard leaves and chili—and then we would go out to the slopes and pick tea. It got very hot during the middle of the afternoon so we would rest for a while and people would eat the food they'd brought out with them, fried *tofu* squares and sauce. I only used to eat two meals a day, in the morning and at night. I went without a proper lunch to save money, and used to fill up with fried *tofu*.

As I picked tea, I dreamt about building a little house. It wouldn't be very big or sturdy, just a wooden house with a zinc roof and a wooden floor. And while I was picking, I met Sein Aye. Sein Aye is my wife. She wasn't from our village but she lived in my area in a village in another township. In Namhsam, we got on very well, though, as if we were from the same place.

At first it was nothing special, we just knew each other vaguely. There were lots of other girls like her and boys like me picking tea. One day

145

though, we were both picking out on the slopes to the east of Namhsam. It was boiling hot, and since it had just rained the mountain-side was quite slippery. We'd been out picking since very early in the morning, earlier than usual because we were about to finish this hillside. Altogether there were about two hundred of us. There were groups on different slopes. You could see each other and call across. But if you wanted to go across to the other mountain side, it would take a whole morning because there was a big ravine between the two.

I was singing a song with my group as we picked, when suddenly I heard screaming about two hundred yards away down the mountain slope. At first I didn't know what it was. I glanced over thinking it was a couple of people shouting to one another. Then I realised that one of the girls in our group was sliding down the slope. I crouched down to see what was going on. Sure enough, there was a girl in white about two hundred feet down the hillside.

'Who is it?' I asked the others.

'I don't know. I think she's one of the ones from See-potara village'.

Our group was mostly old men and young girls and no-one moved to go and help the girl who'd slipped. So I put down my basket of tea-leaves and went down the mountain-side. The slopes were slippery from the rain. I had to tread very carefully, and grab hold of the tea-bushes on the way down. About half-way I slipped and slid nearly twenty feet before I could stop myself by grabbing onto a bush. Little by little I made my way down to the bottom of the slope on the edge of the ravine. When I reached the bottom I saw that there was actually a winding path up the mountain side.

As soon as I saw her, I realised it was Sein Aye. When I got close, I checked to see if she was still breathing. She was, and she didn't seem to have any serious injuries to her head or legs. She was just a bit bruised from sliding down the mountain. I said her name and she seemed to come to and recognise me. I picked her up in my arms and carried her back up the mountain path. Since it was getting dark, we called it a day and went back into Namhsam where I took her to Dr Nyunt Hlaing. He said that there was nothing much the matter with her, she had just got scared and fainted. So we were all quite relieved, and after about three or four days, she came back to work.

Sein Aye's mother had also come along for the tea harvest. The two of them were *myauq-thu* or 'northerners'. Round our parts if a man works in the fields, you call him a *taun-thu* or 'southerner'[2]. If a woman

---

[2] *Taun-thu* means peasant or hill farmer. *Taun* also means 'south'. *Myauq* means 'north'. Upper Burmans make a pun on this double meaning (see also *A Snapshot on Sagaing Hills*).

does it, you call her a 'northerner'. What it means is that she is coolie labour and doesn't own her own land. So she plants and picks beans for other people. That year because of the drought, there was a poor harvest, so she had come up with her daughter to pick tea.

I'll get to the point. Sein Aye and I fell in love. It was nothing particularly special. We just decided that we would get married if the next bean harvest went well. We would go back the village, build a little house and farm our land. We would save up and buy a pair of oxen.

But we spoke too soon. The drought returned that year. We couldn't afford to build a house or buy a pair of cows, and we had to sell our land as well. But Sein Aye and I decided we couldn't wait so we got married anyway. I had no job at the time. We'd had to sell our land to pay for the wedding. We had no house. So I decided to go to the city and find work. I went to Shwebo and found a job as a trishaw-peddler. We moved to Shwebo and I worked there for three or four years.

We had two children, which meant I needed to earn more money. You remember that to start with, we'd decided we would only get married if things started looking up. The problem was, Sein Aye's mother died and left her all on her own, which was difficult for her, so we had to get married quickly.

There were four of us in Shwebo, and then my mother came to stay so that made five. I had to work hard to feed them all but no matter how hard I worked, there never seemed to be as much as I expected.

Luckily, through a friend, I managed to get a job as a labourer in the railway workshop in Ywataung. The wages were nothing much, but at least we got a room in the staff quarters. It had wooden walls and floor and a zinc roof. That was enough for me so I took the job. Gradually I was promoted and learnt how to fix the engines and got trained and went on to become a skilled mechanic.

While I was at the workshop, my wife gave birth to Siamese twins. Just before they were born, she fell sick and we had to send her to hospital in Mandalay. It cost a lot of money so I started to steal bits and pieces from the workshop and ended up getting fired and charged with Section 6(1) of the Public Property Protection Law.

While I was in jail, my family was left without anything to eat. Food wasn't their biggest problem. They could just about scratch a living. My daughter sold sugar-cane lollies and betel and cigarettes at the toll-house on the Ava Bridge. It was just about enough to keep them from starving. But it was still difficult for them to manage. We'd lost our place to stay in the compound when I lost my job.

When my bosses saw how poor my family were, they took pity on them and said that they could stay in an old goods wagon in the compound. But when the carriage was hitched up to the train, they went along with it. They went up to Kawlin and Katha. In Kotaungbo and Chat-thin, the wagon would be unhitched for four or five months at a time and they would live there in it. Wherever they stopped they would sell betel or cheroots or if it was the right time of year, *thanakha* logs or water.

When I came out of jail, I had no idea where my family had got to. I went up and down the line looking for them, and eventually ran across them in a small country halt. I joined them living in the railway wagon. Later on, the brakes went on the carriage and it was hauled into this siding where it's been for the last five years. My youngest child was born in this wagon. My mother died in it.

So, you see, this wagon is now our home. My youngest child has never known anywhere else. They say that you can tell a person's life by looking at his home. I read that once in a book. A home is a record of a person's birth, marriage and death. Well, in that case, this old wagon must be home for us. After all, my mother died on it, my youngest child was born on it, and when my children get married, they'll marry in it, I should think.

I used to dream of having a little house of my own—and now I've got one. My life is tied to the fortunes of this wagon. Remember my name, won't you *Saya*? It's Aung Maung.

[April 1988]

148

19

LAUNDRY MAN

I met him in 'University Laundry', a shop near Rangoon University campus. It was about twelve foot by forty or fifty, and these days must be worth quite a bit of money. There was a low glass-fronted cabinet along the front of the shop and three or four upright cupboards along the walls. The cabinet contained piles of ironed and folded clothes. One of the cupboards held women's blouses and the other one men's clothing. However, they were far from full, with a number of empty shelves. In the glass cabinet was a big rusty old iron that looked like a museum piece. On a table at the back, a worker was ironing, and behind that was the house where the family lived from which wafted the smell of fried onions and curry. He was about sixty. His name was U Aung Kyi. He was skinny, medium colouring and had bright piercing eyes like a village schoolmaster. He wore a stiff collared white shirt with a pinni jacket and a neatly tied cotton longyi.

I was about eighteen when I arrived in Rangoon. I've been working in a laundry now for over thirty years—maybe thirty-five. I come from near Thanatpin, near Pegu. My father started off as a tailor. He owned his own Singer sewing machine. He used to make the sort of shirts and *longyis* which young people wore in those days, and he also used to tailor side-buttoned jackets and so on for rich men. That was what he was doing when I was born.

My mother died when I was quite young. I was an only child. About a year after she died, my father married again and had four more children. I went to live with him. I didn't want to stay with relatives, so obviously I had to go and live with my father. It was down to me to look after my stepmother's children. I brought them all up myself.

That was all during the Japanese occupation. After the war, when I was about fourteen, I went to live in a relative's house in Thanatpin and attended school. Middle school, that was. My father could only manage to send me money now and again so I used to help out in my relative's house. When I was in ninth standard, the civil disturbances broke out around the country. My father left Thanatpin district and went underground. I never saw him again after that. I heard that he'd died in the jungle but I don't even know whereabouts.

My mother was already dead of course, and now I didn't have a father either, so I was left an orphan all on my own. My stepmother married again after my father left and I lost contact with her. I decided to go to Pegu because I thought I might be able to find a job there. I was taken on in a cheroot factory. Just unskilled labour, spreading the tobacco out to cure.

The job didn't suit me so I decided to move down to Rangoon. A friend of mine said he was going looking for a job so I upped sticks and went with him. We bowled up in Rangoon and had to bunk down with one of his relatives who lived in a squatter's shack near Third Street in Kamayut. I seem to have spent most of my life bunking down with people's relatives. Certainly I never lived much with my own parents.

When we arrived in Rangoon, we had to turn our hands to whatever came our way. I got a job working in the Kamayut *dhobi* laundry where people sent their clothes to be washed. You probably remember the one I mean. It was run by old Hindustani *dhobies*.

They used to go to the university hostels and pick up the dirty laundry and deliver back the clean clothes. That was my job. It was my first time inside a University hostel of course. I used to go to a hostel near Judson Hall. Other *dhobies* did the hostels on the main campus.

I used to pick up and deliver the laundry to the old *dhobi*. Sometimes I'd do a bit of the ironing with the big brass flat-irons. They were incredibly heavy and the glowing charcoal inside made them extremely hot. It was bearable during the cool season and the monsoon but during the hot season, the combination of sun and heat made me drip with sweat. I could only manage to iron the easy things like the *longyis*. Shirts were too complicated for me. Collars had to be just so, and I couldn't get the hang of putting the creases into shirts. The old *dhobi* and his two hired Indian staff did those bits. After all, they'd been doing it all their lives and it was hardly surprising they were experts. They could knock off a shirt in no time at all.

I stuck with that job for about three years, going and picking the dirty shirts up from the hostel and dropping off the clean ones. Then I got married. My wife's father had opened up a laundry just near Hledan. But he didn't go and collect from the hostels like the *dhobies* did. They already had the university sewn up. My wife's father—my father-in-law— used to serve the neighbourhood people. In those days, the neighbourhood was nowhere near as crowded as it is now. Over in Htantabin ward there was a jasmine grove. At night there was only a dim streetlight over by the bridge at the end of Hledan. You had to be careful you weren't mugged. From about seven o'clock onwards, there was no-one around. In those days it was only pony-carts going between Kemmendine and Hledan and by seven o'clock the horses would be getting tired and the carts would be going home. There wasn't much to do around here so there weren't many passengers for them to pick up.

We had a little hut near to where my shop is now. My father-in-law opened up a laundry in it. He used to wash clothes that the people in the neighbourhood would drop off. When my wife and I got married, I went and worked for her father. Up till then he'd been doing all the ironing and everything on his own. Once I started working there, he had an assistant. I soon learned how to do shirts. With the two of us working there, business started to pick up. As well as people from the neighbourhood dropping their laundry off, we used to get students coming in with clothes, especially from Prome and and Tagaung hostels. The *dhobies* were quite a distance from those hostels so they often didn't deliver there and the students couldn't be bothered to walk over to where they were. Our shop on Hledan was quite convenient for them. By that time, the disturbances had tailed off and the university was open as usual. So we had plenty of customers.

But you know how it is, *Saya*. Good luck never stays with you. Bad luck comes up suddenly from nowhere, and hits you like a thunderstorm. Just as things were going well for the business, my father-in-law had a stroke and died. My wife, my mother-in-law and I were left to cope. Just the three of us. Our livelihood suffered of course.

I had to take over the business. Although I'd often dreamt while I was working for my father-in-law about what I'd do if I was running my own laundry, I hadn't done anything about it. Now I was my own boss, and I could do what I wanted. My ideas weren't that radical. I just thought that rather than simply relying on the passing street trade, we should go and collect from the hostels. In particular, we should deliver to Prome and Tagaung hostels. They were used to me so they would trust me with their clothing. I would promise to do it for them by a particular time and if it was urgent I could do it straight away. To start off with, I picked up the laundry myself, but later on I took on a boy to do deliveries.

Let me tell you one funny thing which has happened while I've been running the laundry. One day I was going to pick up some shirts from a student in Prome hostel. He wasn't an engineering student—I say that because you'll remember no doubt that in those days the majority of students in Prome and Tagaung hostels were studying engineering. But he wasn't. He was an Arts student. When he went to classes, he used to have to go over to the main University campus.

I'll tell you what interested me about him. He was very fastidious about his clothes. He only ever wore sparkling white shirts. He had a lot of shirts of the type that other students wore those days: Victoria Tweed, Ace of Spades. And his *longyis* were all made of silk. When he went to classes, he used to wear a silk *longyi* and a long-sleeved shirt with a stiff collar. He never once gave me a short-sleeved shirt or a cotton *longyi* or a Burmese *taik-pon* jacket to wash. I only ever got silk *longyis* and expensive silk shirts. That's how come I remember him so well.

He used to insist on his cuffs and collars being starched and pressed to a knife edge. And the shirts had to be sparkling white. He'd tell me not to use any of that indigo on them and if I did, he'd notice straight away and get angry. He was really fussy about his appearance. He was good-looking and had a good build, with a broad chest. He was quite tall and fair.

Anyway, in his first year, his shirts were sparkling. They were never very dirty when he sent them to the laundry. Most people, if the collar and cuffs are a bit dirty, they reckon they can get a couple days more wear out of a shirt. Not him. He only ever wore his shirt once before sending it to the laundry. But he never asked for credit. He'd pay the bill each time he sent a shirt. The other students used to pay off their bill at the end of the month and if they were really hard up, they only paid once every two months. Not him though. He coughed up every time. That was how it was for the whole of his first year.

About half-way through the second year, though, he stopped paying the bill every time. Sometimes he would go two or three times before paying. But he never waited until the end of the month. I used to find figures written on his cuffs, or English words. Like 1st century; 13th century, 1789, 1774, 1812, 1914 and so on, historical dates. He'd

153

written it on his cuffs in pencil. It looked like he must be a history student. Sometimes it was English words sometimes it was dates, I don't know what exactly. Maybe he'd written them on there to remind him during exams. I would find bits of paper in his shirt pockets which turned out to be his school notes. He was clearly a very diligent student. When the university re-opened, he brought his silk *longyis* and shirts to the laundry as usual. During the first half of the year, I rarely found anything written on the cuffs. But I used to find red marks on the shoulders, round the neck and on the front of the shirts. I noticed them straight away. I'm sure you can guess what it was. Lipstick, of course! So he's found himself a girlfriend, I thought to myself. His shirts had lipstick stains on them throughout that second year. And I was always coming across love letters in his pockets.

By the third year, no more lipstick stains. No more perfume. His shirts started coming in with yellow stains on them. I reckoned it was whisky. And then they started getting burn-holes in them. I could tell my student was getting into drinking and smoking in a big way. His shirts were no longer their pristine former selves. They were getting dirty, and he'd gone from being someone who wore a clean shirt every day to someone who made one last four or five days. He stopped sending them to the laundry. Just occasionally they'd come in, and when they did, they were stained and burned. I reckon he couldn't afford to have them done any more. In the old days he'd paid up daily, now it was getting to be once a month, sometimes even two or three months at a time. I stopped finding school notes in his pockets. I started finding betting slips from the racetrack.

My student never came back to do the final year. He even left without paying me everything he owed.

Just from looking at that boy's laundry, I could tell that first his heart had been broken and then he had fallen into bad habits. Of all my customers, he is the one I'll always remember best. I've been here a long time and I've seen plenty of them passing through. They leave university and get rich, go into business, become officials or merchants. I see them all again from time to time. But he's one I've never seen since.

But you say you want to hear more about me? OK, now where was I? I'd taken on my father-in-law's business and gradually I was building it up into a popular laundry. I had to take on two or three assistants. I looked after the money and did the accounts and from time to time I did some of the ironing. But once I turned forty or fifty, I found that lifting the big heavy irons was getting too much for me. They weight about fifteen or twenty pounds you know. It was starting to make my shoulders and my arms ache, and the heat was putting a strain on my heart. Eventually I had to lie down. The doctor came to see me when I was recuperating and told me I shouldn't be doing that kind of work any more. He told me to take it easy. So nowadays I don't do the ironing.

How did I get this building? I can assure you I didn't buy this building out of the profits of the laundry business. The laundry has provided just about enough to feed and clothe us and put my five children through school. I've been able to put one daughter through university to become a doctor. A son and a daughter are both engineers. And another son's a schoolteacher. Their education is all thanks to the laundry. The youngest though . . . he's a bit of a waster. He recently got hooked on drugs and now he's in jail. I couldn't do anything about it. Still, I'm sure it'll do him good to have some of the stuffing knocked out of him.

But I put the others through university on the profits of the business. As for the shop, I suppose I was in the right place at the right time. In the old days, we had a thatched hut and bamboo walls. Then do you remember that big fire in Hledan? We rebuilt the shop using timber and a zinc roof. About twenty years ago or so the landlord rebuilt it in brick. The old tenants were given priority so we were able to buy in cheap. I suppose I must have paid about ten thousand *kyats* at the time. Nowadays, it must be worth at least a hundred thousand.

That's how we came to buy the shop. But nowadays, the laundry business doesn't bring in a lot of money. It's been that way for a while. Prices just keep going up. You've got labour costs, and then there's the cost of all the materials: charcoal, dye, washing soda, indigo. And nowadays people don't send their clothes to the laundry. They tend to do their ironing at home and anyway, modern clothes don't need ironing as much as they did in the old days. You get these drip-dry materials where you can just wash and wear. Young people nowadays don't wear proper shirts that much anymore. They all wear sports shirts and T-shirts and jeans. The ones that do wear shirts don't wear good quality ones. They just tend to get one of those fifty or sixty *kyat* shirts that you can buy from the pavement, and then when it's a bit old, they take it down the market to sell it, and buy another one. Some people have just the one shirt and when it wears out they either sell it or just throw it away and get another one. Dyeing and printing T-shirts is a business that's picking up a bit. Nowadays kids like to have things printed on their shirts. But with dyes being so expensive, it's not very profitable.

So all in all, I'm thinking of packing it in. My kids say they'll take it in turns to look after the two of us. They've invited us to come and live with them. But I don't really want to. If we go and live with my daughter, I know that no matter how much my son-in-law says it's not a problem, I'll still feel uncomfortable if I stay there. And the same goes for living with my son. So I'm not going to live with any of my children. I've been thinking. I could sell this place. I'd probably get five or six hundred thousand for it. I could buy a little house on the edge of town and put the rest of the money in the bank and live off the interest.

I reckon the days of the laundry are numbered. If you look around you, you must know what I mean. Even in the middle of town, there aren't many left. In the old days, you had the Bombay laundry, the National, the Madras, the Hollandia. You could get express service in one or two hours, washing, dry cleaning. Every neighbourhood had two or three laundries. Nowadays, some neighbourhoods don't even have one.

I've had enough. I can't work any more. I'm getting too old. I've put my children through university and that my life's ambition fulfilled.

Are you really going to write something about a launderer? Fancy that! Well I've probably given you a rough idea—but there's plenty more to tell. You should come round again *Saya*, and I'll tell you the rest. But the main thing is, *Saya*, laundry is going out of fashion. No-one sends their clothes to the laundry nowadays.

[August 1990]

20

UP ON AN ELEPHANT BUT WITHOUT THE HORSES

I met him in a jungle logging camp, seven miles west of the village where the Shweli river joins the Irrawaddy. He didn't look more than forty-five, average height, brown-skinned, round-faced with gleaming white teeth. He wore a rough cotton longyi, a shirt with a stiff collar and a pinni jacket, with a tasselled Bhamo towel round his shoulders. He spoke softly, with a sweet and gentle voice which I had to strain to catch. His face was soft too, and always smiling; not the face one would expect of a man used to working closely with huge beasts. More like the face of a gentle schoolmaster. I was surprised that he could handle such demanding work.

My name is Mya Wai. I'm forty-six. I was born in Indawgyi Township, Katha District, of Kadu-Kanan stock—but you'd just call us 'Kadu'. We Kadu generally work with elephants.

I climbed on the back of my first elephant when I was six or seven. My father was an *oo-si* and he'd take me with him on his elephant wherever he went. He started off at fifteen as a *sin-pe-kyeik* attendant and moved up through the ranks from *pe-si* back rider, to *oo-si* front rider, to chief rider, and finally camp chief, before retiring.

When I was young, we lived in a village to the west of Indawgyi, although from what I remember, we rarely stayed in the village. We spent most of our time in elephant camps in the jungle. I was born in a logging camp, and my mother died in one, after she gave birth to my younger brother. They were both buried there. I'll live and die in one too. Just like an elephant. You know. When an elephant thinks he's dying, he breaks away from the herd and goes to find his graveyard. After my mother died, my father married her younger sister. Since she had no family, she used to come with us from camp to camp. After my mother died, she was the only one around to look after me.

If we had to go out to find an elephant, my father would take me with him and we'd come back to the camp, sitting high on the elephant's back. Finding elephants was great fun. Early in the morning as dawn was breaking, and the *koels*[1] were calling, my father would knock back one or two pots of Chinese tea and get me up to go into the jungle.

My father was an opium addict when he was young. Under British rule, there was barely an elephant rider who wasn't, or an elephant either, for that matter. The riders would carry it for the elephant but they'd get addicted too. They needed it to overcome their exhaustion and the boredom of having to live in the middle of the jungle. They had to work in all weathers until they dropped. Out in the jungle, even if you had money, there was nothing to do to pass the time apart from smoke opium. So in those days, the British companies used to supply the riders and elephants with opium. Not any more though.

My father was an opium addict until he married my mother. After he gave up, he stuck to bitter Chinese tea, typical elephant rider's tipple, shovelling the leaves into the pot. It's so bitter most people can't stomach it. After he'd woken me up, he'd knock back a pot of tea and light up a cheroot. He'd have fried me some left-over rice with just some onion, oil, and turmeric, no extras. If there was any curry left over from the night before, we'd mix it in.

The night before, when it had got dark, we'd have let the elephants loose to graze. If they were only grazing nearby, my father would take

---

[1] A type of cuckoo, *Eudynamys orientalis*

me with him to catch them. But sometimes it could be as far away as eight or nine miles, which is too far for a child to walk.

When I was about fifteen, I started working as a *pe-kyeik* attendant. A *pe-kyeik* is the person who fastens the steel ropes round the logs which the *oo-si* is sending your way. I did this for about a year and then got promoted to *pe-si*, back rider, the step you have to do before *oo-si*. That's when you get your first chance to ride on top of the elephant, but you can't hold the *hkyun*, the iron hook for goading the elephant, or direct the elephant yourself. The *oo-si* tells you what to do, and you can only do it yourself once you're trained up. After *oo-si*, there's three more levels. The *hsin-kaun*, elephant leader—he controls a team of up to ten elephants, or an entire camp. An *oo-si* gets ninety-seven *kyats* per month. The *hsin-kaun* gets one-eighty-five, and the chief, *hsin-ouq* gets one-eighty-five to two-ninety *kyats*. At the moment I'm a *hsin-ouq*, one level above *hsin-kaun*. I'm in charge of this camp you're visiting.

So I started as a *pe-kyeik* and got promoted after a year. They say the three happiest days of your life are when you get out of the monkhood, get out of jail, and get married. But for an elephant rider, there's a fourth: the day you get given your own elephant. As soon as you become an *oo-si*, they give you your own six-year old elephant. Young elephants are like young men: they're impulsive and vain. But if you grow up with elephants from a young age, you don't get scared of them, no matter how violent they get. You just think of them like you would that old toy cow you used to drag around made out of coconut palm leaves.

My father was born into the elephant business too. He became an *oo-si* at about fifteen or sixteen. He started off in Indawgyi, and then moved to Katha district, Myitkyina, Bhamo and finally ended up based on the Shweli river. He must have known every elephant camp in Upper Burma. He lived on the back of an elephant until he turned sixty. After that, he retired and as his health was failing, he wanted to go back to the village where he was born. Well, I call it a village, but it wasn't really, more like an elephant camp which gradually acquired more and more huts, until one day it was a village of fifty houses.

As soon as I heard my father starting to say he wanted to go home, I knew that he had given up the fight. You know, like an elephant gets sick and breaks away from the herd to go off and find his graveyard. My father was doing the same. That's why I didn't stop him. He left the Shweli river and returned to Indawgyi. Just as I had feared, he died within a month of getting home.

When he died, I was still in the Shweli forest, with a group who were hunting down a herd of wild elephant with tranquilliser guns. The herd went up north from Shweli to Katha and Tigyaing and we followed them, but although we found their tracks, we couldn't catch them. Sometimes the tracks would disappear and we'd lose them. Then they broke off to the east and we came round to the tributaries of the Shweli and followed them back down to the river again. When we got back to the camp, I found out my father had died four months earlier and I had missed his funeral.

An *oo-si*'s life is exhausting and very dangerous. You're up before the dawn breaks, a quick breakfast of leftovers, and then off to find the elephants you released to graze the previous night. Usually they're about ten miles away from the camp. Everyone has to go and find his own. So you've got to plunge off on your own into the deep jungle. Sometimes you've got to go into wild sugar cane which is taller than an elephant, ten or twenty feet deep, and full of wild animals. You could be bitten by a tiger, or mauled by a bear. So you've got to be aware, and keep your eyes peeled, and be brave and have plenty of stamina.

You've also got to be nimble and have keen senses like a tiger, because you're only armed with a spear and a long knife. When we go out after the elephants, there are certain traditions we all follow, like not spitting or peeing on their fetter tracks. Fetter tracks are what we call the trails left where the elephant's been. If an *oo-si* sees an elephant's footprints, he doesn't necessarily know whether it's his elephant or not. But he gets to know his elephant's foot-prints and its habits, like whether he throws the branches he's chewed to the right or the left. An elephant that throws its branches away to the left never throws to the right, and vice versa.

So an *oo-si* will look at the tracks and the way the branches have been thrown, and he'll know whether it's his elephant. If he comes across an elephant dropping, he'll examine it. If the elephant has eaten bamboo the night before, in the morning, he won't be found near the bamboo groves—he'll be off in the sugar cane. And if you find sugar cane leaves in his droppings in the morning, you'll know that by now, he'll be elsewhere. That's how you work out where he's gone.

So an *oo-si* will know by looking at the leaves in the droppings whether his elephant will be in the bamboo or the sugar cane by now. Once he gets to the sugar cane, he can't storm in straight away. There'll be animals in the grove and if he rushes in, he'll startle them and the elephant. So he waits by the edge of the grove and listens for the sound of his elephant's bell which he knows so well he can recognise it immediately. But even if the elephant is close by, he still can't storm in, or he'll frighten the elephant who could turn nasty. So he has to start singing so the elephant will recognise his voice and then he can coax him out gently. The elephant may not make up its mind immediately to come out, and the *oo-si* will have to light up a cheroot and sit there for a while and croon 'Come on, come on, come on out'. If the elephant pushes his way out of the thicket, the *oo-si* has to get him to crouch down, calling out '*Mek, mek*'. If the elephant refuses to crouch immediately, the *oo-si* needs to judge whether he's gone wild or not. Sometimes an elephant can start acting wild if he's come across a herd of jungle elephants. That's why, if he doesn't immediately follow an order, an *oo-si* must decide whether he's gone wild or not. You can't remove his fetters and attach the saddle and mount him until he has accepted your instructions. Once he gets back to the camp, the *oo-si* has a bite to eat and waters the elephant.

In the rainy season, our work consists of taking the cut logs and dragging them down to the rivers and streams. In the hot season, we rest in the camp. But although I say rest, there's no chance to lie down. We may not be hauling logs, but we have to train the elephants, and keep an eye on them, treat them if they're sick, weave the ropes which are used in the monsoon, cut the logging roads—hardly a rest.

I've been living in this elephant camp for about ten years now, as long as my oldest son has been alive. I was married here, to the daughter of an *oo-si*. We never travel around so we have to look to each other when we want to get married. There are about forty houses in this camp, which is quite big. You can imagine how it is at night, once the work is over, and we've got nowhere to go. In the depths of the forest, there's no kerosene, and the only light we have comes from the hearth. We elephant riders take great care of one another and no-one offends against another man's wife and family. We firmly believe that anyone who does will be trampled to death by an elephant. Whenever an elephant rider gets married, he has to make an offering to the *nats*, either Uteinna, or Kawkari. We also make an offering to Kawkari if someone new comes to the camp, over on that *nat* shrine under the banyan tree.

Does my son go to school? Hardly! What school is there for him to go to? Not just him, but all the kids in the camp—where are they going to go to school? There's a school at the village on the river, but generally speaking we can't send them to it, and we have to teach them their ABC ourselves. And a year ago I sent him for about a month to be a novice in the monastery in the village. He learnt a couple of prayers—that's all we elephant men can manage for our sons. Of course, none of us went to school either—we've all spent all our lives in the jungle. All I know is what I learnt when I was a novice in the monastery.

How much are we paid? I don't know how they expect us to manage, *Saya*. Even living in the jungle, you still have expenses. For an elephant guard, it's even worse. They only get eighty *kyats* a month. So they have to top that up by hunting wild game and having their wives weave baskets to sell at the market.

As an elephant rider you're at the bottom of the heap, *Saya*. But we love our elephants. We've grown up with them, and all we want to do is live here and die with them. I've been an elephant rider for thirty years now, and I've lived with elephants since I was a young boy. I've seen elephants with incredible skill, and I've seen elephants who have trampled forty to fifty *oo-sis* to death. I've seen wild elephant herds and elephants in pain. I know more about elephants than I do about people. They are my friends. They are my life.

I want my son to be an elephant rider. Like father, like son. You know that saying about parents wanting the best for their children? You want to see your children ride an elephant with an entourage of horses following on behind. Well, I'll be doing everything I can to make sure my children ride elephants. But I won't be able to afford the horses.

[August 1988]

21

MARIA CATALINA

I bumped into her on the embankment at Moe Bre dam[1]. Her fair skin was tanned by the sun and the wind. She had shoulder length hair, round eyes and a pointed nose. She was quite tall and slim, and wore a bright red woollen sweater, flip flops, and a Kayan black longyi with green stripes, woven on a back-strapped loom. She was carrying a small child on her back by means of a blanket slung over her shoulders and tied around her waist. On her head she carried a basket. I couldn't work out quite how old she was. I thought she was about thirty but she could have been younger.

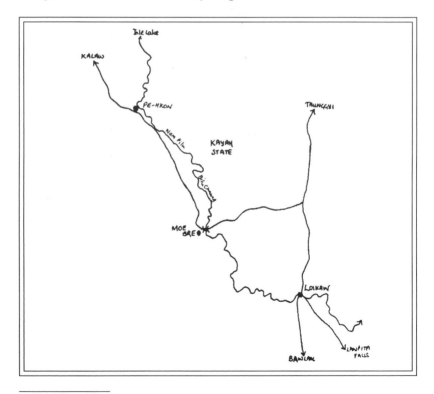

---

[1] One of two hydro-electric dams built with Japanese aid on the Biluchaung stream in Shan State.

My age? Well, to tell you the truth, I don't know exactly how old I am. But I was a young girl when they built Moe Bre dam. Our village is under the water. Before the dam was built, this was all a big valley with mountains on either side. Our village was down at the bottom. When they built the dam they blocked off one end of the valley to catch the water coming from Biluchaung and the other streams and all the villages round here had to move, including ours. The old villages are all drowned in the reservoir now.

Before my father got married, he used to hunt wild game in the hills. We couldn't afford a rifle so he had to make do with a cross bow. Sometimes he'd use snares. When my mother gave birth to my older brother, Kwe Ri, she got sick. I don't know what was the matter but she had to stay in bed. We asked the spirit healers from a nearby village to come and cure her but she didn't get any better.

One day when my father was in the jungle he met an old man who gave him some medicinal roots. He said that if you ground the roots up and gave them to people, it would cure them of anything. But the man also said that if my father accepted the roots, he would have to give up hunting. My father took them and went back home. I don't know what sort of root it was. My father knew a lot about the plants in the jungle from going out hunting. For example if he wanted to catch fish he would grind up *hone*[2] root and sprinkle it in the streams and pools and all the fish would die. There were some other roots which he would grind up with the horns of the mountain goat. If you spread this on the skin, it would make any pain disappear immediately. And there were other roots which you had to grind up with alcohol.

As for the root the old man gave him, he said it didn't need grinding up with anything except water. He said 'Pound it together with water and rub it in and the pain will go away. If you mix it with water and drink it, it will cure the disease'. I don't know what it was. My father said he didn't know either. When he got home, he ground it up with some cold water and gave it to my mother. It worked in no time at all. She'd barely been able to drink water, but soon she could drink *hkaun-ye*[3] and eat millet. A month after taking the medicine, she was well enough to get up and go back to her usual tasks, growing millet, weaving, brewing *hkaun-ye* and polishing rice.

After that, my father had to give up hunting. He became a *nat-saya*. Around here that usually means a sort of spirit healer, like a witch doctor who the villagers all around call out to cure sick people. He would use a

---

[2] A kind of creeper, *Anamirta cocculus* or *Cocculus indicus*, the bark of which is used for killing fish.

[3] An intoxicating liquor made from rice much used by the Karen and Chin.

number of medicinal roots but as a last resort he would always turn to the root that the old man had given him since it always seemed to work. He did this for years.

When they built the dam, they blocked off the valley. We had to move out of our villages because they were going to be submerged. I can remember everything very clearly. My mother was casting chicken bones and making offerings to the *nats* to stop us from having to pull down our house. My father made offerings to the *nats*. He gave them pigs liver and *hkaun-ye*. But it didn't do any good. We still had to move.

Our village had to move out of the valley and onto the mountain slopes. The valley was covered with thick jungle. The government said that we had to cut it down because of the reservoir. But how could we villagers make any impact on it? So the government had to come and chop it down for us. Once they'd cut it down, they dynamited the mountain and blasted away at the sides of the valley and filled it up with digging machines, graders, cranes, rock-breakers, concrete mixers and steam rollers and trucks. The whole valley was hidden in clouds of dust. It looked a bit like a hazy mountain mist. But mountain mist is beautiful and white. This dust was filthy.

If you looked down into the valley you could see people hard at work and hear the banging and clattering of the machinery and the boom of the dynamite. Some people enjoyed watching all the to-ing and fro-ing. Not me. I missed our old village and I missed the dancing and drinking at the parties we used to have. In the winter the hill-side was covered in orchids. My older brother and I would go out to pick them to sell in Pekhon and at the Moe Bre five-day market[4] along with the fish we'd caught using *hone*. When orchids were out of season we would go there to sell *hkaun-ye* liquor and *nga-pein* fish. It wasn't far, just in the next valley over the hill.

I sat on the mountain slopes and longed for our old village. It had vanished off the face of the earth. Once the villages went, my father's living as a spirit healer disappeared too since there was no one left who wanted to consult the *nats*. There were thousands of workers instead. At night they would work under the spotlights so there were a lot of accidents. Lots of them caught malaria too. So they opened a clinic to treat them, with proper doctors and medicines. They would treat the locals if we went there. When I had goitre, my father tried to cure me with the root that the old man had given him. But it didn't work. So I went to the clinic and they cured my goitre just like they seemed to be able to cure the rest of the villagers who went along. Then my father had no-one left

---

[4] In many parts of Shan State, the daily market rotates between five neighbouring towns or villages.

to treat. His roots weren't as powerful as the medicines they had in the clinic. It put him out of a job. He lost his living at the same time as we lost our village. All at the same time they built the dam.

When he lost his job as a spirit healer, he decided he didn't want to go back to hunting. So he went to work on the construction site as a labourer. He earned a daily wage. It was very exhausting work. He'd work on the cranes or the digging machines. Sometimes he'd be on the earth-movers. He had to put the stone in place to build the embankment. The one that we're sitting on. I can't tell you exactly which stones were put in place by my father. They're in here somewhere though.

When they first started building the reservoir, the people round here were all too frightened to go and work on the site. They'd heard that all of the villages were going to be submerged under the water and they thought the *nats* would be angry. We Kayan are very simple people. We are just hunters and farmers. The only tools we know are cross-bows and knives. We'd never seen earth-diggers or drilling machines before. We thought the guardian *nat* of the mountain would be angry when he saw it being blasted away. We were afraid that the soil *nat* would be angry to see the earth being dug up and the forest *nat* would be angry when he saw the trees being chopped down with chain saws. So we didn't dare to apply for jobs doing these things.

Because of this, the government had to recruit workers from elsewhere who weren't worried about such things. But they still couldn't get enough people so they had to persuade us to come and work too. Once we saw that the *nats* weren't angry about the mountains being destroyed and the trees being cut down and the earth being moved, we plucked up courage to apply for the jobs. But it was still a big shock to us mountain peasants to have to work with these machines.

When my father got a job we moved from the mountain slopes to live in the workers' camp. In our mountain hut, once it got dark, the only light there was came from the fire. In the camp though, everything was lit up by electric light.

Ah, yes, let me explain about my name. My name is Maria. Maria Catalina. That's right, it's a Christian name. Most of the Kayan are Christian. The Catholic missionaries came to our area a long time ago. When I was young I had a Kayan name, Nyay Mu. That's Kayan language. But I don't usually use it. I've been Roman Catholic ever since I was a girl. Just like my mother and father. A little while after I was born I was christened and given the name Maria Catalina by a Roman Catholic priest. That's why I wear a crucifix round my neck. This is the image of the Lord Jesus Christ. It's made out of silver.

Once we moved to the work camp, my father started hanging around with the other men in the camp. Before, he was like all the men in our family and had only ever drunk *hkaun-ye*. All the women drink it too. Even the children drink it once they are about three months old. I suppose it's a bit like you all give milk to your children to make them big and strong. In our house after my mother had weaned us, or if she was going into the jungle and didn't have time to breast feed, she would give us *hkaun-ye*.

But when we moved to the camp, my father said he was working so hard he needed hard liquor. My mother used to distil it in our house for him, out of millet. It was very strong. If you held a match to it, it would catch light—'whoosh'!! We still used to ferment *hkaun-ye* for the rest of us. I suppose it was because my father's work was so tiring that he needed a drink before he left. When he came home he'd have another. One day he went to work after he'd been drinking and was killed when he fell off a crane.

That was the day they started to build the sluice gate. My father was on the night shift. He had to leave for work at ten that night. He was sleeping off an earlier bout of drinking. At ten when he had to go to work, my mother woke him up and told him to get going. Before he went, he had another drink.

A couple of hours later one of the Kayan workers from our quarters came and woke us up and told us that my father fallen off the crane and been killed. My mother, Kwe Ri and I ran over to the clinic where he had been taken but he was already dead by the time we got there. After my father was killed, the only one left in the house who could work in the camp was my older brother Kwe Ri. But his pay wasn't enough for us all to live on. My younger sister was attending school. So my mother and I had to brew *hkaun-ye* to sell. We'd also sell orchids if they were in season.

How did I get married? It happened like this. When my father died it was difficult to make ends meet from selling orchids and *hkaun-ye* and we didn't have enough to eat. When we were living in the village we always had enough to eat, no matter what. We could grow millet and pumpkins and gourds in our fields and we could make *hkaun-ye* and keep pigs. But in the camp, we couldn't do those things. We had to buy all our food, including rice and pumpkins. There was nowhere in the workers' quarters to keep pigs. So everything we needed, we had to buy, other than *hkaun-ye* which we could still make at home.

That was when I met my husband. He's Kayan too. I think where you come from *Saya*, you call us Padaung. We call ourselves Kayan. That's right—Kayan women are the ones with the brass rings around our necks. But nowadays we don't do that any more except for festivals and then we only wear two or three rings at a time. So long as they're hinged you can take them off easily. My mother has brass rings round her neck which she can't take off. Hers were put on when she was young. She must have at least a *viss* of copper round her neck which she can't take off.

My husband's name is Seh Ri. He worked on the Moe Bre dam just like my father did. We met in the camp. He used to come and buy *hkaun-ye* from us. That's how we got to know one another. We got married after a while. Not like in our old village. In the middle of our village, we had a 'hall' where all the single boys and girls would go to flirt. We'd say 'I'll come and help you in the fields' and 'Will you come and help me in the fields?'. Then the two of them would go off to the fields to court and get to know one another. But our village isn't around any more and they haven't done that since my parents' time. My husband and I didn't meet in the fields. We met on the Moe Bre dam construction site when I was selling *hkaun-ye* to him and the other workers.

Once they finished the dam, we were both out of a job. They closed down the camp. We had nowhere to go. Our villages were gone, beneath the reservoir. The valley where we used to live was now a lake. We thought about going up to live on the mountain slopes, but we didn't know how to live up there. I'd got so used to the bright lights that I couldn't sleep in the dark. If there wasn't any light, I'd cry all night. Also, since my husband's feet had been crushed when a block had fallen on them, he couldn't go out and hunt.

That's why we decided to move to Pe-khon. We built a hut by the side of the stream on the edge of town. There were lots of other Kayan like us living there now that the camp had been closed down. Since my husband's feet were bad, it was up to me to go out to work. You see, he couldn't hunt or farm so he had to stay at home cooking and looking after the children while I went out to work. Well why not? Jesus Christ has given me two hands and two feet. I don't know how we'd cope if I was in the same position as my husband. But since I've got the use of both my legs, it doesn't bother me if I have to go out to work.

I ferment *hkaun-ye* and sell it near the market in the middle of Pe-khon. I don't know if you've been to Pe-khon or not, but if you have, you might remember there's a cross-roads in the centre of town with a large cross. It's a big crucifix which our church has put up. I've opened up a *hkaun-ye* stall near there. We don't have a house there, unfortunately. Some people can just open up a stall in front of their houses if they've got a patch of land and a couple of benches. Lucky them. I sell *hkaun-ye* to the women who've come to market and kids coming home from school. If they're feeling hungry or thirsty, they come to my *hkaun-ye* stall. It's a bit like the teashops and soft drink shops where you live, *Saya*. They've been brought up on it since they were babies.

On the days when there's a market in Moe Bre I go there to sell orchids. My husband goes out and picks them. Although both his feet were broken, he can still climb high up into the trees to pick them. I go to market and sell them. Moe Bre has engineers living there, and officials, and they all like to buy my orchids.

I'm on my way back from selling orchids in Moe Bre market now. I got up early this morning to go there. It's a long way over the mountains and it's tiring with a child on your back. That's why I come by boat. Providing I get here in time to catch the opening of the sluice gates, I can make it to the market.

They open them up once in the morning and once at night. I think you must have seen them doing it. First they open the lower sluice gate and shut the boats inside. Then they open the upper sluice gate and the water from the reservoir enters and fills up the lock until the water level rises to the same level as the reservoir. Once the boat's gone they do the same thing in reverse. The water is released from the bottom into the river until the lock and the stream are at the same level. That way you can go smoothly up the river. But it's very important that you catch them at the right time of day because if you don't, you end up with a wasted journey and a basket of wilted flowers.

I'm on my way home from the market at the moment. I've sold twenty *kyats* worth of orchids and I'm waiting for them to open the locks so I can go back home. With the money I've earned I've been able to buy my husband some cheroots and I've bought some Chinese snacks for the older children and some salt and some MSG[5].

My name is Maria Catalina. In Kayan, Nyay Mu. I don't know how old I am but I was a teenager when they built this dam. Since they've built the reservoir, it's been easy for us to travel. Maybe you could say that my father gave his life so that this dam could be built for us. Who knows which of those stones were the ones my father put in place? Who can say whether my father fell to his death from this dam for our sakes? All I know is that we live like this now because of my father dying.

Why don't I wear fresh orchids in my hair? Well, sometimes, quite often, I do. But they cost money. So I've bought some plastic flowers in Moe Bre market. You buy them just the once and they last for ever so you save money.

I miss our village. It's all under water now. How much do I miss it? More than anything in the world.

[December 1987]

---

[5] Monosodium glutamate, which literally translates as "taste powder" is also known by the trade name Ajinomoto. It is a staple seasoning for the Burmese.

22

FOREVER WAITING TABLES

She told me her name was Ma Kyin Yi. I don't know if that was the name she'd been born with, but that's the one I shall have to use. She must have been about twenty-five. She was fair-skinned, medium-height with a frizzy perm and wore a cheap batik longyi *and matching top and white sandals. Although she had attractively-shaped eyes, her nose was a little squashed. She told me she was part-Karen, but I would have said she was part-Chinese.*

I met her in a restaurant in a town in Upper Burma. As soon as we walked into the restaurant she greeted us and put us in a private side room. She personally took our order and brought us our drinks, soda water, ice and food, and she returned to sit at our table and serve us our food. She was not a wanton girl like the waitresses and hotel girls of old. She was simply a girl trying to make a living from waiting tables. Since she had read a fair bit, she was familiar with the names of writers. Here is her story as she told it to me.

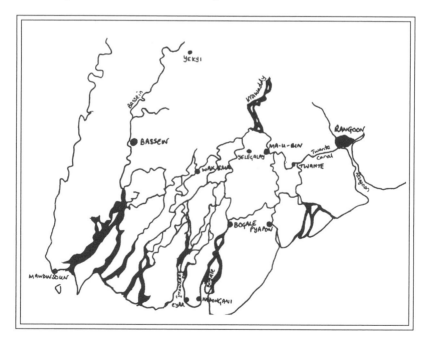

I know—you hear my name and then you look at me and you think I must be Chinese. You're not the only one, lots of people have said that. Well it's sort of true. My father was part-Chinese. But my mother is Karen. You'll be surprised to hear how I got here.

I was born and brought up in lower Burma, in the delta, in a village in Bogale township. You might know it because it's quite big. There are quite a few general stores there which are owned by Chinese, and pawn shops and liquor stalls. My father had a licence to run a liquor stall.

Do you want to hear about my father? Well, we all called him A-teh, not Father. His father was Chinese, born in China. His mother was half-and-half and born in Burma. He told me my grandfather came to Burma from China during the war along one of the trade routes. When he got to Rangoon he did all sorts of jobs. When he first arrived he didn't have a job, so he used to collect cigarette butts down in Chinatown and get the bits of unsmoked tobacco and make them into new cigarettes to sell. He said he could sell them to people like the Chinese opium addicts. He was an opium addict too, my grandfather. After that he had various jobs, scraping out people's earwax, coolie on a steamboat, washing dishes in a teashop.

He also sold noodles on the street. Every night he would sell 'knock-knock' noodles, and advertise them by banging on a piece of wood with a bamboo stick. To start off with he sold them pre-wrapped but later he used to sell them fresh from a tray. But it wasn't his own business, he had to go round selling them for someone else. He would carry the noodles and chopsticks and plates on a tray. He'd walk in front, or sometimes behind the owner of the stall, shouting out 'Noodles for sale!' and knocking on his wooden stick. If they found a customer, he'd put the tray down and the owner would make up the noodles and he would clear up afterwards.

During that time, he married the daughter of the stall-owner. My grandfather was pure Chinese, but my mother was half-Chinese half-Burmese. They had five children, my father was the third, the only son, so my father loved him best because the Chinese always want sons. That's how come my father got to go to Chinese school, but all my aunts were just married off young.

My father learnt Chinese writing and arithmetic in Chinese school, but I don't know what standard he got to. They've got lots of levels in Chinese schools, he told me, but I didn't go to Chinese school, so I can't write Chinese at all.

After he left school, my father went to work in a Chinese wholesaler's. He started off as a tally-clerk, but then he got promoted to accounts clerk. My father worked very hard so the rich Chinaman who owned the trading house trusted him and let him handle the money. My father took good care of the money and the goods and later on they expanded to cover the delta and my father became a paddy agent. At harvest time he would go out with the money bags and buy up the paddy throughout that part of the delta.

One year the paddy business was particularly profitable and the Chinaman decided to build a rice-mill in the delta. He put my father in charge since he couldn't be there to keep an eye on it. My father worked hard at this and then later the Chinaman got licences to run pawn-shops and liquor stalls in Bogale township and my father became a pawn-broker. That's when he met my mother.

My mother is Karen. Her family were paddy-farmers. At harvest time, when they had a bit of spare cash, she'd go and buy some of the odds and ends of jewellery and gold which were unredeemed at the pawn-shop, and that's how she and my father got to know each other. When they got married, the Chinaman gave my father a liquor shop licence, and he only had to pay the licence fee back later in instalments, as if he'd borrowed the money to pay for it.

My father was a very sociable man. After he'd been living in the village for a while, it was like he'd lived there all his life. But although he'd got a liquor licence, he never drank. He didn't even smoke. He told me all this, so that's how I know.

When I was just about grown up, about twelve years old, the liquor stall went bust, and our family started to have problems. On top of that my father's health deteriorated. I've got three sisters and three brothers—I'm the third daughter. But my two older sisters had got married and moved away so it was like I was the oldest daughter.

When my father lost the licensed shop, we didn't have much to live on. He didn't have any other businesses, he didn't have the pawn-shop any more. It wasn't like he could go back and work in the rice-mill because it had been taken over by the Co-operatives and they had all their own people.

So after that we had to sell the liquor out of our house, but we had to sell it as moonshine. The government had its own liquor stalls so they didn't give licences to private ones. That meant we had to sell it illegally.

To start off with, my father sold it himself, but since he wasn't well by then, I started putting the glasses on the tables and waitressing and so on. I suppose you could say I've been waitressing since I was twelve. Later on when my father got worse we used to have to sell the liquor too.

Yes, yes, of course we sold the customers short a little bit!! But we didn't dilute our liquor with water. We sold rice liquor, so it would've been easy for the customers to tell if it was diluted. Our customers were all peasants, so they'd know straight away. They wouldn't drink it unless you could set light to it. That meant we couldn't water it down. But yes,

I'm afraid we did use to cheat them a bit with the measures. As soon as the drinkers were a bit sozzled they stopped paying attention to the amount we gave them. Actually, once they were drunk, they couldn't tell if it was diluted either. Their stomachs were already saturated so they were going to get drunk whether it was diluted or not.

We sold moonshine liquor for about four or five years, but after that we had to close down because the Excise Department were clamping down. By then I must have been about fifteen.

How did I get into reading? I'd been reading stories and comics ever since I was little. We had a still and we used to distil our own moonshine. I've known how to do it ever since I was about twelve—my father taught me. I used to read while we were distilling because I had to sit next to the still all day and keep the fire going and collect the distillate and change the containers. I'd get bored doing that all day long and that's when I got into reading anything I could get my hands on. I passed sixth standard at school.

Soon after I turned sixteen, I got married. My husband was from the Excise Authorities. He was about twelve years older than me. We'd known him ever since my father became a licensee. I don't know if he came to our shop because he was from Excise, but I know he liked a drink. He wasn't from those parts, he came from a small town on the Rangoon-Mandalay railway line. To start with, I'd thought he was single, but later on I found out that he'd got a wife and kids. But by that time it was too late to do anything, because we'd been living openly as man and wife and the village had recognised us as being married.

Later on, he got caught breaking the regulations and he was sacked. I suppose he was lucky not to go to jail for what he did. His supervisors protected him and managed to keep him out of prison. After that, he'd say he was going off to Rangoon to look for a job, but he'd always come back without one. One day he told me he was going off to Rangoon to get a job and he never came back. He left me and his son behind.

Soon after that, my father died. After he died, I had to take on the responsibility of looking after my mother, my sister and my three younger brothers, and my son. He's eight or nine now. When my father died, we pawned what we'd got and took out a loan and opened up a shop in our house. I went up to Bogale and bought Chinese cakes and dried fruits and cigarettes, cheroots and stuff like that. I couldn't buy much because if it didn't sell quickly, I had to wait until I'd sold it all. That's why I didn't go to Bogale regularly. Sometimes I got to go every three or four days, but sometimes I didn't go for more than a week. It depended on how things sold.

I'd take the motor-launch to town and that where I met this clerk. He was the same age as me—I must have been about twenty then. He'd failed his exams and dropped out of school and gone to work on the launch. To start with, I really hated him. He was bad-tempered and foul-mouthed. He was always scowling at me, like I was riding on the boat without paying or something. I used to look at him and scowl back, and sometimes I'd spit loudly and turn my head away.

But one time, I was climbing onto the boat and I was loaded down with things and almost fell into the water. He grabbed me and rescued my bits and pieces which had fallen in. After that we became friends and we started talking and if he wasn't busy on the boat he'd come to the market with me. I suppose that's how we ended up going out together. Then he asked me to come and live in Bogale with him, but I couldn't, because I'd got my mother and my son and my sisters and brothers to look after. That's why I still had to stay in my village.

Sometimes I went with him if he went up to Rangoon. If his boat was being used for the pagoda festival at Mawdin or something then I used to go with him then. We weren't together long, not much more than a year or so. No kids or anything like that. After about a year, he was out drinking and fell in the water and drowned.

I was really depressed then. Here I was, not much over twenty, and already I'd got through two husbands. I was either a divorcee or a widow. I certainly hadn't had much luck with men. About that time, when I was feeling down, a friend of mine who was going to work in Rangoon invited me to go with her. When we got to Rangoon, we stayed in South Okkalapa and I looked for a job. I struck lucky, because those days, it was easy to get a job as a waitress in Rangoon and I ended up working in a restaurant in the city. It was good work. The owner of that particular restaurant didn't want to get a reputation. The waitresses used to get free meals and you got to keep the tips from the clients.

It wasn't a bad life. I used to be able to send money back to my family in the delta. I had enough money to buy clothes and jewellery. I became very popular in that restaurant. Not because of my looks, because there were much prettier girls than me. It must just have been that I was generally friendly. Some of the pretty girls were no good with the customers. They'd only pay attention to the most generous and the richest customers. I treated them all the same. As far as I was concerned, any customer that came to the restaurant, whether they'd got lots of money or not, whether they were good tippers or not, I looked after them the same, and treated them with care. That's why the regulars asked for me, and because I was good with them, I got lots of tips.

Because of this, one of the other girls got jealous of me, and was looking to start a fight. She kept dropping remarks, about how I'd already had two husbands and all that rubbish. To start with, I put up with it, but in the end I got sick of it and we got into a fight. I pulled her hair and slapped her cheeks. Her face all swelled up and stayed like that for a week. She's still got the bruises—and my scars still haven't healed either. After that, the restaurant owner threw us both out. Since I was good with the customers, I knew I could go and work somewhere else. Still, it wasn't so easy after that. You know the reputation waitresses have— you'll have read about it in the papers. They took action against the restaurants and the waitresses were all fired. The ones they didn't close down were operating underground. Because of that, my friend and I came to work in this town, in a restaurant. It's not bad here. We've rented a room locally.

I've had enough of marriage. I've still not got over the last two. I just want to bring up my son properly, get him through tenth standard and manage somehow to send him to university. I don't care if I go under, but I want him to keep his head above water.

[April 1989]

23

JASMINE GARLANDS

I used to see her every morning near a busy tea-shop, hanging around the cars which had stopped in the traffic. She was quite dark, with round eyes and a high brow, straight nose and full lips with gleaming white teeth. Her hair was shoulder-length. She wore a white man's shirt and a short grubby green Tetron school longyi, *and flip-flops. I guessed she was about fifteen or sixteen. She would come up to the cars with a bunch of garlands in one hand, shouting 'Jasmine for sale, jasmine for sale!', so I christened her 'Miss Jasmine' which seemed to appeal to her. I would sometimes come across her at the Myenigone traffic lights, and sometimes at Hledan junction. If she caught sight of me in the car, she would come up to me and say 'Uncle, won't you buy some flowers?' If the lights were still red, I would always buy four or five strings. This is what she told me about herself.*

Since you started it, Uncle, all the drivers at the tea-shop have started calling me 'Miss Jasmine'. I like the name. It's pretty, and it suits me because I sell jasmine. My real name is Tin Tin Aye, though, like the actress. My father chose it because he said I looked like her when I was little. He said I'd got her face. I didn't know who she was when I was young, but now they've shown two or three of her films in our ward— 'Mist Melts Away in Summer', 'Love, Hate', I think they were. But that's just cinema. It's not real. She's a film star, and I'm just a jasmine-seller. We've got nothing in common. Our lives are totally different, our education is completely different, the way we make a living is streets apart. She's the famous Tin Tin Aye, people have heard of her all over the country, but the only people who've heard of me are the drivers round here.

Tin Tin Aye is from Pyapon—people call her Miss Pyapon. Well I'm from Rangoon. I was born here. But Miss Rangoon makes it sound as though I'm something important. Actually, I was born on the edge of North Okkalapa, down by Ngamoeyeik creek. The hut where I was born isn't even there any more. We've moved around North Okkalapa so much I'm not sure where it was.

My father, Ko Sein Lin, was a trishaw driver. He's from Rangoon too. He told me when he was a boy, suburbs like North Okkalapa weren't built yet. He says in those days he lived in U Wisara New Ward. You probably remember it. Dad tells me it's where Resistance Park is now.

Dad left school early and started pedalling a trishaw. In those days, you used to pay two *kyats* a day to the owner. The minimum fare was fifty *pyas*, he said, but it only cost one or two *kyats* to go all the way into town. He didn't go as far as town though, he used to do the patch around Myenigone. In those days, there were only trishaws and horse-carts around Bagaya Road. The horse-carts would go from Sanchaung up to the Shwedagon Pagoda, or across to Shwegondine or into town. For a short trip, you'd hire a trishaw.

Dad would park his trishaw at the Myenigone trishaw stand. He always managed to find enough work there so he never had to go elsewhere. He says in those days the area was full of speakeasys and, uh, I don't know if I should say this, uh, brothels, so it was easy for a trishaw-peddler to make a living. All the students used to come and drink at 'Akyone's' in Myenigone. My mother says Akyone was the name of the chinaman who owned the Bawgabala liquor shop.

Later on, people like my father's family who lived in U Wisara New Ward and all the people squatting in huts around Myenigone were relocated to the new towns, North Okkalapa and South Okkalapa. By that time my mother and father were going out together. They met while my father was pedalling a trishaw in Myenigone, and my mother was selling chicken salad and fried beef outside that Bawgabala shop. In those days my father was about twenty, my mother must have been about eighteen. Then my mother and father were relocated and they each had to go to a different place: my father went to South Okkalapa and my mother went to North Okkalapa, and it became a bit more difficult to make a living. After that, my father pedalled his trishaw around South Okkalapa and my mother worked sewing buttons onto women's blouses in a sewing machine shop near North Okkalapa market. In those days, buttons and trimmings were very fashionable on women's blouses and the work wasn't so bad, it was enough to bring in a bit extra. My mother's father used to be a carpenter but later when he was building a house he fell off the roof and broke his back and after that he couldn't work any more so the rest of my mother's family had to earn what they could.

My father was pedalling his trishaw in South Okkalapa but he wasn't making much of a living because he kept coming over to North Okkalapa every day, which is a long trip if you think about it. There's no direct route, you've got to do a big bend round to the Kaba Aye Pagoda Road and back. Even so, my father says he used to make the trip every day. And when he came over every day, it used to interrupt my mother's work, so later on he took to working out of the trishaw stand near North Okkalapa market. Every morning at dawn he would pedal over there and spend the whole day working out of the North Okkalapa stand, and then when it got dark he would cycle back to South Okkalapa.

I don't know how the news reached my mother's father, but when he heard about my mother and father he was very angry. He didn't want any daughter of his marrying a trishaw driver. In his view, a carpenter's daughter should marry a carpenter. Nowadays, being a trishaw driver isn't so bad. They make an honest living. But my grandfather was old-fashioned, and he was furious at the idea that his daughter was on the way to marrying one.

My mother ended up getting sick of him shouting at her and ran off with my father. My grandfather was so angry he told her not to bother coming back so they had to go and stay with friends who lived on the outskirts of North Okkalapa. My father carried on with the trishaw. My grandfather was so angry he didn't see his daughter until he was on his deathbed, about a year later. After he died, my grandmother took us back.

At home, when my father's earnings weren't enough to live on, my mother and grandmother used to do odd jobs, whatever came their way. That meant selling boiled peas in the morning, selling fresh vegetables when they were in season, washing the old plastic from the factories at North Okkalapa, any kind of work really. By then, there were quite a few in our family. There are six of us children. The oldest is a boy. He stayed at school till seventh standard which he failed, and then he went to work in a car workshop which belonged to a friend of my father's. He got married early and left home. Then there's my big sister. She was no good at school, so she used to stay home and do the housework. She married a driver. She'd go down to Keighley market early in the morning to buy vegetables and fish and that's where she met him. She's left home and moved out to Thaketa.

Next up is my brother. He doesn't live with us. He's not married or anything, but he was so bad my Dad threw him out. Don't ask. I can't count the number of times he's got into fights and been hauled off down the police station. He drinks, see, and when he comes home after drinking he complains to my mother. If my father's there, he doesn't dare come home, and he just dosses down anywhere he can. I've got no idea how he gets enough to eat and drink. Sometimes he goes to South Okkalapa, sometimes he goes to Thaketa, sometimes we don't know where he goes to. Once we didn't see him for four or five months.

He comes back while my father's out and asks my mother for money. She still seems to love him and she gives him whatever she's got, behind my father's back. If she doesn't have any money, she takes whatever clothes and hair-pieces she's got down to the pawn shop. When I think about it sometimes, it doesn't seem fair that she loves the worst son most and lets him get away with murder, and the rest of us who behave ourselves don't get any special treatment.

I'm the fourth child, and then there's one sister and one brother after me. When Dad got older, he couldn't pedal his trishaw like he used to. People don't like to hire old trishawmen, maybe it's because they feel embarrassed about it, or they think old men won't be able to pedal fast enough. Dad's eyesight's no good any more either and you can't pedal a trishaw at night if you can't see properly. Once he's paid the owner for the day's rent, he keeps pedalling all day to pay it off. But he can't cycle during the heat because he's getting old. He often catches a cold in the rainy season, so he can't work then either. He gets asthma and congestion and then we have to buy medicine for him.

That's why I had to go out to work. Yes, you guessed right, I'm only fifteen. My brother's twelve and my sister's ten. It was costing a lot to put us all through school, so I couldn't stay there any longer. I passed sixth standard but left the following year. I've been working since before I left school.

So what do I do? Well what can you do at my age, Uncle? I've had to work since I was ten, and what can you do at ten? You can get work as a housemaid, or you can sell snacks, and that's about it. But I didn't want to do housework, so I started selling fried snacks on the streets. You don't make much money, selling snacks, because you only sell what you can. If you sell out, it's alright, but if you don't, you make a loss. You only take what you can sell and you only make about ten *pyas* on each piece.

You can sell all day and only make about ten *kyats* profit. It's exhausting too, because you're walking the streets, and your legs start to ache. I can stand having aching legs. What I can't handle is having an aching stomach. You get so hungry walking up and down particularly if you didn't get much to eat at home. So you start eating the food you're meant to be selling and you end up not making any money that day. I remember going out one day to sell snacks, and not having had anything to eat at all because we didn't even have any rice in the house. That day I was walking up and down and getting so hungry that I kept dipping into the snacks. In the end we didn't even get back the money we put in that day. When I got back home, my mother beat me.

After that I gave up selling food and now I sell flowers. There's lots of jasmine groves near us in North Okkalapa, and they've been grown to produce flowers all year round. In the evenings, we go and pick up the jasmine flowers. The groves also sell to flower-merchants who collect flowers from groves throughout Rangoon and then sell them on with a mark-up. We buy ours direct from the grove though. We pay seven *kyats* for ten thousand flowers. When we buy them in the early evening, the flowers haven't opened, so when we get them home we cover them with damp muslin. Once they start to open, we can thread them onto garlands.

From ten thousand flowers, you can make about a hundred chains, which you can sell for about twenty or twenty-five *kyats*. With labour costs—which aren't much—and the cost of the cotton thread, we end up with about ten *kyats* profit.

We string the flowers together in the evening and then early the next morning I go and sell them in Rangoon. It costs money to get into town, so I try and save the price of the bus ticket by taking the circular train. I go round the city and get off at Hanthawadi station, and then walk over to Hledan market.

Sorry, what did you say? No, no, I don't sell them in Hledan market itself, but I sell to the people in cars who come shopping there. Some people buy them to take back home and offer to their Buddha images. Some of them hang them in their cars off their rearview mirrors. In one day, I sell about three hundred chains, which doesn't earn me much for a day's work tramping the streets, and I have to buy my breakfast too and pay certain people off. Although I eat boiled peas and fried rice for breakfast before I set out, I get very hungry by ten o'clock from all the walking around, so I have to buy a plate of fried rice and that costs eight *kyats*.

Sometimes I can sell out at Hledan. Early in the morning it's full of shoppers, but later on though, there aren't many cars around so I go down and sell at Hledan junction, and catch the cars when they stop at the lights. If I still haven't sold out after that, I go and sell at the petrol station and go down to Myenigone traffic lights.

I suppose you know, we're not allowed to sell things at the traffic lights. If you do, the traffic police will arrest you. Some of them are quite nice though, and just turn a blind eye. But some of them are real b— . . . well . . . as they say, Uncle, it takes all sorts to make a world, doesn't it? Sometimes, when you're selling in front of the teashops you come across some real bullies. You have to give them a little bit of money or they start telling you not to come and sell in front of this teashop. It's not true for every shop, only some of them. And they're nothing to do with the teashop, either, and it's not like they're traffic police. They just reckon you're an easy target.

Selling at traffic lights is very dangerous, uncle. Some cars leave you a little bit of room to manoeuvre. But some of them keep steaming through even when the lights are yellow. And some cars stop right up close to the car in front, even though they know you can't get between them.

One day I was selling jasmine strings with another girl, Ma Than Htay, and she was up by the side of one car selling them when a big lorry pulled up right next door and she was crushed under it and died on the spot. I was selling on the other side of the road. It was so upsetting. Her jasmine strings were scattered in a pool of her blood. I was so upset I couldn't go back there for a couple of months. I kept seeing those jasmine garlands soaked red with blood in my dreams. I'd wake up screaming.

But I couldn't keep away from that traffic light for ever. It's too good a place to sell jasmine, what with all the roads that meet there. If you get there early on, you don't need to go anywhere else to carry on selling, you can sell out just in the one place. So I had to go back.

If you sell at the teashops, you don't have to worry about the cars. But some of the men are wicked, uncle. They only buy a *kyat's* worth of flowers and they're trying to touch you up and saying horrid things and if you don't play along they get nasty.

Sometimes I get really depressed. I don't manage to sell all my strings and I have to go back and try and sell them near where we live. Whenever that happens, I get really tired because I have to walk around calling out 'Jasmine for sale, jasmine for sale!!' All that walking makes me hungry so I end up buying bits to eat here and there, and I end up spending more money than I earn.

Do I go to school? Not any more, uncle. It's not possible, not for as long as I'm having to work for a living. Dad's not a well man any more. Mum has to spend her time looking after him. And we're trying to keep our brother and sister in school.

I don't really have any big dreams. I just want my younger brother and sister to finish school. But there is one thing I want—a big jasmine grove in North Okkalapa or somewhere. If I owned a grove, I'd grow jasmine all the year round, and open up a wholesalers. You've only got to look at a flower merchant to see how well they do for themselves. Then I'd give work selling flowers to the kids like me who couldn't stay on at school. And one other thing . . . I don't want to have see something like Ma Than Htay with those blood-soaked garlands clutched in her hand ever again. The only jasmine I want to see is jasmine that's white and fragrant.

[May 1989]

24

NO HOME TOWN

He is tall, about five foot ten, and his well-built physique suggests that he was strong and muscular in his youth. He is fifty, going on sixty, but his stomach is as taut as a teenager's. You can see the muscles of his upper arms. His complexion is brown, and dark brown at that. His features are very masculine, wide set eyes, sparse eyebrows and hair, and a heavy jaw. His most noticeable characteristics are his permanent smile and his pleasant voice. We have been friends for many years, and in all that time he has always had a smile on his face. I have never seen him grim or angry. He seems ever smiling, ever ready to forgive the world. I have never once heard his voice register a note of complaint—he always sounds more like he was singing.

I have never met anyone that poor and hard-working who managed to be so carefree. He is like a flower which has survived a thunderstorm, or a bright star shining in a dark sky. I find myself going to talk to him whenever I feel angry. Just talking to him is therapeutic. His name is Ko Htun Sein. He presently works as a porter at a long-distance truck station.

When I was young, *Saya*, my name was Po Sein, not Htun Sein. My mother gave birth to me on the way to the Po Sein Gyi festival so that's why she called me that. My father and mother collected firewood for a living. Maybe you've heard of villages like Kadongani and Eyar, south of Bogale in the delta. Down there, it's all *sundree*[1] forest and after that you come to the sea. I was born while my mother was on her way up to the Po Sein Gyi festival in Bogale, during Tazaungmon. You can get Nattaw roasted rice cakes there. At that time of year, there's not much firewood to gather and there are plenty of festivals in the towns. We were in a sampan on the way to Bogale when my mother started to go into labour. We never made it to the festival.

There were just the two of them in the boat, my mother and father. In fact, before they'd set off, my father had been telling my mother that she shouldn't go because she was almost ready to drop me. But she kept on pestering him to let her go because she enjoyed the festival so much, and in the end he ran out of patience and told her 'Come on then, let's go'. He put an old cotton blanket and his knife in the sampan, and set off rowing. At that time my parents weren't living out in the mangroves, and had gone back to the village for a short while. My mother had spent the whole year out in the wilds without seeing a single festival or hearing a drum, and as soon as she got back to the village, she was longing to go off to Bogale.

About half way there, she started her contractions. They were already quite a long way towards Bogale and it was too far to go back to the village, so my father kept rowing. But it was too far to make it to town, and my mother couldn't hold on any longer. She ended up giving birth right there and then in the boat. That's why I always tell people I don't have a place of birth. I was born on a sampan in the middle of a river.

While my mother was giving birth, my father tied the sampan up against the bank. She couldn't very well do it in mid-stream. He needed to heat up some water and cut the cord. My mother was getting cold so he had to light a fire for her. It was the cool season. All they had between them was one old cotton blanket. He spread it out and she curled up in the bottom of the boat. My mother asked him to cut the cord, but when he looked for his knife, he couldn't find it. He realised had put it on the stern of the boat when they set off, and he must have knocked it off when he picked up the oars. My mother was calling for him to cut the cord but he had nothing to do it with. He climbed up onto the bank and looked for something which would do the job. You can imagine it wasn't

---

[1] *Heritiera fomes*, a hardwood growing in the mangrove forests of the delta

easy to find anything around there with nothing but *lamu*[2] trees and mud flats. My father was wondering what he would do if he couldn't find anything when he came across a piece of old twine tied to a tree stump. He decided it would have to do. It wasn't too frayed so he washed it and tried to used it to cut the cord. But it didn't work, of course. Twine can't cut through umbilical cord. In the end it gave way.

What did my father do then? He searched all over for an old tin can. But, as you can imagine, tin cans don't grow on trees out in the mud flats. In the end he decided he would have to bite through the cord himself. He couldn't manage it at first but after three or four attempts it snapped.

After he had cut the cord and thrown the placenta overboard, he decided they couldn't go on to Bogale because my mother was shivering with cold. He boiled up some water for her in a kettle and gave her some sugar lumps. He wrapped me up in an old *longyi*. Then he turned the boat around and rowed back to the village, because my mother needed to get some hot soup inside her.

Once we were back in the village, my mother sat by the fire and had some fish curry with plenty of chilli to warm her up. Since her teeth were chattering so much, my father even gave her a cup of his rice wine.

Because of me being born on the boat, we never got to see the festival. And that's why when people ask me where I was born, I have difficulty answering. I just say, 'Call me the man with no home-town'.

We didn't stay long in the village before setting out again to gather firewood. Once my mother had been confined for long enough after the birth, they went back to work. My entire life between the ages of one month and ten years was spent out in the mangroves. We'd come back to the village maybe a couple of times a year. But we wouldn't stay long, one or two months at most. Then we'd go back out to the mangroves.

You know what they say about how man is influenced by his surroundings. The saying goes 'If you grow up with hunters, you'll be a hunter. If you grow up with fishermen, you'll be a fisherman'. It's true. I grew up with mangroves and mangroves, to me, are home.

Can you imagine how we use to live out there, *Saya*? We would build a hut in the mangroves and live off fish and prawns. We never ate meat, just prawns from the streams.

. . . Of course I can catch prawns and fish, *Saya*! I've been doing it since I was about five. Where we were was salty, so they were mostly salt-water fish. We caught a lot of salt-water *hilsa*. Some of the fish were beautifully coloured, red, green and blue. Some of them were extremely

---

[2] A mangrove, the sour *Sonneratia acida* which is common in tidal creeks.

ugly. We caught all sorts. You might not believe it, but we didn't go hungry, even out there in the mangroves.

I didn't learn how to read or write as I was growing up. I didn't learn until I was ten, when I went back to the village and went into the monastery. My grandmother wanted to novitiate me before she died, so I had to go back. Once I had had my *shin-byu* ceremony, I stayed in the monastery as a novice for a couple of years learning how to read. Before I left, I learnt the Buddhist scriptures, about Buddha's Eight Glorious Victories and his resistance of the Eight Temptations, and about the Triple Gems. When I left the monastery, I took off my novice robes and went back into the mangroves, back to helping my father like before.

Cutting firewood is tiring work. While my mother and father went off to cut the wood, I would stay at home to guard the hut, do the cooking, and look after my little brother and sister. I wasn't the oldest—I had one bigger brother but he caught malaria and died. The malaria is very bad out in the mangroves and all of us had it, including my parents. In fact all wood-cutters in the delta have it. Some of them die of it.

In the end, my father got a very bad attack and died. After that, we couldn't stay out in the mangroves because my mother couldn't take over cutting the wood herself and we children were too young to do it. We went back to the village, but we had no work there. My mother used to fry food and sell it. We'd help. She married again about two years after my father died.

Once she remarried, I left for the town. I had to. There was no work in the village. A friend of mine got me a job pushing an advertising cart for a cinema. I spent three or four years doing this, sleeping in the cinema, eating at food-stalls and drinking from the road-side water pots. By that time I must have been about seventeen or eighteen. They were advertising for jail warders so I applied and got the job.

Being a jail warder passed the time nicely. You work on shifts. You get a room in the compound. At first I lived there on my own. Later on, I married the daughter of one of the other warders.

I was a jail warder for a long time, about twenty years, and I worked both in jails and in police stations. But then I got into trouble and got fired. Let's not talk about it, OK. Let's just say it wasn't anything really wrong. My bosses did what they could for me but they couldn't protect me from getting the sack.

Once I was fired, we had nowhere to live because we lost our room in the prison compound. By that time we had plenty of children, five altogether, so we had to look for a house. It was only then that I realised just how important it is to have a roof over your head and a place to call your own. Before then I'd always had an easy life, living in staff quarters. Until I got thrown out, I'd had no idea how expensive a room in town could be.

When we'd lived in the mangroves, we'd just put up a hut wherever we happened to stop. A few mangrove branches for house-posts and some palm leaves for a roof—and you could cut them yourself anywhere—and we had a home. In this bloody town, I soon discovered that mangrove branches, palm leaves and even the ground itself cost money. We went round and round in circles looking for a place to live. Even a platform on stilts was difficult to find, let alone a house. In the end my family had to camp out in a monastery *zayat*. There were lots of other people like us who had been forced to live in the monastery.

Later on, we moved out to a neighbourhood on the outskirts of town. It was a rental, not our own plot, or our own house. My daughter had gone to work in a cheroot factory in that neighbourhood and an old widow who was working there had taken pity on her and invited us to come and live in her house. We only had to pay a small deposit and the rent was only fifty *kyats* a month.

We moved out there. There wasn't any electricity in the neighbourhood. There were no street lights. The roads were just mud and dust. At the time we moved out there, our house was right on the fringes, with only three or four beyond it.

Since I'd been fired, I was unemployed. My daughter was rolling cheroots and one of my sons was a 'spare' on a bus. The two of them had to support the whole family. So you can imagine how I felt, *Saya*. There I was, a man of no more than fifty, having to live off the earnings of my son and daughter. I was ashamed. I felt completely worthless. I could hardly bear to swallow food bought with the money they had earned.

So I went into town to look for work. I found a job through a friend who worked at a truck station for cargo trucks going to towns in central Burma. The trucks would pull up at the stop, we would load the goods and get commission for looking after them. That was the job. You'll have seen depots like that all over Rangoon. Since my friend was the manager, he got me a job there as a porter. For fetching and carrying the merchandise, you could earn between twenty and fifty *kyats* a day. Early each morning I would set off with my lunch-box, and not get home until it was getting dark.

My family asked me what my job involved. I lied a bit and said I was in charge of a truck stop. To call a porter at a truck depot 'truck stop manager' is twisting the facts a little. But I was embarrassed to tell them the truth.

I'd been working at the depot for about a year. Whenever my wife or my children said they'd come in with me, I'd always told them not to. I was worried they would see that I was really just a porter. But one day my worst fear came true. I was staggering under the weight of a sack of betel and some boxes when my wife and daughter turned up. You can imagine their faces. They didn't say a word. They'd been on their way to the market. They were so shocked when they saw me. I'd told them I was the manager. In charge of the running of the station. And here I was, lugging boxes, bare-chested and dripping with sweat, dressed in an old *longyi*, with another draped across my back.

My daughter was struck dumb. She finally said 'Mummy! Look!'. I was lugging a wooden chest at the time. I turned to look at them in shock. Then I quickly said 'Go and wait while I finish, I'll be back in a minute'. But they refused to go away. They just stayed and watched me until I'd finished the job.

'You said you were in charge of a bus station', said my wife.

'Well', I lied, 'that's right. Right now the porter is busy so I'm helping out. I have to do it from time to time.'

I don't think my wife believed me. I looked at my daughter's face and could tell that she definitely didn't.

I bought them some tea, and quickly sent them on their way. I've never been so ashamed as that day, *Saya*. When I got home, I didn't know where to look. After that? Well . . . after that, they knew I wasn't the station manager. I couldn't very well hide it any more. Whenever they came to town, they would come and see me there. There was no point in keeping up the pretence.

What about now? Well, as you can see, I'm still working as a porter. I've been doing this for five or six years now. The money's not too bad. Of course, some days there isn't much cargo, but then on other days there is. On average I'm earning twenty or twenty-five *kyats* a day. I may be fifty-nine now, but I can still carry a load. I'll keep on doing this as long as I stay fit. I have to keep working, so that everyone at home will get enough to eat.

[February 1990]

191

25

UP AND DOWN THE RIVER CHINDWIN

*I met him on a motor boat which was on its way up the Chindwin
river. We were passing near the famous whirlpool known as Shwe-sa-
yay. Steep cliffs rose up on either side of the river. On top of one
gleamed a white pagoda. We stood chatting at the front of the boat.
The other sailors called him Uncle San.*

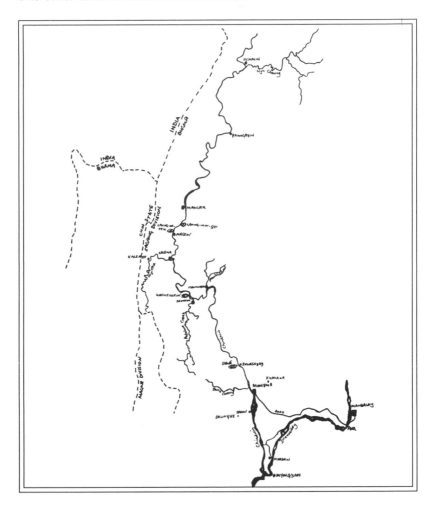

I'm from Sadon village in Salingyi township, on the riverbank opposite Monywa. I've been working on boats ever since I was a lad. I was born in Salingyi but my parents used to move to Maukkadaw each year. They cut wood and collected bamboo. When the water level in the Chindwin dropped, they went back to Sadon but they only stayed there for a short while. I grew up in Maukkadaw. That was where I learnt to swim. When I was four or five I used to play on the sampan and swim in the river. We'd sleep on the sampan. By the time I was about twelve, I'd learnt how to handle the bamboo pole we used on the boat.

Before I learned how to use the pole, I'd do the cooking on board. And I'd fasten the ropes and *weh-that* the boat—that means taking the mooring rope and tying it on shore. Sometimes if the shore was rocky, we couldn't get the boat right up close and we had to stop ten or twenty feet out. I would jump into the water and take the mooring rope and swim over and ram a pole into the bank to anchor the boat.

Later on I learned how to handle the bamboo pole which we used to feel our way in the shallows and near sandbanks. If the boat ran aground, we would use the poles to push off. The boats relied on manpower and the wind. If there was no wind, either we would use poles to push the boats along or we'd pull them along with ropes.

If a boat was carrying three or four hundred bags of rice, you needed to pull the boat along and to push it forward with a pole as well. Pulling the boat along meant walking along the bank dragging the boat. The boatmen used to do that until they came to steep slopes or a cliff where they couldn't walk and then they'd jump on and everyone would have to pole the boat along.

Poling the boat meant putting the front of your shoulder to a sturdy bamboo pole and pushing hard. That's why most boatmen have shoulders as calloused as the backs of water buffaloes. Sometimes the callouses get infected and ooze pus and blood.

The Chindwin is full of shallows, sandbanks, and whirlpools. There are lots of different types of whirlpool. Some of them throw the water up and some suck it down. There are some which chuck boats around and some which spin them. The whirlpools which suck boats in suck in all the flotsam and jetsam as well. You have to steer well clear of that kind.

There's a saying amongst Chindwin river boatmen: 'Upstream in Pay, downstream in Shwe, or Wet-thike mid-way; you're never far from death'. Those are the well-known whirlpools on the Chindwin. 'Pay' is close to Ya-lay-wa. 'Shwe' is the whirlpool called 'Shwe-sa-yay' downstream. Half-way down there's the one called 'Wet-thike'. But there's others too— 'Laung-ka-teik' near Ma-sein village, and 'Laung-min-gyi' upstream from that. Just below Khamti is the 'Toe' whirlpool. And near the inflow of the Patolone creek is the 'Wa-cheik-lein'. When the Patolone creek is in full flood, the bamboo rafts get twisted and broken up by the whirlpool. That's why it's called 'Wa-cheik-lein'—devoured and twisted bamboo. When your boat is approaching one of these famous whirlpools you have to make them an offering. You throw a handful of rice into the whirlpool and that feeds the guardian *nats* and the river creatures.

When you get to cliffs which you can't walk along, there are holes drilled into the rocks. The boatmen stick pegs into the holes and then put planks of woods over those pegs to make a walkway. Then you walk along and pull the boat along by ropes. No-one knows exactly how those holes have come to be there. The boatmen say that they were drilled in the days of the Burmese kings when their military fleets were moving up and down the river. The holes were made by people who were dropped down the side of the cliff with ropes tied around their waists. Some say that that the holes are not man-made, but naturally formed and that there are birds' nests in them. Anyway, that's what they used to do in the old days to pull the boat along. Nowadays, we don't build walkways like that much.

Beyond the cliffs upstream there are villages which earn their living by cutting bamboo and timber. When I was young, our family used to move the whole household up there and cut wood for a living. Some families moved and settled there and made a living weaving baskets and mats.

Pardon me? How did I learn to steer the boat? I was never properly taught, not even by my father. You learn from experience. You have to know the way the river flows. You have to be able to hold her steady. If you don't know the river, you'll be in trouble. You have to know where the shallows, the rocks and the whirlpools are. You need to know the depth of the water. In some places, called *bwets*, the water looks like it's boiling. These aren't whirlpools. The water is bubbling because it's deep. The big, spaced-out bubbles come where the water is very deep. Where the bubbles are small and close together, the water is shallower. The rule of thumb is that the water is three times as deep as the bubble is wide.

These principles form the basis of your knowledge of the currents and the river. If you want to be a boatman, they are the most important bits to master. The rest is nowhere near as important.

Now that we have motorboats, they are much easier to steer and much less tiring. You don't rely on brute force because you have a motor. If you learn how to helm a motor boat, you can get a helmsman's licence.

Where am I from? As I told you earlier, my village is Sadon in Salingyi township. Opposite Monywa. But when I was young, we went to stay further up the Chindwin river where we were working as wood-cutters and basket-weavers. My wife comes from Maukkadaw in Minkin township. She's got a bit of Shan blood because there are a few Shans in the area. We call them Red Shan. But I'd better explain. She's my second wife. When I say my Maukkadaw wife, I mean my second wife.

My first wife was from Kyaukka village near Monywa where the black and gold lacquer comes from. In those days I was just an ordinary boatman. There weren't many motor boats around. My wife used to go and sell lacquerware trays at the pagoda markets in Minkin and Mawlaik. Actually it was her mother who used to take her there. She was about eighteen or nineteen at the time. Just a teenager. They used to go to the markets on our boat.

In those days we had quite a big sampan which could carry about three hundred baskets of paddy. If there was a good wind, we would put up a sail. If not, we had to use poles or ropes to move it along. Sailing upstream from Maukkadaw to Monywa used to take about a week. That's how I got to know my wife.

When we got married, she came to live with us. By that time my father was already dead and as I was the only son, I stayed with my mother. Every time I came home there'd be bad news. My wife and my mother were always arguing. She didn't have a mother herself by then, so I had hoped she'd treat my mother as if she were her own. But I know the way it goes. Mothers and daughters-in-law rarely get on. There always seem to be problems. That much I can understand. But my wife was always insulting my mother. She even called her names in front of me. I wasn't going to put up with it.

She was always getting at my mother. If my mother wanted a snack, some pickled tea or some dried *nga-yan* fish with some oil or some left over rice and molasses, my wife would make an issue of it. If a plate was broken, it was always my mother's fault. When I got home, my mother would tell me what had been going on with tears in her eyes.

To start off with, I didn't take it seriously. I thought it was just typical mother-in-law and daughter-in-law problems. But then I started to hear reports from the neighbours that my wife wasn't looking after my mother properly and that she was even abusing her and swearing at her. I told her to stop it. But it was about as much use as trying to straighten a dog's tail by sticking into a bamboo tube. Once you take it off, it springs back into place.

In the end, it was getting so bad that I didn't want to go home even though I was exhausted from rowing the boat. I told her to stop. It didn't do any good. So I beat her. We argued. In the end, I decided I'd had enough and I divorced her. She took our daughter with her. I heard she married someone else in Paung-pyin not long afterwards.

After we got divorced, I married my current wife. That's her, over there, cooking behind the cabin-housing. Like I said, she's from Minkin

Maukkadaw. She'd been married before. She had a son from the previous marriage. Her first husband was a helmsman like me. He worked on a private motor-boat which ran between Monywa and Kalewa. He was drowned when his boat capsized near the Pay whirlpool, you know, the one I mentioned earlier. She was a widow. I was divorced when we met. I felt sorry for her, having to cope with her son. especially as she was the widow of a helmsman like myself.

When he died, she was selling fried snacks near the jetty. I met her when I bought some off her. She was homely, and she had a good heart, and she was the wife of one of us. Before long we were married. We'd met one more time, got to know one another a bit better and then the third time we'd met, we'd got married. She and her son came to live with us. In the ten years we've been together, we've hardly quarrelled. She's good-natured and she doesn't argue or talk back. If I shout at her, she bites her tongue and doesn't say a word. If I lose my temper though, she tries to calm me down. And I love her because she loves my mother and looks after her and never argues with her. She treats her as if she were her own mother.

I ask you. Just look at the difference between my first wife and my second wife! It's such a relief that my second wife got on with my real mother and with my second mother too. She looks after her. And she is so much more polite than the other wife I had.

Yes, I thought it would confuse you when I mentioned my second mother. It is a bit confusing. After my father died, my mother remarried. I think it might have been because she was upset by the way my first wife was always picking on her. But she died three or four years after remarrying and then my step-father married again. Then not long after that, my step-father died of malaria and left my step-mother on her own. So that's what I mean when I say my second mother. She's not really my step-mother, since she was the second wife of my step-father. She's getting on, and she's about the same age as my real mother, and that's why I feel like she almost is my mother. My second wife looks after my mother—I mean my step-mother. She lives in a hut in our compound and we give her some rice or some curry or whatever we can spare. Young people nowadays don't seem to respect their elders or obey them any more, do they? I'm trying to set a good example. I don't want young people being disrespectful to me when I'm older.

How did I become a helmsman? To start off with, I was an ordinary boatman, like I was telling you. In the days before we had boats with engines, we had sampans which could carry three or four hundred baskets of paddy. The boats that run on the Chindwin and the ones that run on the Irrawaddy are different, you know. Our boats have a low draft with a flat hull. The Irrawaddy boats have a deep draft with a steep hull.

You can tell which boats go on which river as soon as you look at them. The Irrawaddy boats are known as Mye-daw boats because they are made in Mye-daw near Myingyan. The ones on the Chindwin are known as Chindwin boats.

So I started off as a boatman. In the old days, my shoulders were more scarred than this. Then we got motor boats and I started working on them. I started off as a labourer, handling the ropes, then as a cook, then putting down the gangplank, then as a porter. Basically as a general labourer, *Saya*.

Then I moved on to handling the bamboo pole. And sometimes I'd fill in for the helmsman if he was busy. As I knew how to navigate, the helmsman told me about a training course for helmsmen in Mandalay. He suggested I should attend it to get a certificate. So I signed off from the boat and went for training. When I got my certificate I went back to working on the motor-boat. I've been working as boatman up and down the Chindwin river since I was a kid. That's how I learnt to navigate.

Later on, a motor-boat owner from Monywa took a shine to me. He trusted me most out of all his helmsmen so he hired me to manage his four or five boats. He could trust me to steer the boat safely and to make decisions about what could be put on board. That saved him the trouble of talking to the customers. I also used to drum up business for our boat. I looked after the cargo loaded on my boat as if it belonged to me and made sure it didn't get damaged.

After a while, a number of motor boats started up on the Monywa-Kalewa and Monywa-Homalin routes and we faced stiff competition. That meant we had to take even more care with the cargo. We needed to ensure it didn't get damaged or lost and make sure it departed and arrived on time. When we changed our boat into a passenger ferry we had to offer the best service to persuade passengers to take our boat. We put facilities on board to attract passengers like music and benches at the front for them to look at the view during the evenings.

Look at this view, *Saya*. Isn't it beautiful? Of course, for me they're just normal everyday sights. But for someone who hasn't been here before they must be quite special. See those trees clinging to edge of the cliffs. In March they are covered in bright-red *in-gyin* flowers[1] which contrast with the green of the water.

How old am I? Fifty-eight, *Saya*. We helmsmen retire at sixty like civil servants. Once your eyesight starts to go, it's not safe to sail at night. You could have collisions with the cliffs or run aground.

---

[1] The Sal tree or *Shorea robusta,* a hardwood.

I've got four sons, *Saya*. One of them's attending the course to be a helmsman like his Dad. Another one is attending teacher training course. The two youngest are still in school, in Monywa. I've got no idea what they'll do when they've finished. At the moment they don't want to work at all. All the youngest one wants to do is play the guitar. I've got no idea how he'll turn out.

I'm still going strong, *Saya*, even though I'm almost sixty. When I retire, I want to buy my own motor boat. Nothing as big as this one, mind you. I'd like a *pe-daung*[2] passenger boat with a Kubota engine. I'd be able to run it locally.

Saya, I've spent my whole life on the Chindwin. I must have sailed over a hundred times between Monywa and Homalin. But I've never been beyond the Chindwin river. I've never even been to the Irrawaddy. I spent a short time at a jetty on the Irrawaddy when I went to Mandalay for the course. But I went there by bus from Monywa, so that's all I saw of it. I drink Chindwin water. I've sailed the length of the Chindwin. I'm sure I'll end my life somewhere on the banks of the Chindwin.

What are they? That's a troupe of monkeys. There are quite a few on both banks of the river. But they don't cross. The meat of the brown monkey is delicious. So's the blood. Sometimes hunters come down to the river and you can buy it from them. What's the difference between me and a brown monkey? Not much. They never cross the river to get to the other bank. And I've never been beyond the Chindwin.

[March 1990]

---

[2] A lightweight boat designed to carry passengers at speed, seen on most of the rivers of Burma, including in the delta. As the engine is in the rear, it is known locally as *pe-daung* ('back lifted up').

26

COUNTRY ARTIST

I met him in a town in Upper Burma. He was over sixty, thin, with brown skin, greying hair and a moustache, but his eyes were still bright. He wore a faded cotton longyi *and a shirt with the sleeves rolled up. Except when he was talking, he sucked continuously on a cheroot.*

I've been painting since I was a youngster. But I'm the first artist in my family. My father was an advocate. He had one of those titles from the colonial government, TPS. In those days the English gave the Burmese special titles, Burmese titles, but they would shorten them with English initials. Like my father, he was a *Tain-cho Pyi-cho Saun*[1] which becomes TPS in English. *Kyet-tha-ye-saun Shwe-sa-lweh-ya Min*[2] becomes KSM. Then there's ABM which is *A-hmu-tan kaun min*[3] and so on.

I'm getting off the point. My father was an advocate, my mother came from royal blood, she was descended from one of King Mindon's sons. Or maybe it was a daughter. What I'm trying to say is that there were no artists in our family. Or musicians either.

I was their only son. Ever since my youth, from fourth or fifth standard onwards, I've wanted to paint. I must have been born that way. I remember one time, when I was little, I came across a poster by the artist U Ba Nyan. I can't remember what it was called, maybe 'Traditional Burmese Farming' or something. I can't remember the name, but I can certainly remember the painting. In the distance there was this line of hills, and three or four huts. You immediately knew you were looking at a distant village. The hills were lush and green and at the end there was a gleaming white pagoda and a couple of toddy palms. That was the background. In the foreground was a wide expanse of paddy. Some fields gleamed golden, ready for harvest. In others, the paddy had already been gathered and all that was left were stalks. At the front of the picture was a bullock cart, with wheels made out of solid wood, not like the wheels with spokes which you see nowadays. The cart was piled high with straw and nearby two men were bundling straw up into sheaves. At the back of the cart a woman wearing only a *longyi* pulled up over her breasts was handing them up to a younger woman wearing a *kamauk* on top of the cart. The girl was putting them in place with a pitchfork.

I don't know why this scene has stuck in my memory to this day. In the jargon, you'd say that the composition was good and the subject matter was powerful. The subject was a Burmese rural scene, the sort of thing you see throughout the country. The dark ridge, the little village, the pagoda, the paddy fields and the bullock cart, the sheaves of straw and the peasant family team—husband and wife, son and daughter, pure and simple Burmese folk. The traditional Burmese way of working together and sharing the daily tasks among the family, and the devout

---

[1] 'Serving for the benefit of the country'
[2] 'Glorious golden sash-wearer'
[3] 'Good servant'

Buddhist way of life. Of course when I first saw the painting, I didn't think of it like that, broken down into its constituent parts. I just saw it as a whole, and I took delight in a beautiful picture which made me feel serene. It was only when I was older that I realised why it had captivated me so much.

After I'd seen the painting, I copied it into my school exercise book. Later on I drew it in coloured pencil in a sketch book. By then, I was no longer interested in lessons—all I wanted to do was paint.

In those days, magazines like 'Dagon' and 'Thet-hsaun', and the Rangoon University Yearbook used to include line drawings and pictures to fill up the empty spaces between the articles and short stories. They were just ordinary pictures—a jetty, a boat on the river, a pagoda on a hill, four or five boats drawn up on a river bank. I'm sure you know the sort of thing I mean. So I started drawing that sort of picture.

Then I heard that the artist U Hla had started a painting class in Rangoon, and I bought a stamp at the Post Office and sent off for his book. I followed his step-by-step instructions by correspondence course. I must have been about twelve at the time.

There are some religious paintings in the entrances to a pagoda in this town. They're the work of a fresco painter, and not very good. But that painter taught me how to do coloured wall-paintings and I would use these skills when I did my own drawings with coloured pencils. Later on my father bought me some water-colour paints and I moved on to those. I usually painted landscapes. I used to copy pictures and photographs in 'Dagon' and 'Journal-kyaw' magazines, and colour them in how I wanted.

During the Japanese period, my school produced its own hand-written magazine. I was the only one who was allowed to do the illustrations. The cover was my own work. On one of them, I copied U Ba Hpan's picture of Bandoola[4]. On another, I did a picture of an olden-style Burmese woman singer sitting on a royal couch and playing a harp during a cold misty night in the month of Nattaw. We brought out about four or five issues of this magazine and in every one, I'd done all of the illustrations and the cover.

After the war, my friends all passed their Matric and went to University, or got jobs. Almost everyone passed tenth standard. In fact I could have been the only one who failed in the whole year. Once the war was over, magazines and books started to be published again with the usual illustrations. In a Mandalay magazine, I used to come across the illustrations of U Ba Yin Lay, U Aung Chit and U Kyweh Lay. In the Rangoon

---

[4] Maha Bandoola was a warrior of the colonial period.

periodicals, you'd see the work of U Ngwe Kain, U Ohn Lwin, U Ba Kyi, U Ko Lay, U San Lwin, U Ba Lone Lay and so on. My father died around that time, leaving me and my mother on our own. He left us the brick building which was too big for the two of us, so we did it up and then rented it out, which gave us enough income to live on. We had extra room, so my mother's younger sister came to live with us too. Since I didn't have to worry about making a living, I could paint what I wanted. I was about twenty by then. In those days, I was starting to learn more about painting, and read a lot of books on the subject. At that time, some new younger painters were beginning to appear like Bagyi Aung Soe and Hla Soe, as well as the well-known ones like U Ohn Lwin, U Ngwe Kain, U Ko Lay and U Ba Kyi, who were still around and who had already become famous for fine art and commercial art before the war. The new young artists like Bagyi Aung Soe and Hla Soe only emerged after the war. Their painting style didn't bear much resemblance to the old masters. Their art was something strange and new. I'm not saying that it was good or bad—just different.

When I saw these new artists coming up, I wanted to get into the art world. In those days, there was no School of Fine Arts or anything. There weren't as many periodicals as there are today. Nonetheless, I was determined to be a famous artist. I wanted to paint great pictures, and to be a successful commercial artist at the same time. So I asked my mother if I could go down to Rangoon—and when she tried to stop me, I went anyway.

I had a friend in Rangoon who was renting a room in a shack on 37th Street, squashed between two run-down brick buildings. In the days immediately after the war, Rangoon had very few new buildings—most of them were falling down. Some of them had roofs made of zinc or thatch. Some were just shells of three storey buildings, with the people all living on the ground floor, surrounded by the four walls. My friend lived in a shack between two such buildings. In nearby huts there were refugees from the civil war that was raging in the countryside. In the rest of the street were Indian rickshaw-pullers, typesetters, people who sold fried snacks, Indian women pounding spices, toddy shops, brothels—all human life was there!

My friend rented a room which took up a quarter of the shack. In another room lived the owner of the shack and his wife. In a third lived an old fortune-teller and his wife, and another couple with endless children were in the last room. The room rent was five *kyats* a month. There was nothing on the floor and it was always muddy. If you peered in, you could see everything. There were no doors, just a gunny bag hanging at the entrance to each room. To get into our room or the one

203

where the endless children lived, you had to go past the owner and the fortune-teller.

My friend was working as a proof-reader in a newspaper house. He'd would go to work every evening and since they didn't put the paper to bed until around midnight, he wouldn't come back all night and would sleep on the piles of paper at the press. I used to be able to sleep on his single bed at night while he was out, and then when he came home in the morning, I'd get up and let him have it back. He would get up at about two in the afternoon and have breakfast. During the day I'd stay out of the house. He'd tell me I could hang around, but I didn't want to—the room only had a bed and an armchair, not much room to relax. So once he came home, I'd get up and go out for a walk around Rangoon. Sometimes I'd play with the kids outside the hut. Sometimes I'd go down and sit on Pansoedan jetty, or in Bandoola Park or in front of Rangoon Station.

Whenever I went out, I'd take my sketch-book. I'd sketch pavement scenes, or views of the park, or the station. I'd take some of these sketches to magazines, but they never got used.

I started to feel bad about my friend. He was providing me with a place to stretch out and paying for my food. I felt embarrassed. I decided I would have to take whatever work I could get. I started painting sign-boards and car licence plates. The money wasn't too bad. I could earn up to five *kyats* a day, which in those days was a significant sum, more than my friend was earning as a proof-reader.

After that, I met an artist who did bill-boards for films, and went to work with him. I started off doing frames which was really nothing more than carpentry, but I had to take any job I could get. After that I moved on to blending the colours, and then putting the background colour onto the canvas. Then I was allowed to sketch out the outline and little by little I moved up through the levels of painting until I could produce posters which were all my own work.

At about that time, my mother passed away, and I went back to my home town. After she died, I was on my own. I thought long and hard about how things were going for me. I had gone down to Rangoon to try and make it as a famous and successful artist. But I'd ended up living hand-to-mouth and hadn't achieved the fame I'd been hoping for. I'd spent my time doing paintings for other people. I'd never been famous enough to sign my name at the bottom, so what was the point? That was why, instead of returning to Rangoon, I stayed here and got married. Luckily there's a bioscope in town, so painting posters for that earns me enough to live on.

There is one thing I want to say. You can't have it all. If you want fame, you have to go without money. If you want to live comfortably, you have to forego success. People who think they can have both are being too greedy. That's my personal philosophy, *Saya*.

I've been painting posters for the cinema for over thirty years now. I never did become a famous artist. I'm just a billboard painter in a small country town. But the money I get from doing this is enough to live comfortably on. It was enough to bring my sons and daughters up and put them through college. One son and one daughter are doctors, one son's an engineer and the other daughter's a school teacher. They've all had a modern education.

I like to think that that is my reward. I may not be a famous painter. I may only be a bioscope billboard painter in a small country town. But I have managed to bring my children up properly. I may have failed in one way, but I've succeeded in another. Like I said, you can't have everything.

There are very few artists who've managed to be both famous and rich. The few that have were lucky.

[May 1988]

27

A STREET COBBLER

He's between thirty-five and forty, average height, skinny with a sparse moustache and long hair. He wears a shabby cloth hat which seems permanently attached to his head. He prefers it to an umbrella, even in the monsoon. His longyi is faded and he wears one of the sports shirts they sell on the pavements. The most noticeable thing about him is his shoes. He almost always wears down-at-heel flip-flops, with the pattern on the sole worn away. Since he mends shoes for a living, you tend to look at his. It is one of life's ironies that a shoe mender should wear worn-out shoes. He almost always has an old army knapsack with his bits of canvas, leather and velvet, rubber soles and the tools of his trade—his awl, his needles, a sharp pen-knife, a couple of chisels, an anvil and different sized nails. He turns up in our street at the beginning of the afternoon when the neighbourhood is quiet, calling out 'Any old shoes to mend? Any old slippers to mend?' He told me his life-story as he mended a pair of mine.

My name's Kyaw Win. I'm a pure-blooded Hindu, not Burmese, or mixed race. My father is an Indian citizen because he was born there, and my mother is a Burmese citizen because she was born here but her parents were Hindu. My father's Madrassi, but my mother's an Oriya from Orissa. She was born in the delta. Her father was a paddy farmer. She says they used to live near Bassein and Ye-kyi, although this was before I was born, and her father was an Indian coolie. When he died, my grandmother remarried and she and my mother moved to a small town on the Rangoon-Bassein ferry route. Although my mother was Indian race, she might as well have been Burmese. She was born here. She spoke almost no Hindi, She grew up eating *nga-pi-ye* fish sauce, wearing a *longyi* and worshipping Buddha.

My mother told me they opened a stall on the jetty when she was marrying age, selling fried Indian snacks like *baya-gyaw* made out of lentils. My grandmother's second husband died but they stayed in this town since they were settled there. My mother went to school there up to fourth standard. It was a Burmese school of course, she had no way of attending an English one. But she said she was embarrassed to be in a class with children, when she was already a teenager. So she left and went off to help my grandmother on the stall, cooking and selling the food from a tray down town.

As my grandmother's stall became more popular, she was able to expand and open up another stall nearby, this time selling chicken salad, roasted hyacinth beans and slices of dried *mayan* fruit. My mother's chicken salad was a best-seller. She pounded her own Coringee masala spices and went personally to select chickens in the market.

Who came to eat at the stall? Well, there were *gazaw* shops nearby, and some illegal shebeens, like you usually find on a waterfront. You remember in those days the boats were manned by Indian sailors, called *kalasi* or lascars. The waterfront was lined with drink stalls, selling toddy and *gazaw* liquor and country spirit. It was their customers my mother used to sell chicken salad to. That was how she met my father.

My father was a first generation Indian immigrant. He worked as a *kayani*, a clerk for the Inland Waterways. They say in those days they were loads of Indians working on the boats and the trains. I can't remember that far back myself.

He would do the run up to Mandalay and then up the Chindwin and back down to the delta. When they got to our town, the crew would disembark and go for a drink. My father said he stayed off the strong liquor though.

He met my mother when he bought a plate of chicken salad off her. She was sixteen when they got married. You know what they say about sailors—a girl in every port. So my father would leave my mother behind when he set sail. He'd send her money every month of course. But he had another wife. I never saw her, although my mother says she did once.

I was born in that town, but once my grandmother died, my parents decided we couldn't stay there any more, so my father moved us all to Rangoon. We stayed in Thingangyunn in the big compound of this house which belonged to one of my father's friends. We built a little hut there. My mother no longer had her stall. My father still worked on the boats and was only home about four or five days a month.

One day my mother and father had a row. I was about ten at the time. I can't remember exactly what it was about, probably money. My father was drunk and beat my mother up and then stormed off to his boat. My mother was upset and cursed him and went off and got drunk on *gazaw*. I had no idea what was going on. I ate, played and went to bed as usual.

My father stayed away for quite some time. He stopped coming home every time his boat docked and stayed on board instead. But he did send us money. My mother was too proud to go and see him. She just used to stay home and get drunk on *gazaw* with a woman who lived nearby. Every evening they used to get together to get sloshed.

Once this started happening, money became quite tight, since we didn't have any savings to live on. So my mother sent me to work for an old Indian cobbler who worked near the compound. He was old, but he was still a very skilful shoemaker, and could turn out a well-made pair of leather shoes. The workmanship was so good, it was even better than a machine could produce. But since his eyesight was beginning to fail, his seams sometimes went a bit crooked and sometimes when he was cutting off the extra leather he would stray from the line. He was going blind and his hands were getting shaky, so he wasn't as accurate as he used to be. So my job was to spot the shaky seams and wiggly cuts and correct them.

I would cut the shapes out of the leather once he had marked them out and he would teach me all he knew about cobbling. There was so much to learn. How to use the needles and the awl. How to cut leather and stitch seams. How to use a hammer and anvil. And how to replace heels and build up a worn down toe. After three or four years of apprenticeship, I was turning into a good cobbler. I still couldn't make a pair of shoes from scratch like him, but I knew how to mend old ones.

I'll tell you about this one customer. He was an old Anglo-Indian who worked on the trains and lived near us in Thingangyunn. He always used to wear very good shoes. He only ever wore John White or Rowe & Co shoes—those days there was still the Rowe Company who made them, and they had a store on Dalhousie Street. They were foreign, of course.

In those days, we hadn't heard of trainers. Everyone wore pumps decorated with strips of ribbon. Then there were 'half shoes'—slip-ons. There were also canvas shoes, made from local canvas. Where was it made? In the Thamaing Textile Factory, of course. It only came in two colours, red and white. There was none of the multicoloured stuff you get nowadays.

So, like I was saying earlier, this Anglo only ever used to wear John White or Rowe & Co shoes. They were very well-proportioned and had pointy toes. They were made out of the best cow hide with accurate stitching. They were also tough and would last for a long time without falling apart or wearing down at the heel. The seams were stuck together with good quality glue and could last a lifetime.

He used to wear his shoes for about five years, and then we would have to build up the heel a little bit, or put a new one on. If you gave them normal usage they would last. The colour would fade a bit, so you'd need to polish them. In those days we used Kiwi shoe polish. We had black, white and brown. About once a month we would give his shoes a polish and if he gave them a rub with a bristle brush every time before he wore them they would stay shiny. That Anglo never went to anyone else but us.

Eventually, Rowe & Co closed down and he couldn't get hold of his Rowe or his John White shoes any more, so he asked my master to make him some. We bought best quality leather for them, from a shop on Maungtawlay Street. You could get goatskin or cowhide there. Cowhide is better for making shoes, goatskin is too soft, better for making purses and handbags. Cow-hide is the best. Ordinary leather is very thick and rough and better for making suitcases.

So the Anglo kept coming back to us to have shoes made, and us alone, because he said our shoes were such good copies of John White and Rowe & Co shoes. We only made him his leather shoes, though, because when it came to canvas shoes, he wasn't interested in wearing local canvas. He used to order Dunlop shoes from India.

My master would make the shoes personally of course. I just did what he told me. But when his soles or his laces needed fixing or his Rowe shoes had holes, I could do that myself.

I was very sad when the old man died. He was a talented cobbler.

My father still hadn't come home. Typical sailor—a wife in every port of call. I don't know how many he had all told, and I never asked him. Meanwhile, my mother was addicted to *gazaw*. It didn't stop there either. She was addicted to harder liquor. She said if she didn't drink, she couldn't sleep properly, and she would get the tremors and not be able to do anything. Just like a proper alcoholic.

My father eventually came back, but my mother was drinking every day and every day she would fight with him, and in the end he stopped coming and we later heard that he had gone back to India for good, so that was the last we saw of him.

At the time the old man, my master, was still around. But he died shortly afterwards. He was about seventy. He had no children or grandchildren and we had been looking after him. When he died, he left all his tools to me.

There were a couple of anvils and five hammers, a couple of knives for cutting leather, a couple of chisels, some iron bars, awls and various other bits and pieces for mending shoes, all kept together in a pine chest. He also left behind four or five pairs of old shoes. That was the sum total, and they were not particularly valuable. But the knowledge he had left me to go with them was worth more than the tools, and together, they have kept me fed and clothed to this very day.

After his death, I went out to look for customers. He had had his own customers who would come and bring him their shoes and then I would mend them under his instruction. Now that he was gone, I had to find my own customers. You know, he was like a father to me. All my real father did was give me life. The old man was the one who brought me up and taught me everything I know. It's thanks to what he taught me that I've never starved.

Once he died, the old customers who had him make their shoes stopped coming and all that were left were the people from the neighbourhood who wanted a sole fixing or a thong stuck back down. That kind of work isn't enough to live on. Each job brought in only five or six *pyas*. So I loaded the tools into a shoulder bag and set off to find work in town. I'd work in various places, Maungtawlay Street, Pansoedan, Bo Aung Kyaw, Anawrahta and Maha Bandoola Streets. I'd set up shop on a small bench on the street corner.

I used to get business, but their custom wasn't regular and people who have good quality shoes don't want to bring them to be mended by a cobbler with a road-side bench and a bag full of tools. You see, some repairs can't be done on the spot. They can take a couple of days, so you don't trust people like me with your good shoes. After all, if I didn't turn up the next day, where would you be? So the sort of customers I got were all people who had quick repairs to do, or whose shoes had broken while they were out.

That kind of trade isn't very profitable. In a day, you might earn fifteen or twenty *kyats* total. It's not enough to cover my own food and travel expenses, not to mention my mother's drink habit.

After a while, more expensive shoes like trainers came in. Trainers are incredibly expensive, fifteen hundred, two thousand even three thousand *kyats* a pair. You've got the brand names like Adidas and Nike, Puma, Dunlop and lots of others whose names I can't remember. Some come from Singapore, some from Hong Kong, some Taiwan. The most expensive and the best are Adidas and Nike. All the young people are wearing them nowadays. And the problem for me is, with those kind of shoes, if they get ripped or get holes in them, there's no way you take them to a roadside cobbler. You take them to a shop. So I decided to set up in a shop near Maungtawlay Street with a former pupil of my master's. He had enough money to invest in one. It was still only a roadside stall but it had a proper roof and walls so people would be prepared to come and leave their shoes there. The owner knew my handiwork, being a cobbler himself. In Rangoon, all the shoe-makers know who's good and who's bad.

With a proper stall, we used to pick up custom from people who'd come with their expensive shoes. Some shoes just needed a bit of glue, so we'd charge forty or fifty *kyats*. If the stitching needed repair it could cost upwards from a hundred. After all, these were shoes which cost over a thousand. And people could leave their expensive shoes with us without worrying that we would take off and leave, because they could see we had a proper shop with a number and a signboard.

This man asked me to come and work in his shop for a daily wage of fifty *kyats*. That made fifteen hundred *kyats* a month, which was a lot more than I could have earned working by myself from a bench. As far as I was concerned, he was offering me a good deal.

I'd go to work with a lunch box and eat at the shop. Sometimes if we hadn't cooked at home, I'd just bring some rice and buy curry locally. He stood me tea twice a day. So I had no expenses other than the train ticket there and back from Thingangyunn each day. I left work on the dot every day and it all suited me very well.

I repaired shoes at his shop for about a year, earning fifty *kyats* a day. Then I asked for a rise. Why? Because his shop had become very well-known and successful. It regularly received forty, fifty, sixty even a hundred pairs of shoes a day. There were only two trained cobblers there, me and another man, plus a couple more workers who used to do the easy gluing and mending. But me and the other worker, Mu Tu, were the only ones allowed to repair the expensive shoes which belonged to the rich customers. We were run off our feet. Every day we were doing about five or six hundred *kyats* worth of work—each. Sometimes we must have brought in almost a thousand *kyats*. For the most expensive shoes, the lowest charge was fifty *kyats*. That would just be for stitching. If they needed gluing or strengthening in some way it was a lot more. You're talking one hundred, one fifty. So each one of us was bringing in at least five hundred a day in charges—a thousand between us. That was why we asked for a rise.

The owner said he couldn't afford it. Once he said that, since he wouldn't play ball, I decided to quit and strike out on my own. And here

I am. I don't stay in one place any more. I walk the whole of Rangoon, but generally in the Burmese quarters. Why don't I work downtown anymore? You don't get regular work down there. Sometimes you're busy, sometimes you don't even make enough to cover the cost of your food. And there are so many shoe repairers down town, the customers are spread too thinly.

Let's say, for example, you're mending shoes on a bench in Mogul Street. You don't pick up any custom from people in Latha Street because they'll go to a cobbler nearby. People from Pansoedan and Bogyoke Street and round by the Sule Pagoda don't come as far as Mogul Street when their shoes need fixing. Downtown, you only go out of your way to get your shoes fixed if they're expensive shoes, otherwise you just get them fixed any old place. So nobody's going to walk all the way to Mogul Street to get them fixed at my stall.

That's why I go out walking in the neighbourhoods to get customers, usually to the Burmese townships. On Mondays and Tuesdays I visit Kemmendine and Sanchaung. Wednesdays and Thursdays I go to Yegyaw and Pazundaung. Fridays and Saturdays is Mingala Taungnyunt and Kyaukmyaung. Sundays I go to Kamayut and Ahlone. That's because it's easiest for me to get there by train and on Sundays the train isn't so crowded.

These are all Burmese neighbourhoods, so you don't come across many shoes. Mostly people round here wear slippers. Sometimes they're made of leather or rubber. There aren't many shoe repair stalls around the neighbourhoods and they can't be bothered to go into town and get them fixed so they wait for me to come round.

I do okay like this. I earn between fifty and seventy-five *kyats* a day. On average I get at least three or four *kyats* a pair of shoes. About the price of a cup of tea. Some people try and bargain down the price by one or two *kyats*. If there are only a few repairs I might be prepared to do it for less. But if there's a lot of work that needs doing, I stick at five *kyats*. If they try and bargain me down, I say to them, it's only the cost of a cup of tea. If I put it like that, and just point out it's only the cost of a cup of tea, they relent. Altogether I make between fifty and seventy-five *kyats* a day.

Am I married? No, not yet. I'm still single but I do have a girlfriend. She lives in Thingangyunn. But she says she's ashamed of me because my mother's an alcoholic. She says if I can get my mother off the booze, she'll marry me, otherwise we'll have to wait until my mother dies. So, what should I do? Am I supposed to pray for my mother's death? I've tried to get her to give up. I've put her in to Tadagalay Psychiatric Hospital a couple of times. She was off alcohol for six months. But she started drinking again because she said she was depressed and couldn't sleep properly. I took her up to Tadagalay for the third time but the doctor just shouted at her and said 'We've already cured her twice!! What's the point of getting her off the booze if she just keeps going back to it? She's had her chance!' I think the doctor was pretty angry. 'If she just goes back to drinking every time we get her off, it's wasting all of our time!!' he said.

So nowadays, I give my mother enough money for a bottle a day. I feel sorry for her. She tells me she doesn't want to drink either. But she says she can't manage without a drink. Her hands start to shake and she can't sleep or work. Actually she doesn't need to work, apart from cooking for the two of us. She's turned fifty-five now.

What about me? No way, I don't touch the stuff. I just have to take one look at what it's done to my mother. She really is pitiable. She just can't give it up, even when she tries, she has to keep drinking. But I tell her not to drink more than a bottle a day. I told her I'll buy that much for her.

When I said this, she wept and said 'My son, you're having to suffer for all my sins'. So she tried to give up. But since she couldn't get the doctor's help, she just had to go cold turkey. She gave up, but then she couldn't eat or sleep, she was up and down all night like a yo-yo, reciting prayers. She only slept one or two hours a night and she started to lose weight. So I gave up saying anything about her drinking.

One day I came home to find she'd been hitting the bottle. She was up cooking. When she saw me, she said she couldn't help herself. She was weeping buckets. I couldn't tell her off. I said to her 'If it's that bad, you may as well stop trying to give up'. I've never tried to get her to stop again.

I know how disgusting her habit is, of course I do. But I'd just rather she was happy. We all have a duty to look after our parents, and I'm going to do the best I can for her. But I do sometimes wonder if I'm doing the right thing, letting her carry on like this.

[January 1991]

213

ရန်ကုန်အင်းခြေဖုံးစာရွက်ဆိုင်။

CHAPTER V
SHATTERED DREAMS

28

TRANQUIL POOL

I met her in a well-known tea shop near the Rangoon university campus. We chatted for hours. She had sparkling eyes and a thin mouth. Her skin was so pale I wondered if she was anaemic. Her round eyes and dark eyebrows, her sharp nose and her tightly drawn lips seemed, I thought, to reflect her determination in the face of adversity, her pride, her intelligence and her courage. You could tell her personality from looking at her face. She wore no make-up or lipstick and her hair hung naturally. She kept pushing it back when it fell in front of her eyes. She wore a Kenzo shirt, a turquoise longyi and white high-heeled shoes with a coconut-coloured sling-bag over her shoulder. She was so skinny that she seemed taller than she really was. She gave the impression of someone who, if something shouldn't be said, would keep it to herself, but would tell things straight if needs be. Her name was Thida. She was twenty-seven.

I'm Saturday's child. I was born at sunrise. When I was born, they called me Nilar because of being born on Saturday. But later my father decided he didn't like the name and called me Thida instead. Thida's a good name. Do you know what it means? Cool like water. I think it is a very good name for a girl. The Thida in the Ramayana opera was reliable, calm and courageous. It's a name that brings peace. You should know that, because I remember you put it in the foreword to your novel, *Linkadipa*, remember? 'Thida exemplifies tranquillity'. Do you remember saying that?

But my name is just about the only tranquil thing there is about me. My life has been pretty devoid of peacefulness. I'm not saying that because I want you to feel sorry for me, *Saya*. I would never want that. I can't stand people like that and I've met a few, I'm sure you have too. They always want to tell you how hard their lives have been. Egotistical, narcissistic, intent on telling you how wretched their lives are. I'm not that kind of a person. I take the vicissitudes of life as they come without any rancour. I don't like to wallow in self-pity.

Do I use unusually long words, *Saya*? Perhaps it's because I like to read. I tend to pick up the words I read. I like poems too, and I like to go for long walks in the rain. If I can't sleep on a moonlit night, I'll go for a walk. Maybe I am a bit crazy. A bit eccentric. Maybe.

I've been writing poetry ever since I was little. I like reading generally, but above all I like reading poetry. And I like writing poems. I started off when I was little by learning my favourite poems by heart and then writing them out.

In my family, there are five children. I've got two older sisters and two younger brothers. I'm in the middle. My oldest sister is a doctor. She's married to another doctor. She doesn't live here any more. They've both moved abroad. The rest of us left still live in Rangoon.

My father was a civil servant out in the districts. In the old days it was called the BCS—Burma Civil Service. Before I was born, he was stationed in various towns and districts as a Township Officer and Sub-Divisional Officer. I was born in a town out in the districts when my father was a Deputy Commissioner, except in those days they called it District Commissioner. My father was an honest man, and he worked hard.

If you want to know about me, I'd better give you some background about my parents first so that you can get the full picture. My father's father was a clerk. His son was clever and made it to college. Rangoon University. In those days, once they passed their degrees they usually sat for the BCS exams. My grandfather wanted his son to become a Township Officer or a gazetted officer. He was just a clerk and he was in awe of the officials who used to come round. So he wanted his son to have what he never had, the status and the respect.

My father sat the BCS exams and went on to serve as a Township Officer and then Sub-Divisional Officer in various places. He was twenty-six or twenty-seven when he got promoted. While he was moving from town to town, he met my mother. She was the daughter of a Deputy Commissioner. She's younger than my father and he first met her when he used to go to her house on business or for social calls. My father was very old-fashioned. He didn't dare to ask my mother out. Anyway, he wasn't really interested in taking girls out, or in going out drinking or dancing. The sort of things that officials in the districts used to get up to in those days. They would go to the club and play a little poker or billiards. Or they would go and play golf. That way they rubbed shoulders with the leading lights in the town and got themselves seen by the senior officials.

My mother was at convent school in Rangoon at the time. As a convent school girl, she was very Westernised and spoke fluent English. The nuns wouldn't let them use Burmese at school. She used to board there. She came home during the holidays in the hot season and during October and at Christmas. That was when my father first met her. To start with, he wasn't interested in her, probably because she was so much younger than him. He was about twenty-seven at the time, and a Township Officer. She must have been seventeen, and in her final year at school. Basically she was the daughter of his boss, so he treated her like a little sister.

Also he still had a sweetheart back in his old town. Her father was a clerk as well, just like his father had been. They'd been childhood playmates, and schoolfriends and neighbours. But she'd had to drop out of school when her father died. She'd gone and worked in a clothes shop in the market. My father said he'd always been in love with his childhood sweetheart. But what with one thing and another they'd never been able to get married. He had always meant to marry her one day and they were staying faithful to one another.

Let me tell you a bit about my mother. Her father was District Commissioner. Her mother had died when she was little. Her father had re-married, to an older woman, and as so often happens, my mother did not get on well with her stepmother. They were always arguing. So my mother was packed off to a convent school in Rangoon. Even when my grandfather got transferred to the capital she stayed on as a boarder.

My grandfather wanted his only daughter to do well at school and grow up into a proper little lady. But unfortunately my mother didn't live up to his expectations. She was always getting into trouble and the school kept sending him letters. I think it probably had something to do with boys. So my grandfather and his wife decided to marry her off quickly to my father. He was about twenty-eight, she was about eighteen. They got married and had us five children.

My father married my mother out of duty to his boss, but he didn't really love her. His heart was still with his childhood sweetheart. But after they'd been married for a while, these things were forgotten, as so often happens. After I was born, my father got promoted to Assistant Secretary and was transferred to Rangoon. It was moving to Rangoon which started the problems which began to plague our family. Up till then we'd been quite happy.

You remember what Rangoon was like in those days? Lots of parties and dances to go to. My convent-educated Westernised mother went to them all with great gusto. My father was a workaholic. He'd leave the house at seven in the morning and not get home until eight or nine at night. Even then, all he thought about was work. Sometimes he didn't see his children from one day to the next. He'd leave the house before we got up, and by the time he got home we'd be tucked up in bed.

While my father was obsessed with his work, my mother spent all her waking hours at parties and Embassy receptions and dances. We hardly saw her for more than an hour a day. We'd be packed off to school in the morning and when we got home we'd be lucky to see her for more than an hour before she rushed off to a reception. She'd spend the weekends playing poker at gambling dens. This was what started my parents fighting.

My father was promoted shortly after I was born. It was really that promotion which started all the problems. But the rest of the family have always said that it must have been me, that I must have brought bad luck into the house because I was Saturday born. That used to really annoy me. How could it have been my fault? It was obvious that coming to Rangoon had been what started my parents fighting and it didn't have anything to do with me or anyone else. That was just the way it was.

My father and mother divorced when I was in my last year at school. My father had been a simple hard-working man. But now he started drinking. I think it was to drown his sorrows. He'd be coming home drunk every night at about nine or ten, or even past midnight. And the drink was affecting his work too.

On top of acquiring a reputation for drinking he started to get a name as a womaniser. We heard gossip that he'd been spotted around town with a secretary from his office. One day my mother decided she'd had enough, so she followed him to the office and confronted him and the other woman, using language which made everyone blush.

My father said he'd had enough of her as well, and so the two of them divorced and he married the secretary. He gave us the house and the compound. He took nothing for himself other than the clothes he was wearing because he said that it was all his fault. But he couldn't afford to support us on his salary.

I was in my final year at school, my elder sister was at medical school and my middle sister was at college. My brothers were in eighth and ninth standard. My mother rented out the house to an Embassy and we did up the servants quarters at the back and moved in there. The rent was four thousand *kyats* a month which was enough for us to live on and finish our education.

My mother started working as a broker. She sold gems and acted as an agent for houses. She met a broker who was several years younger than her and he moved in with us. When we told her it was wrong, she just moved out and lived quite openly with him somewhere else.

So the family split up. My honest simple father had run off with another woman. My not so simple party-loving mother had taken up with another man. I was ashamed of them both. The five of us were all quite close together in age and none of us had the authority to take charge. My oldest sister did the best she could, but neither my middle sister nor my brothers would listen to her. My sister took the four thousand *kyats* rent and worked out how it should be spent on food, clothing and our school expenses. We three sisters did the cooking. But the boys were completely useless and didn't even bother to wash up their own plates or do their own laundry. If they'd been just a little bit more helpful, we wouldn't have minded working hard. But they were completely selfish and refused to lift a finger. They would complain and break the plates if they didn't like the food we cooked and if they did like it, they'd scoff the whole lot before the rest of us had had a chance to have any. So then there would be arguments and shouting and sometimes we even traded blows and damaged the furniture.

My brothers and my middle sister were the worst trouble-makers. The older one was always bringing girls over to the house and when we told him to stop it because it wasn't right what with not having any adults in the house and with us being unmarried, he told us to go take a running jump. He said, if we didn't like it, there was nothing to stop us from going out. This was the house which our parents had given to all of us and here he was behaving as if he owned it. I couldn't believe it.

The youngest brother was no better. He became a heroin addict. He used to hang around with a thoroughly dubious crowd and sometimes he'd bring them back to the house and they'd sit around playing tapes and guitars and making a racket and doing whatever they felt like. My middle sister was as bad. She took after our mother, always going off to Embassy parties and hanging around with this man and that and getting into trouble. To tell you the truth, she ended up having to have an abortion.

Meanwhile the younger brother was taking things from the house and selling them to fund his habit. We got sick of him taking our stuff.

My mother had moved to a different town. My father came round from time to time, or sometimes he'd buy us clothes or presents and send them round. Home life was getting to be hell, *Saya*. A day never went by without something bad happening. But I had to stay there until I got my degree because I didn't have any money to move out and live somewhere else. My big sister said she would move out with me and we could share together. But then she met her boyfriend and got married and moved out to live with him. That left the four of us. I'd had enough. I felt like crying the whole time. None of my brothers and sisters took a blind bit of notice of one another. They all just went their own sweet way.

About a year after my big sister left home, I graduated with a Zoology degree and went looking for a job. My father helped me get a job in his department. I only earned three hundred and twenty *kyats* a month basic pay but that didn't matter. I was desperate to move out. My three brothers and sisters wanted to sell the house and split the money between them but the house was in my mother's name and she wouldn't do anything about it.

Nowadays I'm living in a hostel. It costs a hundred *kyats* a month. We're not allowed to cook so I have to live off take-aways. It costs me about two hundred and fifty *kyats* a month for a cup of soup, a plate of curry, some fried snacks and some fish sauce. It's not too bad when you consider how much food costs nowadays. How do I manage then on my salary? I don't. I only get three-twenty flat pay. So I top that up by giving Chemistry home tuition. I've got four or five students so I earn about five hundred *kyats* a month which means I can get by.

There's no way I'd move back home and live with my brothers and sisters and listen to them bickering all the time. I'd rather be on my own. I have been to see them once or twice, but there's always something to argue about whenever I go round. So I'm fed up of it. The three of them still live there. My sister does what she pleases. She lives off take-aways and works as a tutor at the University. Neither one of my brothers has a proper job. The older one does a bit of brokering cars and gems. The younger one survives on the little bit of money he gets from my parents. But he says it's not enough and he's having to drive one of his friend's taxis. I don't know how much he gets from that. He never graduated from high school.

I don't see how my family's problems can be my fault, *Saya*. Maybe you can put the blame on my parents. It could have been because my mother was too Westernised, too much of a party-goer. It could have been my father's fault for drinking and having a mistress. Maybe it was both of their faults for getting re-married. But it could have been my brothers' and sister's faults too, for being so selfish.

But while things may have been difficult for me, I don't really want to apportion the blame to my parents or my brothers and sisters. I don't want to end up bitter and twisted. I just look on it all as fate. I do my best to be good. I want to build a life for myself now and go my own way. I've got the courage to do that.

Well, it's been good talking to you. But now I've got to get off to my next tuition. I'm sorry if I've been boring you with all my problems. But if you want to hear the full story, I'd be happy to tell you sometime.

[September 1988]

29

ABANDONED

We'd been out of touch for over thirty years, but I was always hearing news about her and her family. She had been Miss Rangoon University and was famous for her looks, for having a good time, and for having an endless stream of admirers. It was probably all quite true. To my knowledge, she'd had at least four or five boyfriends and when she broke up with them, it used to break their hearts. Some would end up getting thrown out of university without finishing their degrees. Some would take to the bottle. Some were so distressed by the fickle nature of womankind that they abandoned society and lived the life of a recluse. She was the most popular girl in college. She attended all the dances and parties and the stories about her and a certain foreigner which appeared in one particular newspaper at the time could have filled a book.

It came as a big surprise when she married an extremely ordinary man from a farming family in Upper Burma. He was not like the other students. If he hadn't won a scholarship, his parents would not have been able to afford to send him to university. While she was very westernised, he was thoroughly Burmese. She was the most popular girl in college. Her name was on everyone's lips. She had been through Convent school and spoke fluent English. He was tongue-tied trying to speak a word. When he tried to speak English, he would start croaking 'Aaah . . . aaah . . . aah' like an old bird, which was why we nicknamed him the 'Country Crow'.

We were all stunned when she married old Crow, after she'd had the pick of the boys in college. Some people reckoned that she must have had to marry him because someone else had got her pregnant. But she paid no attention to that and the two of them settled down quietly. People said that it would never last—they would split up before she'd even had a chance to blacken the bottom of her rice pot. But those people were proved wrong. They lived happily together and it looked like she really loved him, and he loved her. They had children, and we were pleased when we heard how they had turned out well, all going on to university and medical school. I heard she and he still had a happy home all the way into her fifties. It was then that I bumped into her again for the first time for years. I didn't even recognise her until she greeted me.

Her appearance had changed drastically. She had lost her looks and figure completely. Where once stood a fair-skinned luscious slim young girl, there now stood a worn-out plump old woman with dry blotchy skin. Her arms and face had once been golden like sagawa *flowers. Now they were flabby. She came and sat herself down next to me and cheerfully told me about how she had got to where she was today. She kept laughing at her situation. She didn't seem a bit remorseful about her past or seem to resent the cards that fate had dealt her.*

I t'll take me ever so long to tell you[1] all my news. It could even run to a novella. I know you've all been thinking that my life has all been perfect. Not a bit of it. From the outside it might seem that way. But really it's more like a cockerel who fluffs up his feathers to make himself seem bigger. You might think he's a two *viss* chicken. But underneath, you'll find he's a shrivelled old rooster.

I married my husband after university. You know that much. We had children—my oldest girl, she's a doctor now, my oldest boy's an engineer. Works on a boat. He's even married a foreign girl. Gave me my first grandchild. I can't see him coming back to Burma somehow. The oldest girl's not married yet, she's out in the districts working in a hospital. The middle son and the youngest daughter are just so wild I've had to wash my hands of them. He comes home to his bed once in a while, when he feels like it. Sometimes we don't see him for weeks. One time when he didn't come home we asked around and found he was locked up in jail on a drugs charge. He's upset me so many times, I've just given up caring and left him to his fate. His father feels the same.

But that's enough of them. I'm meant to be telling you all about me
. . . .

You probably remember what everyone said when I got married. They all thought it was peculiar. I'd been such a socialite at university, with so many friends, and there I was marrying this cold fish who was so old-fashioned and never mixed with anyone. I know they all thought I was the lucky one and he'd had the wool pulled over his eyes. I know some people were even saying that I was only marrying him because I was shop-soiled goods. They felt sorry for him. They thought that once we got married, I'd carry on going out and having a good time and leave him at home with the babies.
.

---

[1] The speaker uses the English 'You'—a sign of a convent-educated middle class Rangoon resident.

After we married, we had to move out to the districts. He was working for the government. Out in the sticks he became a changed man. At university, he'd never so much as sniffed a glass of whisky, but in the districts he took to drinking like a fish to water. It was all part of the lifestyle for a government official. They all trekked off to the club to play golf and get drunk. I didn't mind that much. After all, that was just the way it was, the way you were expected to behave when you were with your colleagues. I didn't get much of a chance to socialise myself. I had the children to bring up and the house to look after so I didn't have much free time. But if I was at a loose end, I'd get the other wives round for a game of poker.

I suppose people thought of us as being like Ma Ma Myint and Ko Tin Maung in that film 'Love to Share'. Do you remember that film from when we were young? Tin Maung played a straightforward, honest husband. Ma Ma Myint was his pretty young wife who liked parties and ended up running off with another man.

That wasn't me by then, though. Nor was my husband the Ko Tin Maung character. He was always getting drunk and picking fights with me about my old boyfriends from university. We used to fight like cats and dogs.

That's where the similarity with 'Love to Share' ended. I was the housewife who still loved him and wanted to stay married. He was the one who went off and had a good time and broke up the marriage. Definitely role reversal.

Where I am living now? I'm out in Parami. On the surface, at least, my life looks like it's turned out well. I've got a nice house, with a garden and a car. All mod cons. Three or four maids. An easy life.

But while it may be easy, it still isn't complete without my husband. I've lost the love of my life, you see. Where is he? Where do you think he is? He's living with his mistress. Not even mistress number one either. By my reckoning, he's onto his third one at least. His third declared mistress that is. Goodness know how many more there's been who I don't know about.

Of course he looks after me. He gives me five thousand *kyats* a month housekeeping. I don't know how he manages to give me so much and I don't ask. That's his business. He's retired from government service and works as a rep for a foreign company so they pay him in dollars. It's all above board and legal. I suppose that's how he can afford to give me so much. Also we jointly own two houses and we rent them out to an embassy for a thousand dollars a month so that's two thousand altogether which goes into our joint bank account. So I suppose you could say we've got no worries when it comes to money.

But, like you writers put it, I'm starved of love. My heart has been broken. Still, what does it matter? I'm sure I'll manage. When you get to my age, people think it's funny if you're still talking about love and heartbreak. You know what the young people say—he's caught measles. I caught it when I was younger and now I'm immune. It's him that didn't catch it until he was middle-aged.

His mistress? Yes I've met her. I've known about her all along. She was one of the three secretaries he hired to work in his office when he became a rep. I said to him at the time 'One is enough, surely?' But, no, he said, he needed three. He couldn't manage with just one. To cut a long story short, he seduced her and now they live together somewhere else.

What's she like? Oh, she's pretty of course. She's young. Attractive. Chic. Flirtatious. As the young say, she's trendy. That's why he fell for her. Not like me. She's not a grey haired fifty year old woman who's over the hill. Well, enough of this. I just wanted to show you how strangely it's all turned out. At university, there I was—fashionable, fun-loving, and there he was—quiet, ordinary. Look at us thirty years on. He's completely changed and I'm still in the nineteenth century.

[August 1989]

30

CONFESSION

I'll describe her face as if it were a garden. Her lips were rosebuds and her cheeks were golden sagawa *flowers. Her nose was a posy. Her eyes were as blue as bluebells. She was as tall and straight as a pine tree and with her every movement she swayed like a willow. She was still only young, not more than twenty or twenty-five. She wore a matching* longyi *and blouse which had an embroidered pattern on a mauve background, and white high-heeled shoes. Over her shoulder she carried a fashionable sling bag with narrow straps which hung at her waist. Her hair was short and curly and blew around in the breeze. In short, she had the sort of beauty which would cause any man to take a second look. I won't mention her name.*

Where should I begin? Shall I start from when I first met 'Uncle'? Or should I go back to before that? Okay, I'll go back as far as I can remember. That way you'll get the whole picture and you can edit out the bits you don't want and fill in the rest. I'll just tell you as much as I can. My father worked as a night-watchman in a factory. Neither he nor my mother were from Rangoon. Originally, he was from Central Burma and she was from Taung-zun near Thaton. Their two families moved to Rangoon when they were young, and they met here. They got married here, got jobs here. I don't know exactly what my mother was doing, but once I was born, my father got a job as a guard in a factory. They had four more children after me and my father kept on working as a night-watchman throughout that time. In fact he's still not retired yet, even now. I suppose he's not old enough yet.

We lived on the edge of town, quite near to the factory in quarters they provided. I went to school. I stayed on till eighth standard but then I kept failing so I had to leave. I tried to take the exam once I'd left but even if you're going to school every day, it's difficult to pass. Sitting it once you've left is much harder. We couldn't afford to send me to tuition either. Do you have any idea how much it costs? We couldn't even afford food, let alone tuition classes. All we had to live on was my father's salary which was hardly anything . After all, what does a night-watchman earn? Not a lot. So making ends meet was a struggle, and we were pretty hard up.

Do I read? Yes I like reading novels and stuff. In fact, I often read three or four a day. I like cartoon books too. I really enjoy reading, but I can do without those books you get about poor people and how they have money troubles. If I'm already depressed about being poor, the last thing I want to do is read stories about more depressed poor people. I can see all that just by looking around me. I have to put up with being poor every day. Why should I want to read more about it? I'd much rather read books that'll cheer me up, love stories and stories which bear no resemblance to my own life. Those are the sorts of books I find interesting. Sure if there's nothing else to read, I'll read other books. But I think you understand what I'm trying to say.

So I think you get the picture don't you? We were struggling to get by on my father's salary as a night-watchman. That's why my mother decided to set up a stall outside the factory gates selling cigarettes. Since I'd left school by then, I used to go along and help her. She didn't do badly right from the start. Little by little she began to earn enough to help us along. At least she'd be a bit in pocket by the end of each day.

In those days, my father's monthly wage would only last four or five days, maybe a week. After that, we'd run out of food in the house and there'd be no money left. We'd borrow a bit here, a bit there. from friends. If we couldn't borrow money, we'd have to borrow oil and salt and *ngapi*, and sometimes even rice. My father went out peddling a trishaw during the daytime but even that wasn't enough to feed the seven of us. I hope you'll excuse me for telling you this, *Saya*, but sometimes I couldn't even afford a blouse and had to go around with my *longyi* hoiked up around my armpits. Otherwise I'd have to wear my mother's clothes. Sometimes I even wore my father's shirts.

One day, one of my mother's cousins dropped by for a chat like she often did. She and my mother would gossip about what had been going on and about the family. Sometimes they'd eat pickled tea or the snacks she'd bring along. While they were chewing the fat, I used to take over at the stall, although sometimes I'd join in. My Aunty lived in South Okkalapa and she'd be full of the latest goings on in the market in Number 10 Ward, and in what was called St John's market in those days. Nowadays it's Mingala market. She was up on all the news because her business took her around all these places. She used to buy clothes in Number 10 Ward market and come and sell them in neighbourhoods like ours. People would buy them on credit, and pay by the month. If she knew them, she'd give them two or three months credit.

She hadn't brought along anything to sell that day though. Instead of the usual raucous gossip with my mother, they were talking together in whispers. I thought they must have been talking about grown-up things, so I didn't try and join in. I just sat on the stall reading my cartoon book.

Suddenly I heard my mother say 'Well, you'd better ask her y'self'. Since they were quite close, they used to use very familiar language with one another. 'Surely it's not up to me?' said my aunt.

'Look', said my mother, 'I'm not going to ask her, she's my little daughter. And if her father found out, he'd kill me. You can ask her if you want, but there's no way I'm going to.'

I was starting to get interested in this curious conversation. I kept pretending to read my comic, but I was straining to catch what they were talking about. But after that they stopped talking like this and went back to gossiping as usual.

After a while, my aunt said goodbye to us all and left. But just before she went, she turned to me, looked me up and down, and said 'You know, my little niece, you're getting more and more beautiful by the day. I think you're even getting pretty enough to be a movie star'.

About a week later, she turned up again. This time, I didn't know what to think. She'd brought me material for a matching batik *longyi* and blouse which must have cost a good three hundred *kyats*. I was over the moon, particularly as it was my favourite colours, pinks and browns. My aunt said that she'd brought it for me because she'd made a good profit that day and she hated to see her pretty little niece wearing an old green school *longyi*. I was only young and I cared a lot about being able to wear nice clothes. She gave me my present and then went off into a huddle with my mother. I paid no attention, because I was too wrapped up thinking about my new brown *longyi*. I decided to get it sewn up in time for *Thadingyut*, and then I could wear it when I went out with my friends to the Festival of Lights. I thought to myself how great it would be to show it off in front of my friends.

Just before she left, my aunt came over to me for a chat. She told me how many clothes there were down in Number 10 ward market and how every time she went there and saw them all, she always thought of me. My mother was sitting nearby at her stall with a miserable expression. Then suddenly my aunt came out with it:

'So, does my little niece have a boyfriend yet?'

'Oh Aunty, whatever do you mean? Of course not. Not even a shadow of one', I jokily replied.

Then she said, 'In that case, why don't I find you a nice husband? I could set you up to live very comfortably. Not just you. Your mother and father could live comfortably too. How about it, eh? Why don't I go and find you one?'

'Aunty, are you trying to marry me off?'

'Not at all, dear. Someone with a face like yours should be able to pick and choose her husband. But if you want me to find you one, you've only got to say.'

Although she was being serious, she made it sound like it was all just a bit of fun.

'Oh Aunty, I don't know. If that's what my mummy and daddy want for me, of course I'll say yes. You'll have to ask Mummy', I said lightly.

So my aunt called across to my mother and asked 'What do you think? Your daughter says it's all up to her mother'. But my mother said nothing and just kept on puffing on her cheroot.

My aunt continued 'I just want the best for my niece, you know. I've got a very good husband in mind. He runs a motor launch in the delta. He doesn't just own one, either, he's got three or four. He'll take good care of you. He's rich you know, and you'll be able to support your parents. You won't want for anything. And since he runs a motor launch, he's not always in Rangoon. He comes and goes. So you'll be boss in your own home. You won't even have to stay there if you don't want. You could always come back home and live with your parents when he's not around. He'll buy them a little plot of land and they can build a house. He'll want his in-laws to look respectable. If you agree, I've already seen a plot of land in South Okkalapa, just close to the market. So, what do you think?'

She was trying to talk me into it. I hadn't had a chance to think it over, since she'd just sprung the idea on me out of the blue. So I couldn't give her an answer there and then. I didn't know if the man she had in mind was nice or nasty. But I felt sorry for my parents and I wanted a good life for them and me and a chance to put my younger brothers and sisters through school.

'I'm only saying all this because I want the best for you, dear. Don't think there's any other reason, will you? There's nothing wrong with this man. I can fix it all up for you if you tell me to. He's told me that I'm to look out for a suitable wife for him so that's what I'm doing. You know, you'll not want for anything if you marry him. There is one thing, though, he is . . . older than you, but . . . .'

She looked at me to see my reaction. I didn't know what to say. Earlier on, I'd been able to answer her back because I thought it was just a bit of fun. Now that she wanted a straight answer, I was struck dumb.

'What do you think? Should I tell him about you? Like I said he's a bit older than you. But, well, you know what they say about husbands and wives, eh? And ten years age isn't that big a difference really'.

That day, she ate in our house before going home. As she left, I watched her bending my mother's ear. My mother just listened to it all glumly. Then I heard her say 'It's got nothing to do with me. Let her make up her own mind'.

About a week later, my aunty turned up again. This time she was dressed smartly. She said to me, 'Let's go off to Mingala Market and buy a few things for you. I'm sure you've been there before, haven't you?' Had I heck? To me it was just a name. I didn't even know where it was. 'Go and put on that nice pinky-brown one-set I gave you. And with all the shopping we've got to do, it might get late. If it does, you can always sleep over at my house and go home in the morning'.

My mother said I could go, so I set off with my aunt and we shopped till we dropped in Mingala market. She bought me a sling-bag. It must have cost two or three hundred *kyats*. But my aunt said it was on her. 'If he's got time', she said 'your would-be husband said he'd drop round my house. Then the two of you can get to know one another'.

We tramped all over Mingala Market and by the time we'd finished it was about three in the afternoon. We went back to South Okkalapa to find the house locked. My aunt and her husband lived there alone, they had no children. He worked for Myanma Oil and Gas Enterprise. I'm not too sure exactly what he did but sometimes he used to go off up-country.

When we got back to her house, we cooked up a curry from what we'd bought down the market. I helped her out. 'It's still early', she said, 'You can go home after you've had your dinner. But if it's dark by then, you can always sleep here'.

I wasn't bothered. I helped her with the housework and when we'd finished, I picked up a comic and sat down to read. About five o'clock, a car pulled up outside her house. It was an expensive model, I think it was a Toyota SE. A man got out. He was dark-skinned, fat, balding and wore a batik shirt outside an Arakan *longyi*. When I saw him, I thought to myself that this must be some other visitor of my aunt's. Then I suddenly realised the truth. 'That's your future husband', whispered my aunt. I was so shocked, I felt like crying. I just couldn't believe it. Look at him! How could that be my husband-to-be? He was at least sixty. Excuse me, *Saya*, but he was old enough to be my father—older even.

What could I do? I didn't have time to think. I wondered if I should run away. My aunt exchanged one or two words with the man and then said, 'Well, I've got a few errands to run nearby' and disappeared.

I won't bore you with the details, *Saya*. From that day onwards, I became this man's mistress. My aunt was right. He was a rich man. He owned several motor launches. He gave me ten thousand *kyats* to be getting on with. The next morning he dropped me off at the end of my road in his car. Ten thousand *kyats* isn't to be sniffed at.

From then on, he gave me three thousand *kyats* each month. He didn't live in Rangoon, he had a home out in the districts and maybe once or twice a month he'd come up to Rangoon. He had a wife and kids back home.

Later on he bought us the house in South Okkalapa and we moved there. On three thousand *kyats* a month, we were able to live comfortably. Round there, I was just a normal single girl. But once or twice a month, I became his mistress.

We were together like this for about a year. No, maybe it was longer. But after about a year he suddenly snuffed it. I don't know why, exactly, but it could have been high blood pressure or heart disease. I read his obituary in the newspaper, because my aunty showed it to me. So that was the end of that.

With him dead and gone, things were back to the way they always had been, living from hand to mouth. We went from an income of three thousand a month to struggling to survive on my father's pitiful salary.

So because of what my aunt had got me into, I ended up a woman of easy virtue. But I wasn't cheap. I'll be quite frank with you. I could work ten days and earn enough money to keep us for the rest of the month. So it was always going to be hard to resist.

It was during that time that I met him. He's the man of my life, *Saya*. I call him 'Uncle'. He's about twenty years older than me. He's got a wife and children. One day he came to visit me, through a contact. Although he's somewhere between forty and fifty, you'd think he was only about thirty. He's an assistant engineer, working on boats, so he often gets to go abroad.

He was too much. Sometimes he'd visit me and we'd just talk and he'd tell me that he loved me. To start with I thought there was nothing in it. But after he'd visited me three or four times, I realised he really cared about me like I was his proper mistress. Since I told him I liked reading, he used to tell me about the English books he'd read and the films he'd seen. One time, he told me about a film he'd seen when he was a student. It was so sad. It was a film about a prostitute. At the end, she's on a bridge when she gets hit by a car and dies. What was that film called? What was it again? It was called after the name of the bridge. A bridge in England. What is it? Oh yes, I remember. 'Waterloo Bridge'. In the film, the actress is on the bridge and she's knocked down by the car, like an execution. It made me cry so much.

It didn't take long before we were in love like boyfriend and girlfriend. But he used to say to me 'Look, I can't afford to keep you like your motor launch magnate. I'm no millionaire, I only earn money when I get a job on board ship. So don't rely on me—get yourself a nice boyfriend who can look after you properly'. He often used to say this, and every time he did, it made me sad. I really loved him. I don't know why. I suppose it was because he understood me, and loved me and cared about me.

He used to come and visit me about once a week. Sometimes we'd go out for a drive in his car. We went out together for about a year. During that time, I never expected him to give me any money, but if he had any, he'd give me whatever he had. He used to say to me 'If I was your only customer you'd be a poor girl. So I don't mind you working if you want to'. But I didn't go with anyone else while I was with him.

After about a year, he got a job on a ship and went overseas. Every time he disembarked at a port of call, he'd send me a postcard. He and I weren't serious or anything. During that time, my situation was more precarious, and I had to go back to my old job. While I was working, I met this boy and married him. Although I say boy, in fact he was the same age as me. He used to come and visit me and we grew fond of one another and we ended up getting married.

I sent my 'Uncle' a letter via his shipping company to tell him I'd got married. I got a reply. He said that although he was sad because he was apart from me, he was happy that I had settled down properly. It made me very sad to read his letter. He told me to look after my husband and take care of my house and my marriage. I realised that he really cared about me and that just made me respect him all the more.

He wished me a happy marriage. Unfortunately his wish didn't come true. My husband was arrested on a drugs charge and given a three year sentence and sent off to do hard labour. To be honest, I didn't love him.

But because I was young and silly, I thought I did. Really, the only man I have ever loved is my 'Uncle'.

I wrote to tell him I had split up with my husband. Soon after, he came home and got in contact with me again. We rebuilt our lives the way we had been before, just like young lovers. But the other day, he came to see me and said he had something he had to tell me. He said that his wife had found out about the two of us. She waited until they got out of the house before mentioning it. She suggested they should go for a drive and a walk in the park. Then she said 'I've heard this and this about you, is it true?' He couldn't deny it. He admitted, 'Yes, there is this girl, and I love her. I care about her. I don't want to break up with her'.

He is a very honest man, *Saya*. He says exactly what he thinks and he never lies. He wouldn't lie to his wife. He wouldn't lie to me. He admitted that it was entirely his fault that he had betrayed his wife, and he told her that if she wanted to throw him out, he could accept that, but he did still love her. But he didn't want to break up with me. He would still do his duty by her and his son, and support them. But he couldn't leave me. He told his wife that she could do whatever she wanted to punish him.

It was all my fault. So when he'd finished, I said to him that he should leave me and go back to his wife. I didn't want to be responsible for breaking up his marriage. But he wouldn't listen.

Now I'm depressed, *Saya*. I don't know what to do. I don't know if I should do something which will hurt him or if I should leave him and go and live somewhere else. Sometimes I even wonder if I should throw myself under the wheels of a passing car on Thaketa bridge, just like that film.

Saya, really, I do love him. He might be older than me, but he really understands me. He is forgiving. And he protects me. But I wish that he wouldn't come to see me any more. I don't want to be the reason his marriage falls apart. So I often think about that film he told me about. 'Waterloo Bridge.'

[September 1990]

31

BITTER-SWEET TASTE OF SUCCESS

It must have been about twenty years since I'd last seen Ko Myo. He was about fifteen years younger than me. I was about thirty-five when I first met him, and he was about twenty. His parents were already dead by then and as an only son, he had no other close relatives. His parents had been poor and never had steady jobs. In summer they used to open up a stall by the road selling cold drinks, sugar cane juice, lime juice and so on. During winter and the monsoon, they would find something else to do, like selling coconut noodle soup. They didn't have their own house so they lived in the garage behind the house of a niece whose business was more successful than theirs.

Ko Myo was in middle school when his parents died. They died in quick succession, within the space of a year. After his mother died, his father stopped working and spent most of his time drinking or working as a labourer in the gem tracts. But he never seemed to earn as much from mining as other people did, and one day he never came back. There were rumours that he'd died of malaria or been killed by other miners. Either way, he died and his family were reluctant to discuss it, and so gradually he was forgotten.

Ko Myo stayed on at school and lived at his cousin's house, working for them in return for free board and lodging. In those days he was skinny and tall with a light skin. Twenty years later, he had developed a pot-belly and his face was florid. If he hadn't been so tall, he would have been a fairly fat man. Our next encounter was in an Upper Class carriage on the Rangoon-Mandalay express. He was knocking back whisky from a bottle of Johnnie Walker Red Label. When I first saw him I thought he seemed vaguely familiar but I didn't realise it was Ko Myo until he said my name.

Brother, don't you recognise me? It's Ko Myo—you know, Myo Swe. Long time no see. But I've kept up with what you've been writing. Not everything mind. I do like reading though. Whenever I pick up a magazine, I always check if you're in it and read your piece first. I've read your 'Tales of Ordinary People' in *Kalya* magazine. They aren't bad. They're certainly different. But do you mind if I give you my honest opinion? I'm saying this as a reader rather than a critic. I find them a bit dull, a bit repetitive. I think it's because you only write about dull people who no-one's ever heard of.

I mean, it's not as if those are the only type of people in the world, is it? So why don't you write about people from different walks of life? Why don't you interview famous artists or actresses, for example? That would be good. Or what about a society lady? Those wouldn't be ordinary people. They'd be the sort of people everyone had heard about. OK, maybe not people who are known through the country. But at least they'd be people who were well-known in the circles they move in. Why not? Why don't you write about them, eh? (I thought to myself that he had probably drunk quite a lot of whisky). They've got stories to tell. They've got feelings too. I'm sure they must have.

Of course, it's up to you who you write about. Whoever you do write about, ultimately they're all stories about human beings aren't they? Everyone has a story to tell. I've got a story. I've been wanting to tell it to you for ages. I never came to see you in Rangoon because I was too busy. I never made the effort to see you. I'm not telling you that you have to write about me. It's up to you if you want to. If you do write about me, you can write it like I'm an ordinary person, or however you want to write it. It's up to you.

You're probably surprised to see me looking like this. I never smoked when I was younger and now look at me. I don't even smoke cheroots now—only cigarettes—and only 555 International. You can see that I drink as well. Only Scotch Whisky. And usually only Black Label—I rarely drink Red Label[1]. Do you think I'm boasting? Do you think I'm trying to impress you? I'm not. I promise you I'm not. Definitely not. I've got nothing to boast about. After all, you know how I grew up, with no proper home and no money. I used to camp out in someone else's house and work like a slave in order to get regular meals and graduate from high school. You know how it was. You know how I grew up. You know I don't need to try and impress you.

---

[1] 555 are the most expensive brand of cigarette in Burma, made in England. Johnnie Walker Black Label is superior in quality and price to Red Label. Both are regarded as the signs of a rich man.

I'd better tell you how I've come to acquire these bad habits. No really, I want to. I want to tell you how wicked I am nowadays. In the past I never smoked. I never drank. Now look at me. Smoking, drinking and even . . . I've got to admit it. I even spend the night with call-girls. I've worked hard to get the kind of money that lets me do that. And now I've got it. I've got my own house in my own compound in a lane off Inya Road. I've got my own car with a driver. I've got servants. And if I want a call-girl to sleep with, I can get one. I bet you're thinking 'This man has got everything he could possibly need'.

Maybe you're not. Maybe you're thinking that I can't cope with being rich, you know, like people say. I can. Honest. But what I can't cope with is not having true peace of mind. I don't behave like this because I enjoy being rich. I do it because I'm trying to forget the poverty in my emotional life. I'm doing it to forget.

I've got everything I could possibly need. But you know what Rockefeller said? 'A rich man is a man who's got nothing but money'. He was right, you know. He should bloody know what he's talking about, if anyone does. 'A rich man is a man who's got nothing but money'. Damn right. I've got everything I need. Except love.

You probably think I'm starting to sound like a spotty adolescent. I'm just trying to put it simply. I've lost my marriage. Sure, I've got houses in Rangoon, Mandalay, Maymyo. But none of them are what you would call 'Home'. They're just houses, not homes.

I'd better tell you how it all happened, because it's been a long time hasn't it? The year you moved away from the neighbourhood, I passed tenth standard. I passed but I didn't get any distinctions. I got married the same year. My wife was from a poor family like me. But her father died too. She was at school with me, same class. She was good at school. We both did tenth standard at the same time but she got three distinctions and I didn't get any. She was working at the Electric Power Corporation.

We fell in love. Her family couldn't afford to send her to university. I could have gone if I'd wanted. My cousin said she would pay for me to go to college. If I'd stayed on living with her, I'd have eventually got a degree. But my girlfriend couldn't. Her relatives had had to support her even to get her through high school. So she had to stop after that, even though she'd have liked to carry on. Her mother was trying to arrange a marriage for her. She was very beautiful. I'm not just saying that because she was my girlfriend. Anyone would have told you the same. Even though she's in her forties now, she's kept her looks.

She didn't want to get married. She wanted to carry on studying. And she didn't like the man her mother had found for her because he was a lot older than her. In the end, she was coming under pressure to get married, so we had to elope. We didn't have a red cent to our names. I took her to a friend's house in South Okkalapa outside Rangoon. My friend and his wife didn't have any children so it was OK to stay there. We had nothing to our names. No mattress, no pillow, no blanket, no saucepans. My friends looked after us and lent us a blanket and a mosquito net. We couldn't go on like that though, so my friend lent us his wife's gold necklace and we took it to the pawnbroker. We bought blankets, pillows and a mosquito net and spent the rest of the money on saucepans, because we couldn't carry on eating their food. We couldn't afford to move out to our own place. But at least we shouldn't take advantage of their hospitality.

My friends were very kind to us. They gave us the money we needed to go to the Registry Office to get married. They had a whip-round. Have you ever heard that happen before—your friends have a whip-round so that you can get married? I'm sure it was a first. They knew how hard up we were so they did all that for us. They all wanted to help us out because they knew that we had been forced into eloping. That kind of thing makes you feel good about people doesn't it? They collected enough to pay for the marriage certificate and the lawyer and the payoffs for the officials at the court.

My friend was so good to us he even gave us his wife's necklace to buy blankets and a mosquito net. I didn't really want to accept it. But if I'd refused it, we'd have been stuck without a bed or a blanket or anything. We were having to share their blanket. I felt very bad about it because his wife was pregnant and if she caught a cold or anything it would be our fault.

That was why I had to accept the necklace and take it down to the pawnbrokers so I could buy some things to set up house. We carried on sharing the room but we ate separately. But then, we were so in love that we were prepared to put up with that kind of thing. Like in the song: 'When you're in love, you can be happy in a palace or a tumble-down hut'. We were happy no matter what. We could walk in the scorching sun and feel like we were walking in the light of the silvery moon. We could walk in the pouring rain without umbrellas and not feel a thing.

I used to go into town and try to find a job. My wife would go with me. We would walk around in all weathers looking for a job. When we found a vacancy, both of us would apply in case one of us got lucky. Sometimes we didn't even have enough money for the bus fare into town so we'd have to walk. One time the strap came loose on her flip-flop. So I gave her my shoes to wear and I went barefoot. When people saw us, they smiled. But we didn't care. Providing we were together, things like that didn't bother us. When we reached town we found a cobbler who fixed the shoe and she gave mine back to me.

She was the first one to find a job. Sales assistant in one of the Trade Corporation stores. She was pretty and well-spoken so the manager took a shine to her. At least with one of us earning, things got a bit easier. But I still couldn't find anything. I'd take her into town every morning and then go looking for a job. Since I still couldn't find one, I joined forces with an old friend and started selling second-hand books in Pansoedan Street.

I'd make two or three *kyats* a day. In fact it was his shop and I was really just helping out. When he took a break I'd sit in for him. When he opened up I'd help set the books out and when it closed I'd collect them up. That was all. And when we closed up, I'd go over to pick my wife up and we'd go shopping down the market and then go back to South Okkalapa. But it was enough, with my wife's pay, to let us rent our own room.

My wife was very ambitious. I suppose you could even say she was greedy. She's clever. She wanted to get a degree. She wanted to have a nice house and nice clothes. I can't hold that against her. All women want to have nice clothes and do better for themselves. So she tried hard and it was because of her we could afford to rent a flat. She tried to make some extra money on top of her pay from the store. She used to buy gold and with her savings we were able to rent the flat.

She'd got a distinction in English in tenth standard. So she said she wanted to go on and study at university and major in English. I did my best to find a job so that she could do it. I looked and looked and eventually I got one. Guess what as? Nightwatchman. I ask you, a nightwatchman at an office of the Rangoon City Development Committee? But I wanted her to get an education. So I was prepared to work as a guard.

I encouraged her to quit her job and go to university. She worked incredibly hard and she was naturally clever anyway. She was in the top three every year. But she wasn't satisfied if she only came second or third. She wanted to be top. In the third year she didn't come top and she was so upset she cried and I had to comfort her.

As for me, I was just happy she was doing so well. It didn't bother me if she came first or third. Why shouldn't I be happy? I could see my clever wife doing well at university because I'd worked hard to send her there. I was very proud of her and proud of my own sacrifice. I didn't mind that I couldn't get a degree. I was happy if she could be successful. Her success was my success.

After she graduated, she applied for a job with the Civil Service and had to sit the written exam. She came out top and got a job without any problem. There was no need to pull any strings. At her interview she impressed them with her looks and her personality and they gave her a job straight away.

She got a job as a civil servant. She said she didn't want to have any children because they would get in the way of her career. So we made sure she didn't get pregnant. While she was working, she went to the Institute of Foreign Languages and learnt German and also did Japanese after work. It tired me out just watching her. But she wasn't tired at all. She said she was happy. Let me show you just how hard she worked. She used to get up early in the morning at about four and cook the rice and have a shower before going off to Japanese at seven. Then she would go the office and work selling things here and there.

Then she started working at home as well, trading in diamonds and in real estate. She'd go off to language classes after work and not get back until after seven in the evening. But even then she still wasn't tired. She'd have a shower and eat dinner and then settle down to study some more.

She told me I should stop working as a nightwatchman. She got me a job through one of her connections as a driver in one of the offices. Not the office she worked at. She could have got me a job there of course, but she said it would be embarrassing for her if I was working there as a driver. She was right of course. It wouldn't have looked good if the husband of one of the officials in the office was employed as a driver.

One time she got a hefty commission after finding a house for a foreigner, and she used it together with some gold which she sold to buy me a Mazda taxi[2]. In the morning I'd drop her off in the office or at language class and then spend the day driving the taxi and pick her up in the evening. It all worked out very well.

Once she'd mastered the art of brokering houses and diamonds, she moved onto cars. She could tell immediately who had owned the car, what had happened to it, how many accidents it had been in. Sometimes she'd go down to the car-brokerage street herself with a sling bag to check the cars out. I asked her how had she found the time to study all these things. She said that it wasn't difficult to pick up once you'd got the hang of it. Easy for her perhaps.

She bought and sold about three cars while she was working as a car broker. We used to use the cars ourselves and then re-sell them and make a profit. We didn't need to live out in Okkalapa any more. We moved into town and bought ourselves a flat on one of the main streets. We had about four or five changes of car and eventually ended up driving one of the latest Toyota Corolla models.

---

[2] Blue 600cc Mazda taxis are assembled in Burma and are a common sight in Rangoon. Government employees often have first option to buy them.

During that time she got a job as a 'rep' for a foreign company. One of her foreign contacts got her the job. She couldn't do it under her own name because she was still employed by the government. So she used my name. We got a telephone installed in our house and hung a signboard up outside with the name of the company we were representing. We got a lot of commission that year because the company won a lot of orders from the government.

Later on she resigned from government service and concentrated on being an agent for foreign companies. She was very successful because she had lots of contacts. She took on several more companies. One time one of her bosses came to Rangoon. He was a European. He must have been about sixty. When he left, he invited my wife to come and study his business so she went and stayed in Bangkok and Singapore. She stayed there a couple of months and came back with even more contacts. Since she could speak English, German and Japanese, she was very good at making business contacts.

When she came back, we earned even more commission. We had so much money we didn't know what to do with it. We bought a plot of land out in Bawdigone ward and built a house, but then we got a good offer for it, so we sold it again. We did that several times, buying land, building a house and then selling it. Eventually we built a house in one of the lanes off Inya Road, and we also built one in Parami. We lived in the Parami house and rented out the house in Inya Road to a foreigner for dollars.

My wife also bought several plots of land in Mandalay quite cheaply and then when the price of land went up, she sold all of them except one. You know how land prices are in Mandalay nowadays. It costs an arm and a leg. Even an empty plot is worth millions of *kyat*.

Then my wife sent me off to Singapore to learn more about business. I spent about a month with her boss's company. To tell you the truth, I spent about a month sight-seeing. I only studied a bit. I went to Bangkok, Hong Kong and Japan as well.

I came back and she went off to Singapore on business again. This time, she was there for a long time. She must have been gone about five months. I phoned her and asked when she was coming back. She said she couldn't come back just yet because she still had work to do.

Meanwhile, I started hearing stories about her. Nowadays there's a lot of coming and going between Burma and Singapore so news travels fast. I was hearing stories about my wife and her old boss in Singapore. In the end I went out after her myself. She told me she couldn't come back yet. So I confronted her and asked her if the stories I was hearing were true, and she admitted they were.

We decided to separate. I don't think she even wanted to live in Burma any more. I think she must have been smitten with living abroad. We didn't have any feelings for one another by then but we had to work out how to divide up our property. Since she was the one in the wrong, she gave me the lion's share. I got two thirds and she got a third. I think she asked her relatives to look after it for her.

So now she's still abroad and I'm still here. I've got plenty of material wealth. But it's here in my heart that I'm empty. It's not because I still love her. Far from it. I've totally forgotten about her. How can I love her if she doesn't love me? I don't need her any more. If I want, I can get girls who are much younger and much prettier than my old wife.

She's hurt me though. I sacrificed a lot for her, so she could get an education. I worked as a nightwatchman and as a driver to look after her. Then she just turned her back on me without thinking about everything I'd done for her.

The whole experience has taught me a big lesson. I suppose you could say it's made me philosophical. When we started off together, we didn't have a red cent to our name. We even had to rely on the generosity of friends to help us get married. It was them who paid for our wedding certificate, our wedding reception, even our mosquito net. And we thought that we would stay together for the rest of our lives even if we had to live in a tumbledown shack. We thought that we could live off gruel and still love one another. Instead, we became rich and successful and that's why our marriage collapsed. That's the lesson I've learnt.

Nowadays I'm not that bothered about it any more. I just live from day to day, drinking and having a good time. It's the only way to go, in my opinion. Maybe I'm wrong. But in my view if you just live to have a good time, you can't go wrong. Well, I've gone on far too long. You probably want to get some sleep. Good night then.

[December 1990]

CHAPTER VI
SEEKING REFUGE

32

MADAM ZERO MEH YIN

I was reminded on my way to see her of the poem by U Pone Nya which describes a red footpath strewn with wormwood flowers running through a jasmine grove. There was no jasmine grove on the road to the meditation centre nor wormwood either. But the earth track was bright red, typical of the soil of the area. There were red fields as far as the eye could see, and steep red-brown hills, red valleys, and red roads. The muddy track was scattered with gravel and lined with two rows of champac trees. Above my head and scattered over the red road and in the rough grass at the side were white champac flowers. The air was thick with their scent.

Although the meditation centre wasn't far from the town, it attracted very few passers-by. Low hills encircled the centre and a stream rose from a spring somewhere in the hills and flowed down nearby. To the east rose Pyet-kha-shwe mountain and behind that the Myinsaing range, site of ancient Myin-saing city and the blue mountains of the Shan plateau. Long before I reached the centre, I could hear dogs barking, birds singing, crickets whirring and the sound of a gong.

The place was peaceful as befitted a meditation centre. The rooms for meditation were made of brick, ten foot square, scatted over the slopes of the hills. There was a central room where sermons were given and nearby were wooden cabins with thatched roofs and walls and floors of bamboo matting where the nuns and yawgis stayed. Around the cabins grew star-flower trees[1], silky oaks and champac.

I heard that she was in Webu Meditation Centre while I was in nearby Kyaukse so I decided to track her down. She didn't know who I was so I asked the person who took me there to introduce us. She didn't show a flicker of interest when he explained I was a writer. But when he told her where I was born and who my father was, she sat up in amazement.

Her name was A-may Yin[2]. She was a little over eighty. She was thin, about five foot four and you could tell that at one time she had

---

[1] Star-flower or Indian medlar, *Mimusops elengi*.

[2] *A-may* means mother. Young Burmese particularly in Upper Burma use this term to refer to women over sixty.

been quite fair-skinned. She had a strong jawline, big ears, wide-set eyes and a sharp nose. Her most noticeable feature was her eyes which were brighter than one would expect of a woman in her eighties. Her brown yawgi clothes made her look paler than she really was. I noticed that the palms of her hands were reddish.

When I was young, Madam Zero Meh Yin the bandit queen, as she was known at the time, had been a household name. Her exploits put her on a par with the legendary Amazon women. When I heard that the self-same Meh Yin was now residing at the Webu Meditation Centre, I decided that I had to go and see her. It was there that I persuaded A-may Yin, the yawgi, to recount to me the legendary exploits of Madam Zero Meh Yin, the bandit queen.

Are you really Ko Gyi Tint's son!!? If I'm eighty-two, Ko Gyi Tint must be about ninety by now, because he was always several years older than me. When I was young, we used to call boys who were older than us Maung Gyi or sometimes Ko Gyi. Since his name was Tint we'd call him Maung Gyi Tint or Ko Gyi Tint. He came from a village quite close to ours. There wasn't much more than a creek between the two. To the west of his village was a farm called Oak-po-ya, and beyond that was a broader creek called Chaung-kan-pa, and on the other side of that was the Mya-thein-dan pagoda. Near that pagoda was our village, Pauk-yin.

That was where I was born. Pauk-yin. My father was a traditional healer and a peasant farmer. He used to grow groundnuts, sesamum, corn and so on. My mother used to help him out. She was a coolie really. She used to hire herself out as labour during the harvest season, and the rest of the time she looked after the house.

I had one brother and one sister. I was the youngest. My sister Meh Khin died when she was only young. My brother was called Ko Shin. He was a real wimp. He wouldn't say boo to a goose. You'd ask him to go to some village or another and he'd be too scared to go on his own. When he was in the monastery, if there was a fight, he'd be sure to get it in the neck. He cried out to be bullied. He would look after the cattle, and other boys would beat his cattle and he never used to say a word to stop them. After a while he asked to be let off doing that kind of job so my mother used to get him doing the housework, fetching water and helping out with the cooking. My father often used to beat him for being so wet. But it didn't do any good. He never changed.

I was the complete opposite. I was very quick-tempered. I never let anyone bully me. If they tried I'd retaliate. I'd use my knife, or the pole we used to carry water buckets on our shoulders. If I didn't have a weapon to hand, I'd bite them. I only ever played games with boys. I never played hopscotch or marbles or skipping rope with the girls. I was up the trees with the boys, playing hide and seek and trying to hit birds with my catapult. I was a good shot and I used to borrow my father's bow and arrow and take it out into the paddy fields. I didn't aim at anything in particular, just the trees or a mango or a jackfruit. When my father discovered I'd used up all his arrows, he beat me. So I made arrows myself and took them out for target practice.

I liked to ride. My father used to breed horses. We had some good horses in our area. There was this breed called 'Madras', Burmese horses crossed with Gurkha horses. They said that it was because some officers from the Gurkhas had come to our area and let their horses out to stud and that was how we got such a good breed.

My father didn't think much of Ko Shin because he was so soft. He used to call him a poof. But my mother loved him and said he was a good boy. My father loved me best. He thought I was tough and strong. So he taught me how to ride. By the time I was eight I was already quite a little equestrian.

We had one horse called Pyay Gyaw who was very bad-tempered. Only my father could ride him. Anyone else, he'd buck them off. There was a big creek near our village called Kan-par-gyi. It was wide with steep sandy banks. My father used to take me there when I was little and teach me how to ride bare-back. Sometimes the horse would buck me off. Then my father would feed it some jaggery from his hand and talk to it. I don't know if it was because the horse understood what he said or because he was pacified by the jaggery but after that the horse stopped throwing me and he was all right to ride.

My father put me, his eight-year old daughter, on the back of this horse and sent him off along the creek. The horse began to gallop, although the sand slowed him down. I was terrified. I hung on to the reins for dear life. I didn't have a saddle or anything. I wasn't up there too long, not more than about a mile. The horse reached a bend in the creek and threw me off. It didn't hurt that much because he threw me into the sand. My back hurt a bit. When I came round I saw the horse standing nearby. It looked like he'd realised what had happened and he was hanging around waiting for me.

My father arrived and gave the horse some jaggery and said something to him. Then he told me to give the horse some jaggery and to nuzzle him with my face and stroke him. He told me to treat the horse as if it were human. 'If you treat animals as if they are your friends, they will be your friends', he said. He must have been right. The next morning I went and gave the horse some jaggery and some boiled chickpeas. I nuzzled him and stroked his nose and talked to him. He acted like he understood what I was saying and from that day on he never got rough with me.

After that I went out to the creek to practise riding with that horse. My father told me to practise first without the saddle and then side-saddle and then crouching in the saddle and eventually to ride standing up on the horse. When I stood in the saddle, it was as if the horse knew what his mistress was doing, because he ran steadily and didn't gallop. I stood on his back with my arms outstretched for balance. I fell off into the creek three or four times but each time I fell off he stopped and waited for me. Eventually I could go quite a way standing up without falling off.

Later on my father specialised as a traditional Burmese herbalist. I used to go behind him on his horse when he was called out to treat someone or when he went out looking for plants. When I was young, he'd injected me with some of his medicines to make me strong and invincible. For the medicine to work, you had to keep the five precepts and avoid eating the flesh of four-legged animals. I don't know if you believe in all that or not. All I know is that when I was young it seemed to work. I was protected against knives and sticks. I don't know about bullets though because I never got shot at. But knives and sticks just used to bounce off my skin as if it was made of leather.

I also learnt about traditional medicines because my father used to take me out with him and teach me about them. As well as teaching me that, and teaching me how to ride a horse, he also taught me martial arts, especially fencing with a stick. He used to teach me, and then challenge me to a match. But I only did that when I was little. I stopped practising soon after.

Then my father died of malaria. He came home from the jungle but the malaria bacteria had got into his brain and killed him. I was about seventeen. My mother was widowed. The only thing Ko Shin was good for was cooking and housework. I hadn't got an education and I didn't know enough yet about medicine so I had to work on the rice and sesamum harvest with my mother.

About that time, I fell for a boy from a nearby village. He was just a peasant too. He was looking after his father's fields because his mother was a widow too. His name was Ko San Win. He was my first boyfriend. He was a brave boy and decent and honest. In my view, those are the three most important characteristics in a man. I'm not that educated. But in my opinion, one—a man should be courageous. He should stand up and speak out when something is wrong. Two—he should be decent and upstanding. He shouldn't stir up trouble and he should help others when they are in trouble. And three—he should be honest. He shouldn't take advantage of other people, and he should make sacrifices to help others.

Ko San Win was that sort of a man. Basically, that was why I fell in love with him. When I was young, I was good-looking by peasant girl standards. I had quite a few boys after me. One of them was the son of the headman. He was a trouble-maker. He was always trying it on with the girls from our village. One day I was on my way back from collecting water when he propositioned me. He was drunk. I swore at him and chucked my water pot at him and ran off. I left him there soaked to the skin.

News got out that the widow's son had lobbed a pot of water at the headman's son and drenched him. The whole village knew, and so did the nearby villages. It was pretty embarrassing for both him and his father. But I thought that since everyone would know that it was his fault, they wouldn't dream of punishing me. That's what I thought anyway.

In fact, they were just waiting for a chance to get me back.

That year, January came round and it was the Mya-thein-dan pagoda festival. Everyone came from the nearby villages. I arranged to meet Ko San Win there. That was the usual thing for teenagers round there to do. There was a troupe from Ban-kyi playing, but I can't remember what they were called. We stayed for the *a-pyo-daw* scene. Then we made our way down to the creek like young lovers.

It was cold, the middle of winter. So the two of us wrapped ourselves up in the towel which I had brought along. When we got to the bank of the creek, a gang of men emerged from the bushes shouting. They asked my boyfriend 'Who do you think you are? What makes you think you're so special that you can go out with someone from our village?' They had all been drinking and they were brandishing bottles of country spirit. As soon as I saw them, I realised that the leader was the son of the local head-man.

Ko San Win told them, 'We're in love. We're going to get married'. But they didn't care. They weren't listening. The headman smashed the bottle in his face and then when he fell down, one of them knifed him. He groaned, and keeled over. I threw my arms around him as he fell, but the headman's son grabbed me and tried to drag me into the bushes. I struggled to break free. But he was a man, and stronger than me and he had a knife. He dragged me into the bushes and tried to rape me. I was struggling and he was holding the knife to my throat and shouting at me 'Shut up! Do you want to die?' So I gathered all my strength and kicked him. As he got up from the ground, he tried to stab me. I tried to grab hold of the knife, just like I'd learnt in my martial arts lessons. I finally got hold of it. I've no idea how I managed it. He was grabbing my arm so I thrust the knife into his chest. He gasped and fell. When they heard him, the other four who'd been standing around Ko San Win's body came running over. They all had knives. I picked myself up and ran off into the jungle, scared out of my wits.

That night, Ko San Win and the headman's son both died. I didn't dare go back to the village. I went and stayed with some relatives in a village nearby. I told them I was too scared to go home because I didn't have anyone to go with. I was OK for that night. But come the morning, I didn't know what to do. I didn't dare go back to my village or I'd be arrested for sure. The news that I'd committed murder had got round and the police were out looking for me.

I got in touch with my mother and spent about a month hiding out in the fields. But I realised I couldn't hide that way for ever. In the end I gave myself up. I was charged with the murder of the headman's son.

Ko Gyi Tint was my defence lawyer. He told the court that I was not guilty of murder because I'd been acting in self-defence. But the judge said that it was murder, not self-defence, because I had stabbed the victim several times deliberately with a knife. So I was sentenced to life imprisonment which in reality meant ten years.

I appealed. Ko Gyi Tint represented me. Since I was a woman, the appeal court reduced the sentence by a third to six years. In the end, I only served just over four because I got remission. I was about twenty-two when I got out of jail. My mother was already dead by then. Ko Shin was the only one left. He was scratching a living, despised by everyone, running errands here and there.

I didn't want to stay in the village. I was afraid that the headman might try and get his revenge. And even though people from the village were sympathetic, I was uncomfortable about staying there. So Ko Shin and I moved to a village near Ban-kyi.

I won't go into all the details. We moved village and I married a widowed landowner who lived there. He had quite a bit of land and he used to deal in groundnuts and oil and sesamum. But his health was poor. I looked after him since he had taken care of me. One day his luck ran out and he died. Then his relatives accused me of killing him to get at his money. One of his sons got drunk and insulted me. I stabbed him, but I escaped just before the local ward boss arrived to arrest me. He didn't die but the police wanted to charge me with grievous wounding.

I realised I was in trouble. So I went to a cousin of mine, Ko Kyaw Yan, and asked him for help. He was the bandit supremo in the area. He was well known round those parts. To start off with, I just went to him to seek refuge because I was in trouble. But I stayed a while and ended up fencing his stolen property. Well, you know how it is. You grow up with hunters, you become a hunter, you hang out with fisherman you become a fisherman. In my case I hung around with villains and became a bad woman.

I could ride. I could fight. I eventually became deputy chief of the bandits. I was smart and I was young and my name was soon well-known in the area. I was particularly notorious because I was a woman. We would ride into a village with me up front on a horse. I had a revolver at my waist and a rifle on my back. Generally we never touched the poor, we only attacked the rich. What ever we took, I used to sign for. I hadn't been to school, so I used to sign my name with just a circle, a zero. That's how I got the name 'Madam Zero'.

One day we raided a village but the police had got word of it and were lying in wait. We got into a fight with them at a cemetery near the village. They caught me and charged me with armed robbery and the previous stabbing cases. I went to jail. Your father didn't represent me that time. We were in a different district so I had a different lawyer. I got seven years altogether. That was my second time in jail.

When I was released, I went to see Ko Gyi Tint to pay my respects. Were you there at the time?[3] Yes, I think you might have been. You must have been about ten years old. You were wearing shorts. I think I was about thirty at the time.

When I paid my respects to Ko Gyi Tint, first he prayed, then he asked me, 'Meh Yin, are you still sinning?'

I said to him, 'Ko Gyi Tint, I'm not really a sinner. It's other people who make me sin. Are my oppressors the sinners? Or is it me?'

He was nonplussed. He considered this and said, 'You're right. But you have to defend yourself against your oppressors within the bounds of the law. You know how it is. I have to tell you that. I'm a lawyer.'

I didn't say anything. I just thought to myself, 'Money sometimes silences the law. And the law sometimes relies on money'. Have you heard that saying? But I bit my tongue because your father was basically a decent man.

After that I went home and lived peacefully for a while. But it didn't last long. The police were always coming and harassing me. I was on their 'Wanted' list. Every time there was a robbery in the area, the police would take me into custody and interrogate me. When they couldn't find any evidence against me, they'd let me go. This happened four or five times and I felt like it could always happen again.

Then my cousin, the bandit Bo Yan Kyaw, was killed in an ambush. His men came to me and asked me if I wanted to take over as leader of the gang. I'd had enough of going straight, so I went back to robbing rich villages. We became known as Madam Zero Meh Yin's Gang. The government put a price on my head and I became a fully-fledged outlaw. That put an end to my chances of living a normal life. From then on, I was stuck in the jungle.

---

[3] Mya Than Tint was born in Myaing in 1929.

When the British retreated, I was still living in the jungle. Anarchy reigned and there were lots of gangs like mine. But I made sure we operated by certain rules. No robbing poor villages, only rich ones. No killing except in self-defence. No molesting girls. If I caught any of my gang breaking the rules, they were punished severely. Some got the cane. Some were executed.

After the Japanese take-over, the Japanese came and recruited my gang. But although we collaborated with them, we never joined them properly. When the British returned, we went back into the jungle and became outlaws again. They eventually caught up with me and charged me with murder and armed robbery and all the rest of the offences committed by my gang. I went to jail and didn't get released until a long time after Burma became independent.

When the civil war broke out, I was recruited by the Red Flag Communists. But I soon fell out with them and gave myself up. That was when I took up meditation. It suits me. I used to be a sinner and a murderer. But since then I've visited meditation centres all across Burma. Religion has been my life for thirty years now. I've decided that I'll live out the rest of my days here at Webu.

Did I ever get married? Yes. Three times. My first marriage was to the land-owner. The second and third were to members of my gang. Both of those husbands were killed in fighting or killed by the government.

They called me 'Madam Zero Meh Yin' because I signed my name with a zero. At that time 'Bo Bo Aung'[4] by Khin Maung Yin was at the top of the charts. That was partly why they called me Madam Zero. Originally it was other people's name for me. But in the end, I started using it myself.

[July 1990]

---

[4] Bo Bo Aung or Master of Victory was a legendary sorcerer and master of runes during the reign of King Bodawpaya (1782-1819). He was said to have possessed a magic 'wa', or zero, which he could proliferate into infinity.

33

THE PRODIGAL SON

I met him in the Christian Leper Colony in Moulmein. He must have been about thirty. He was quite short and spoke with an accent. As he looked like most lepers, I will spare you the details. But he wasn't infectious. Dr Saw Wa Tu, who took me round the hospital, explained that the bacteria in his body were already dead by the time he was diagnosed. The damage to his flesh was not a direct result of the leprosy but was a side effect which occurs when a patient ceases to take care of his personal hygiene after contracting the disease. Once the disease has been cured, he said, there is no reason why the patient cannot rejoin society. Dr Saw Wa Tu introduced us and told him to tell me his life story.

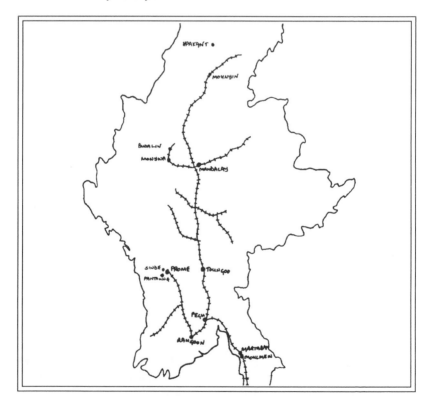

My name is Saliang Ha Zayu Nyein Aye. I'm a Chin. My parents are Christians and so am I. I've got seven brothers and sisters. I'm the fifth oldest. My parents and my brothers and sisters work at Sinde, opposite Prome. I contracted this disease when I was about eleven. It started off as a patch on the instep of my right foot. The patch of flesh dried up and I couldn't feel anything. Then the flesh started to crack open. I didn't take it seriously at the time because I was just a child and I didn't know what it meant. I didn't even tell my parents. At that time I was at school. I got as far as sixth standard.

In 1979, when I was about eighteen, I joined the Heavy Industry Corporation in Sinde as a labourer. With my level of education, that was the only job I could get. I couldn't carry on in school because my father was getting old and we had a lot of mouths to feed. We didn't have much money, so I couldn't attend school much and because I couldn't go, I lost interest in going and in the end I just left. It was a vicious circle which stopped me from getting an education.

About three years after I started working, I began to get pains and numbness in my leg. Ever since then, I've had a miserable life. My skin fell away and I felt embarrassed and avoided contact with other people. I got short-tempered and angry with everything and everybody including my brothers and sisters. I felt like everyone was out to get me. I stopped talking to people and spent the days curled up in bed, or out in the jungle far away from everyone else. Sometimes I felt angry, and sometimes I felt like crying. (Dr Saw Wa Tu interrupted at this point to explain that these were the symptoms of depression).

One day I was so depressed I set out for Prome. I met a group of men on the ferry between Pantaung and Prome and they bought me some food and gave me tea and cigarettes. They were excellent cigarettes. Once I started smoking them I felt so much better. Even cheerful. The first few drags made me a bit dizzy and sick. But I didn't realise it was the cigarettes doing it to me. They gave me one after another and I smoked them all. After four or five I felt wonderful. I just wanted to smoke more. It felt so good just smoking those cigarettes and sitting half-asleep on the ferry. When we got to Prome, they bought me some food. They asked me where I was off to and I explained that I was sick of living at home and I was running away. They told me off for that. When they were young like me, they said, they'd had itchy feet too. But what I needed was a job. They asked me if I wanted one. I said sure I would. So they told me to come with them to Prome railway station.

The Rangoon Express was leaving at about ten that night. They took me to the station and told me to wait there while they went off to look for some people. They left one of their group with me, and after a little while they came back carrying various bits and pieces which they dumped down next to me. Leather suitcases, bags and so on. I thought it must be their things, and they wanted me to keep an eye on them. Then they gave me another packet of cigarettes and I smoked them and felt drowsy.

When the train left, they gave me fifty *kyats* and told me to come back tomorrow. The following nights I looked after their bags again. It didn't take long to work out that they were pickpockets. Actually they were thieves rather than pick-pockets. They'd steal handbags, baskets and so on. The cigarettes they gave me were laced with Number Four, heroin. They'd give me fifty *kyats* a night, or sometimes even a hundred or one fifty. I never asked them how they earned it and they never told me. I just gradually got the picture. One time though, this Indian-looking gang member who was about thirty threatened me with a nine-inch knife. He said he'd use it on me if I even thought about snitching on them. But why should I? They gave me money and cigarettes and I could smoke my cares away.

So I spent about three or four months like this. My family knew I was out on the streets living wild but they weren't around to tell me to stop. I stopped listening to the priests too. In the past I'd gone to church every Sunday. Not any more. I turned my back on God and spent my time with criminals, breaking the law and hanging out in brothels and gambling houses. At that time, my disease wasn't too serious.

Later on, I moved to Rangoon and carried on the same sort of activity and hung out in the same circles. From there I went up to Mandalay and did the same again. I stayed with my criminal friends. But even Mandalay wasn't enough for me, and I decided to go up to Kachin state, to Hmaw, Kachin state, where the jade comes from. Places like Hpa-kant. I stayed there about six months. When I got there it was the rainy season. It sure can rain up there. All day, all night. The mountains are wreathed in mist. It all made me homesick for my family. But by then, there was no way I could go home.

I worked in the mines, but I used to get tired very easily. My health wasn't very good, so I often caught a fever and had to rest up in bed. From time to time, I'd get malaria. I couldn't stay in bed for long though. As soon as I was better, I had to go back to work. But then I'd get malaria again. During that time, the pain in my leg got worse. My whole instep was cracking open and the lower part of my leg was getting numb. Then I injured my good leg with a pick-axe and the wound never healed and became septic.

It was winter by then, and freezing cold. I didn't have enough warm clothes, just an old denim jacket they'd given me and a blanket. At night I used to sleep by the fire huddled in the blanket, with a belly full of Kachin liquor to keep me warm.

I spent three months of monsoon and three months of winter there. Six months in all. But I ended up with almost nothing apart from regular meals. Even then I sometimes didn't get anything to eat if it was one of the days when I couldn't work. We were self-employed and on the days we didn't work, we didn't eat. Sometimes though, we'd be able to sell off some of the gems we'd found to get money for food.

The gems we found weren't very good though, so we couldn't get much for them. Sometimes I went so short of food I was like a man on a life-raft without a drop to drink. What could I do? I had a fever almost every night, so I couldn't work. I had spent all my savings. I sold all the spare clothes I had. I couldn't afford my Number Four. I didn't even have enough money for food. At first when I came off Number Four I used to buy Kachin liquor, but later on I couldn't afford that either.

In the end I decided I'd better go home. The pain in my leg was becoming unbearable. I sold whatever I had left and set out for home. First though, I went to Mo-hnyin where I had a friend who dealt in Number Four. He and I had worked together in the mines. But when I got there I discovered he'd gone to jail because of his drug-dealing. I spent about a month hanging around there doing nothing particular just a bit of stealing from time to time. Then I returned to Mandalay, but I couldn't find any of my old friends there either. They were either in jail, or they'd moved away to where the grass was greener.

Instead of going home, I set off for Monywa and Budalin. I was like a tramp, going wherever my feet took me, doing odd jobs or stealing. Sometimes I got food from monasteries or money from the Christian associations. I lied to all of them. You can see how low I had fallen, lying to both Buddhist and Christian priests.

Meanwhile my leg was getting worse and worse. I had a fever almost every night. So I decided to go home. I went back to Mandalay and caught the 10.30 a.m. down train which arrives in Toungoo at about 9.30 p.m. I hadn't eaten since the previous day and I was starving by the time we reached Toungoo. My stomach felt like it was twisted up in knots. I wanted a drink but I didn't even have five or ten pyas to buy a glass of water. I couldn't bear it any longer so I got off the train and went to look for a water pot in the station. I found one but it was empty. Then I saw a water pot just outside the station. I went over to get a drink. It was so good. I knocked back four or five mugs one after another. I turned back to the station and found that the train was pulling out. I ran to catch it but I couldn't run fast enough because of the pain in my leg. The train pulled out and left me stranded in Toungoo station and all because I had to have a glass of water.

I spent the night in the station. The next morning, a goods train carrying sugar cane pulled in. I was so hungry, I can't remember how many pieces of cane I ate. I only stopped when my mouth and gums started to bleed. At midday a goods train pulled in to load up with teak and I climbed on board. I hadn't eaten for three whole days. On the fourth day of not eating, we reached Pegu. We had to spend the night there because the train couldn't go on to Rangoon. The wheels were too hot. On the fifth day we were still stuck in Pegu station and I was getting desperate. I didn't know what to do or where to go. I felt sick. Another train pulled up in the station. I saw that it was going to Moulmein.

I was so sick and hungry and feverish I could hardly move. I hadn't eaten for almost a week. My eyes couldn't stand the glare of the sun. I crawled onto the train. I had wanted to go to Rangoon. But with no trains going there I had no choice but to get on the Martaban train. I was starving and desperate and my leg was agony.

I'd never been to Moulmein. We arrived at about 4 p.m. I wandered aimlessly around a market called Mee-laung-pyin. A vegetable seller gave me a couple of cucumbers. He had been going to throw them away because they were going off but he gave them to me when he saw me. He probably thought I was a beggar. I gobbled them up. I felt like a new man. I'd never eaten anything so delicious. I ate every last bit, even the rotten portions. It was like all my Christmases had come at once. After all, I hadn't eaten for a week.

A woman called me over and asked me to help her carry her basket over to the bus. She gave me two *kyats*. She must have thought I was a porter. That suited me fine. I'd got myself a job. I worked as a porter in Mee-laung-pyin market for about five days. But my leg was getting worse and worse and I could only walk with great difficulty. I couldn't carry baskets. So I took myself off to the People's Hospital. Outside the hospital I asked a boy if there was a leprosy clinic nearby. I wasn't ashamed. I knew what was wrong with me. He told me that it was in the southern part of town. I followed his directions and arrived here. I believe that boy was sent by God to help me in my pain. I asked a man if there was a men's ward there and he said there was. I was so happy. I felt like I had escaped from Hell.

However, it was a Saturday and the hospital was closed for the weekend. There was nothing else for it but to wait until it opened. I went and sat down under a rain tree. A couple of Christian boys from nearby, Saliang Ngwe and Aye Hlaing called out to me and I explained to them about my disease and how I had got there. They felt sorry for me and let me stay at their home until the hospital opened on Monday.

It took three months for them to cure the disease. They had to operate on my aching leg. I can't tell you how happy I am now. I feel like my life has begun all over again. I believe that this is all the work of God. He sent the little boy to show me the way to the hospital. Up until then, I had been thinking of committing suicide, although I knew that if I did I would lose my soul as well as my body. I'd been contemplating suicide because poverty and disease had isolated me from society. But God has rescued me. The Bible says that the Lord created all living creatures. Things change and are renewed. God gives each their own ability. We must all learn to live according to our own ability, in accordance with God's wishes. I have had to suffer from this disease, but I no longer feel ashamed. The Bible says 'I will look after you as a mother looks after her child'. I have given thanks to the Lord for helping me return to the family I left over three years ago. Thanks to him, I have a new mind and a new body, and I am beginning a new life and a new year.

[May 1990]

34

FROM RIFLES TO ROSARIES

I considered writing a whole story about her. Some of her life is already included in my travelogues. She was about sixty when we met, but she didn't have a single grey hair or a bad tooth. Her skin was fair, her tall figure was like a girl's, as slim and straight as a pine tree and her eyes shone. Her dainty mouth and her eyes were an apt reflection of her character, I thought. She looked supple and strong-willed and her quiet gentle voice revealed her courage. She seemed both gentle and capable of tolerating a lot of hardship. Her qualities were rare in a woman. To look at her, you would have thought that she was just an ordinary housewife living an everyday life in the kitchen, grappling with the task of looking after a husband and children. In fact she was a talented horsewoman, a straight shot and skilled with a knife. But you would not have gleaned an inkling of that from her calm and gentle mien. We got talking huddled around a brazier, eating sticky rice packed tight in a bamboo tube and drinking strong bitter tea. Her name was Eh Nan Mai Sai, or Daw Nan Sweh.

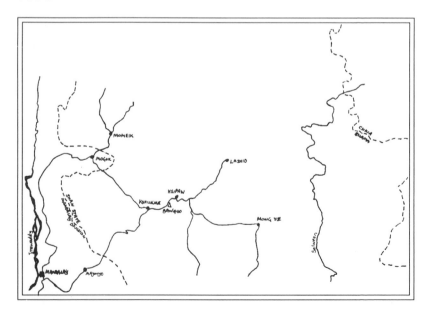

If I tell you my life-story, you'll be shocked, *Saya*. So you should be. I know I look like a defenceless little old lady but I had a tough life before I got married. It surprises a lot of people. My father's name was U Kar Lein. My mother was called Daw Yweq Laing. U Kar Lein was his name from the village. Later on he worked for the Sawbwa, the Shan Prince, of Mong Yai and changed his name to Khun Byan. When he went on to become a *htamoun*, he changed his name to Sao Naw Lone. *Htamoun?* That's the village chieftain, *Saya*, the Sawbwa's right hand man.

My father could ride a horse and shoot. He could use a knife and knew martial arts. I look like my mother. She was as slim as me, as fair, and lived quietly, like a typical Shan girl. She would work in the fields, or stay at home doing the cooking.

My mother and father were nothing alike. He was a tall, stocky, strapping man with a bushy moustache. I never once saw him in a *longyi*—he always wore Shan trousers. In his youth he'd been a wrestler. He loved fighting. He usually joined in if there was a wrestling match in our village during the pagoda festival. Because he was so good, there were very few men who were willing to take him on. So in those days, he used to wrestle at the Bawgyo Festival in Hsipaw, where he picked up his habits of drinking and gambling.

You know what the Bawgyo Festival is like, I think. It's held during Tabaung and gamblers come from across the Shan States, from all over the country even. My father used to go there regularly and that was where he took up gambling. His main game was Thirty-Six Beasts. I don't know if you've ever come across it. At pagoda festivals in Shan state, and particularly at the big gazetted festivals like Bawgyo, there are always people playing Thirty-Six Beasts[1].

My father was hot-tempered. He was built like a giant. He was a fighting man and he wouldn't put up with anyone insulting him or if he suspected they were cheating him. One year, he went down to Bawgyo to gamble. It's a busy festival, because there isn't much to do in the mountains at that time of year. People had come from all over the country as usual. My father told me that one night he was playing Thirty-Six Beasts and doing pretty well. All the promoter's money and the stakes

---

[1] The game of Thirty-Six Beasts originated during the prewar period in the Shan States and has since spread throughout Burma. There are thirty-six animal figures (goat, horse, butterfly etc), one of which is wrapped in a bundle and placed on top of a pole. The man running the game then gives hints, usually in verse, as to what the hidden animal is. These tips can be interpreted in a number of ways. If you bet correctly on the hidden animal, winnings are paid out at odds of 26-1 rather than 35-1.

from the other players were ending up in his pockets. He said the promoter's eyes were on stalks.

To tell the truth, my father never understood a great deal about gambling. He was simply a lucky man. The promoter and the touts would try to give the punters tips on which animal would come up. But he just ignored them and bet on whatever he felt like. This apparent recklessness alarmed the promoter and the others, with good reason. No matter what tips the promoter gave, my father just picked the animals he wanted. Since they kept turning up, his winnings were mounting up.

The promoter started to get worried. '*Sayagyi*', he said 'you told us you didn't know how to play, but look at all the money you're winning. If you're this good, let me give you some tips. I dare you to take them. If you win, I'll give you all I've got and close up shop for this year'.

My father replied 'Look, I'm not lying when I say I don't know how to play properly. It's pure fluke, that's all. You can give me tips if you want, but I'll still just bet on what I want to'.

By that time, no-one else dared to play and my father was left playing against this one man. Everyone was waiting to see who would win. Really, what the promoter had said was all talk. He didn't have any money left to pay out. His offer wasn't sincere—he just wanted to win back everything my father had won off him. But it was difficult for him to get the better of players like my father who ignored the promoter's tips and bet on whatever they wanted.

Since he was flat broke, the promoter knew he would have a problem if my father bet on something which won. So he secretly told one of the touts which animal he would arrange not to come up. The tout was one of his men—you know how it works.

The tout then went and told my father that he had a sure-fire tip about which animal would win. He suggested they place a joint bet, with each of them putting in half the stake. At first my father wouldn't agree to it. He wanted to place his own bets and do his own thing, even if it meant losing. So he refused to place a joint bet. The tout then invited him to one of the liquor stalls to discuss it over a drink.

My father was already a little drunk from earlier on, and once the tout had bought him a few more drinks, he got even drunker. Once he was drunk he agreed with the tout that they would place a joint bet of ten thousand, with each of them putting in five. They would bet on the animal which the tout had got as a tip, and not the one my father had originally planned on choosing. They placed the bet and the promoter ran the game, and the animal they had bet on didn't turn up. Instead, the winning animal was the one my father had intended to pick originally. My father got angry. If he had had a chance to choose the one he wanted, he would have won. But because he'd believed what the other man had told him, he'd staked all his money and now didn't have a penny left. He was very upset. But there was nothing he could do. The tout was behaving as if he was very disappointed too. He said he had only chosen that animal because he'd got such a surefire tip. He said that he'd got hardly any money left either but that he was very embarrassed that my father had lost because of him. So he would give my father the money to get home, and buy him another drink. My father was already pretty drunk and he didn't go back to his lodging house, but bedded down in a hut near to the gambling area.

While he was snoozing, two men came into the hut. When he opened his eyes, he saw that it was the promoter and the tout. The two of them were sharing out the money which they had won off my father. They must have thought my father was sound asleep drunk. But my father can hold his drink well, and he wasn't as drunk as they thought. He could hear everything they were saying and soon found out that they had got him drunk in order to trick him out of his money. When he discovered that, he lost his temper. He shook off his drunkenness and leapt up brandishing the knife which he always carried at his waist. Although there were two of them and only one of him and each of them had a knife too, my father was stronger and the better fighter and overwhelmed the two of them. After a struggle, he stabbed the tout, who died on the spot. The promoter fled.

My father suddenly realised what he had done, wiped the blood off the knife, sheathed it and ran off into the jungle. He told me he had no idea where he was going. One day he turned up at my mother's village. After a month of living in the jungle, he looked like a real hunter. As well as his knife, he was armed with a single-barrelled rifle he had stolen. He spent about four or five months hunting in the forests near my mother's village. That was how he met my mother and fell in love with her.

My mother's father was the *htamoun* of the village—the headman, remember. After my father married my mother, he kept a low profile. He changed his name too, to Khun Byan. Later on, the police discovered that my father, who was still a wanted man, was living in the village and they came to arrest him. He admitted to my mother and her father that he was guilty of the charges against him. But his father-in-law loved him as if he was their own son. They depended on him as they had no sons of their own. He could see that my father was keeping a low profile and staying quietly at home. He knew that my father respected him; he listened to what he said; he helped out with the *htamoun* work and so on.

Since they wanted to arrest my father, my grandfather took him to the Sawbwa and explained the facts of the case. My father vouchsafed that this was the truth. He explained that, although he was guilty, he didn't believe that it was his fault; the other two had driven him to it. They had got him drunk in order to trick him. He had been driven by anger to commit the offence. The Mong Yai Sawbwa took pity on my father and only sentenced him to a year in jail. At that time, my mother was pregnant with me.

I was born before my father got out of jail. Since he had behaved himself in jail and people respected his character and because of his father-in-law's influence, he was appointed a *kyawt*, and later on, since my grandfather was getting on and couldn't carry out his duties any more, he became a *htamoun*.

As a *htamoun*, my father looked after his district well. He delivered taxes regularly to the Sawbwa, and was loyal to him. It was the Sawbwa who gave him a new name 'Sao Naw Lone' which was more fitting to his status as a *htamoun* than Khun Byan. 'Sao' is a name you pass down the family line.

My father was promoted from *htamoun* to chief tax collector. When he had been a *kyawt* he was in charge of ten houses. Once my grandfather passed away, he was promoted to *htamoun*, and then after that, he was promoted to *hein*. *Hein* is a more senior headman. My father was appointed *kyawt* by his father-in-law, but he was made *htamoun* and *hein* by the Sawbwa himself. And after *hein*, chief tax collector.

At that time, I was about ten years old. My father had wanted a son, but instead he had had two daughters—I was the older one, of course. My sister died when she was little. I think my father used to treat me as if I was a son. When I was still young, he taught me how to ride a horse. When I say young, I mean I was only four or five years old.

My father was an expert at gauging the character of a horse. He could tell which horses were good-tempered and which were bad just by looking at them. When I was about five years old, he bought me a good-tempered horse and taught me to ride. He taught me how to ride side-saddle, astride and bare-back, and without reins but with blinkers. Since the horse was good-tempered, it was quite easy. I think my horse understood a lot of what I said. If I said 'stop' for example, he stopped. After I had learnt to ride on a good-natured horse, he gradually got me to ride on wilder and wilder horses. By the time I was ten years old, I was able to ride horses which had fairly foul tempers.

My father didn't stop at teaching me how to ride. He taught me how to shoot, and how to fight with a knife. Before my father had been appointed *kyawt* he had carried a single-barrelled rifle. In the Shan States, almost every hunter carries one. When he was promoted, the Sawbwa presented him with a double-barrelled rifle and he taught me how to use it too. I already knew how to use a single-barrelled gun. Sometimes my father used to invite me to come hunting in the jungle. We would set off, father and daughter, each on horseback. We weren't looking for big game, just small animals. Near where we lived, there wasn't any big game. My father had taught me to shoot by throwing a rice wine bottle into the air and having me shoot it before it hit the ground. After a lot of practice, I used to be able to hit it six or seven times out of ten.

One day my father had to go up to the *haw*, the palace of the Mong Yai Sawbwa. I can't remember why he had to go, but he took me with him. The Sawbwa's palace was incredibly grand, with white umbrellas and thrones and big fans made out of Himalayan yak's tails—all the royal regalia.

When we went into the palace, we had to wait at the back. At the front sat the ministers and courtiers, the *myo-sa*[2], *myo-sa-gyi*, and *myo-ouq*, who were receiving the instructions and counsel of the Sawbwa. Suddenly the wife of the Sawbwa, the Mahadevi, spotted me and called out 'Hey, Sao Naw Lone, is this your horse-riding, sharp-shooting daughter you've been telling me about?'

My father nodded. 'In that case, why don't you leave her here with the court? If she's as talented as you say, she shouldn't be left in the jungle to rot. Leave her here at the palace, where she can get on in life'.

I'll keep it short, *Saya*. After that, I was only able to go back briefly to the village to say goodbye to my mother, and then I returned to the palace.

I lived in the palace as the Mahadevi's attendant. If she wanted to see some horse-riding, I'd ride for her. She was always chewing betel, so I would prepare it for her. She liked spices from India in her betel quid, and cashew-nut paste to freshen her breath. She used to order a year's ingredients at a time from Mandalay.

At about that time, there was a big palace fracas. The younger brother of the Mong Yai Sawbwa was dissatisfied with his lot and attacked the Sawbwa. My father was on the side of the younger brother. The Sawbwa retaliated and the younger brother and my father were forced to hide out in the jungle. My mother went with him and they fled to another area. I was left behind in the palace. I think I was about fourteen at the time.

Although my father had become an outlaw, I remained a palace attendant. I was pardoned, as were some other relatives of the younger brother who hadn't been involved.

Not long after these royal ructions, the Second World War started. We call those times the 'disturbances'. Ruffians and outlaws and Chinese and Indian soldiers came into town. Burmese soldiers would pass through too. I was only young, and I didn't have a clue which was which. All I

---

[2] Literally 'town-eater'— one who was granted the revenues of a town by the king.

knew is that they were soldiers. Outlaws and bandits attacked the palace and set it on fire. The Sawbwa and the Mahadevi and their children and retinue had to flee, like refugees.

We would arrive at one place only to find that it wasn't safe, and so we'd move on to another and the same thing would happen and eventually in this way we ended up at the Salween River. The river-banks have many natural caves. Some people say that they were carved out of the rock by soldiers during the reign of the Burmese monarchs. The locals called them the 'Ogress Caves' for some reason. We had to live in them for four or five months.

I was only young so I found all of this disruption and moving around from place to place quite fun. From time to time I wondered what had happened to my parents, but most of the time I was kept busy roasting the barking deer which we caught in the jungle, and listening at night to the tales which the royal guard would tell us. During the day we would go down to the river to bathe and wash our clothes. It was great fun—I never felt like we were refugees.

We had plenty to eat of course. There was endless fresh meat running around in the jungle, and if you didn't want to eat that, we had plenty of tinned and dried meat and fish, as well as lots of rice, oil and salt. We had enough food for more than a year. When we moved camp, we needed fourteen or fifteen elephants to carry our provisions. The people travelled either by horse or by cart, and where we couldn't go by cart, we went by foot.

After about four or five months, the Japanese captured the Shan States and set up a government. They invited the Sawbwas who hadn't fled with the British to come back to their lands. Since some Sawbwas had already taken up the offer without any problems, we decided to return.

The roads were bad and we couldn't get all the way back to Mong Yai, so we had to stay a while in Kun Hein. The Sawbwa and Mahadevi's retinue was sadly diminished by that time, Some of them had run away, some had died of malaria and some had already gone home so it was left up to just a few of us to do the cooking. Since there was no palace, we had to set up camp in the circuit house.

One day I was on my way down to the landing stage to collect some water when I saw a man eating in a restaurant near the jetty. I looked at him carefully, because I was sure I had seen him somewhere before. In those days, whenever you met a stranger, you had to look at them carefully and decide whether they were good or bad. I thought I remembered seeing this man somewhere else. He kept turning round and looking at me too. Then he suddenly called out 'Hey, Eh Nan, is that you?' and as soon as I heard that voice I realised it was my father. He told me that he was still an outlaw and he was on his way back to Mong Yai. I asked about my mother, and he said she had died of malaria about a year before. I begged my father to come up to the circuit house but he said he couldn't. He said he was still on the wrong brother's side and the Sawbwa might kill him. He told me I should go back alone and he would go back to Mong Yai. The Japanese were also trying to wipe out the outlaws, so even if the Sawbwa didn't kill him, the Japanese might.'You go on', he said, 'I can't come with you'.

It was a tragic parting, Saya. If you wanted to write a story, you could write one about a daughter separated from her father. The father is an outlaw wanted by the Sawbwa. The daughter is part of the Mahadevi's retinue. The daughter wants her father to go with her. The father can't go with her because he's a wanted criminal. The father asks the daughter to come with him, but she can't go because it would mean betraying the trust of the Mahadevi. What's more, the father is being hunted by the same Japanese for whom the daughter would have to cook dinner that night.

It was certainly a day of coincidences. That same day the Japanese had arrived at the circuit house, saying they were looking for outlaws. We were living in a small house near the main circuit house which was where guests stayed if they came, which wasn't often. Anyway, that day I had to cook for the Japanese. I took their food up to the circuit house. The Mahadevi had told me to take the food up to the Sawbwa and the Japanese, who were talking on the upper floor.

Under the circuit house, there was a man, tied to a post. It was getting dark, so I couldn't see him properly. I had just put the cooking pots and tiffin carriers onto a tray and was about to take them upstairs when I heard the man hiss at me 'Hey kid! Over here!' I was about to run upstairs in terror when I heard the man say 'Hey kid, I'm a good guy. Help me out of here. I'm one of Khun Byan's gang. They're going to kill me. Please, help me get these ropes off. If you do, I'll never forget you'.

Khun Byan was my father, of course. When my father and his group had fled, they had gone wherever their feet took them, picking some companions up along the way and dropping others. Only a few hours ago I had met my father down by the jetty. Now the Japanese had arrested one of his men. But I felt sure that my father would have managed to escape.

I waved to the man and then ran quickly upstairs with the food. Then I came back down, undid his ropes and took him up to a place on the hill where he would be safe. By the time I came down from the hill, it was already dark. The Japanese and the Sawbwa had discovered that both I and the man had disappeared and they were out looking for us by torchlight. Nearby was the tomb of the Sawbwa's mother. It had been looted earlier on in the war and was now empty. I spent the night curled up in the tomb and as soon as it grew light, I fled. I ran from village to village, taking rides with bullock carts or with anyone I came across. After three or four weeks I reached my grandfather's village in Mong Yai district where my father had been *htamoun* and that was where I stayed. My father had not turned up. I didn't know where he had got to. That time at the jetty in Kun Hein had been the last I'd seen of him. My mother was dead. But I still had other relatives.

I lived with them, and kept an ear open for news of my father. After the war, the Japanese retreated and the British returned. I heard that my father was in charge of a village called Kun Pain in Momeik district. That would have been under the Sawbwa of Momeik, of course. I set off for Kun Pain, and found that my father had married again and already had young children.

While I was staying with him in Kun Pain, when I was about eighteen or nineteen, I met my husband-to-be. He was originally from Kyaukme district but he grew up in Lashio. He's eight years older than me, and before the war, he was a schoolteacher. During the war, he moved to Momeik district and became a merchant. He used to come regularly to Kun Pain and that was where we got to know one another.

By then the war was over. The Mong Yai Sawbwa heard that my father was in charge of Kun Pain village and invited him back to Mong Yai. He forgave him for what he'd done in the past and made him a *myo-sa*. My father died in Mong Yai, a *myo-sa*.

Once the British returned, my husband went back to teaching. He still did a little bit of trading of tea and so on on the side. He managed to save up some money from the business and when my father died, we inherited some land in Kun Pain, above Momeik, which we sold. With the money from that and from what we had saved, we managed to buy a tea warehouse in Mandalay, but it didn't do very well. We were only ordinary country folk and we couldn't compete with the big merchants in Mandalay. On top of that, the internal disturbances in the country were always a worry. We decided it would be better to return to our old district so we moved back to Momeik and settled here for good.

I've sent my children to college. I don't know if it runs in the family, but we've ended up with three daughters and no sons.

Nowadays we live off my husband's pension and remainder of our inheritance. It's enough to get by on. Being an old couple out in the country doesn't cost much. Food is cheap round here. Our main cost is putting our daughters through college. The oldest is now a schoolteacher but the other two are still studying.

No, *Saya*, I don't ride horses any more. I used to do it from time to time if I had to, up until I was about thirty. But once I'd passed thirty, I gave up. I think that beyond a certain age, it starts to look undignified. As for guns, I never touch them. Although we've got a licensed double-barrelled shotgun in the house, it's only my husband that sometimes takes it out. I don't even touch the thing. Nowadays, instead of guns, I handle prayer beads. Every day I use beads to meditate on the thousand virtues of the Lord Buddha.

So what do you think of all that? To look at me, you'd never guess I'd been through so much, would you?

[February 1989]

35

A DAUGHTER OF BUDDHA

I met her in a nunnery somewhere in the Sagaing Hills. She must have been about thirty-five. She was as tall and slim as a pine tree, clothed in a nun's robes and her newly shaven head gleamed almost turquoise. Her eyes twinkled beneath curling lashes and dark eyebrows. She had a strong nose and pretty pink lips, and a mole on her fair golden cheek. Her hands had straight and slim fingers and her nails and palms were slightly pink. She looked serene. She sat facing me with a poise so relaxed it reminded me of the way a silken handkerchief falls to the ground.

I 'll tell you my life-story since you're related to one of the senior nuns, Daw Nyanatheingi. I've already told her all about it. I've explained it all to her, a bit like Catholics confess to their priests. I'll say it all again for the second time, but I intend this to be the last time too. I can't see why I should need to repeat it after this. Now that I've become a nun, I regard the previous chapter of my life as closed.

I'd barely given a moment's thought to becoming a nun before I came to this nunnery in Sagaing to meditate on the Triple Gems[1]. But while I was here, I decided to join the nunhood. My name is Daw Thilasandi. The senior nun gave it to me.

I was born in a town in the delta. My name used to be Win Win May. My mother was pure Burmese but my father was half Chinese. That must make me a quarter Chinese. I was the oldest of ten children. Three brothers, seven sisters. One of my brothers died young. My father was upset because he put more store by sons, which I suppose was down to him being part Chinese.

That didn't stop him wanting the best for his daughters, or stop him from giving us the same education we would get if we were boys. He wanted to make sure we could all look after the business. He worked as hard as he could to get us an education. He wasn't educated himself. Before he married my mother, he worked as a clerk in a private company. In those days, he earned enough to live comfortably.

We lived in the delta. The trading company he worked for was doing well. After he married, he carried on working there while the first four of us grew up. There was a school in the town and we all attended. But when I was about ten, the company was nationalised. I was in fourth standard at school. He started to have problems with his job. The company was taken over by the Trade Corporation and my father became a government employee. He couldn't afford to keep us all on the small salary they paid him, and the family kept growing. So he resigned and started out on his own.

He had to start small. He went to see a chinaman in our town who owned an ice-cream factory and asked him for a job. The man gave him an ice-cream cart and sent him out to sell ice cream as a sort of agent. My father wasn't afraid of hard work. He'd be out there in all weathers selling ice cream. That's how he managed to put us all through school.

When money started to get tight, he asked himself whether we should drop out of school and go out and get jobs. But since we were still only

---

[1] The Buddha; the *Dhamma* (the teachings of the Buddha) and the *Sangha*, (the monkhood).

kids, there wasn't much we could usefully do. Also, I'd always been good at school, ever since I was little. I used to work hard. So he wanted me to carry on in school, and he used to say that they were relying on me to get an education. He didn't want any of us to end up without one like him. So he told me that since I was the clever one, I should stay on at school until I'd finished.

So thanks to him and his ice cream I sat tenth standard and passed first time round, and even got three distinctions. But because there were some changes to the educational system going on at the time, I couldn't get a place at medical school or on another vocational degree and I ended up going to Rangoon University and studying chemistry. At the time I started, my brother and two younger sisters were both in high school so my father had to keep on working because if they did well in their exams too, he felt he would have to make sure they could go to university too.

I told him not to work so hard. I said I could just as easily do nursing training and get a job instead of doing a degree. Or I could get a government job or go and work in the Trade Corporation. But he wouldn't hear of it. He told me that as I was the oldest and I was clever, there was no way I could quit college and get a job. He said he hadn't worked this hard for me to be a drop-out.

It cost a lot for me to live in Rangoon. On top of the fees, they had to send me about four hundred *kyats* each month. And when I first started, I had to buy books and clothes, and there was the cost of travel to get there. And you have to pay all the fees up front, don't you? I added it all up and told my father that it would cost him about ten thousand a year to send me to Rangoon. That would make forty thousand for just doing a degree. If I did a Masters, it would come to even more. So I kept telling him there was no point in me going. I wanted him to save the money he was spending on me, and invest it in some other business instead. But he was having none of it. He just told me to shut up and said that my job was to get a degree.

I want to give you an idea of how hard he had to work. He used to get up early and go off to the ice-cream factory. He'd stand in line with his cart and pick up his order. If you wanted a lot, you had to go early, particularly in hot weather. In summer, my father used to start queueing at four in the morning. Business was brisk in the hot season, but the work was exhausting. The opposite was true in the cool season and during the monsoon. He wasn't so tired, but he didn't make much money either. So he had to find other ways of topping up his income. We used to buy waste paper and turn it into paper bags at home to sell to the grocery shops. Everyone at home got involved in making them.

When I was in my fourth year, my father started getting sick quite often. That year I got good enough marks to do a Masters Degree but I decided not to. I wanted to get a job to help my father out. I didn't care whether I got a government job or a job in a self-help school out in the countryside[2]. By then even my younger sister was at university. My father couldn't manage to send three children to university simultaneously on the income from his ice cream stall. So I decided to drop out of university rather than do a Masters Degree. But my father wouldn't hear of it.

My younger brother hadn't done very well at school and had failed tenth standard. He was too busy having a good time and hadn't bothered with his exams. My father was annoyed about this, and declared that sons weren't worth the bother. He decided that he would only educate his daughters and told my brother to find himself a job. Luckily he got one as a ticket seller on the private ferry boat which went between our town and Rangoon. As for my sisters and me, my father put us through university and he told me I should do my Masters.

I got engaged shortly before the end of my fourth year. I'll just call him 'my fiancé'. I'd rather not mention his name. He started university at the same time as me and I first met him because we were in the same group for practicals. We were friends from then on.

I shouldn't really be telling you these sort of things while I'm wearing my nun's robes. This has to be the last time I talk about this—I can't see any reason why I'll need to talk about it again. We got to know one another during our practicals. I guessed he was interested in me though he never told me so. But I could see the signs. He used to come to my dormitory when he had no classes and during the evenings. We just used to talk. It was all quite innocent. Neither of us said how we really felt about each other. We both tried to hide our feelings. I never did anything which he might have interpreted as leading him on or which might have made him think that our friendship was anything more than just that.

Even though we told each other a great deal, I never told him about my family. I wanted to keep all that to myself. That I was an ice-cream seller's daughter. That I had eight brothers and sisters. That it was my responsibility to make sure they could all get a good education, so I couldn't let myself get distracted with love affairs. Also, my boyfriend was the only son of some very well-to-do merchants in Rangoon. They had a big house and a compound in Windermere Road, and owned a flashy car. So in my view, there was no question of the two of us becoming any

---

[2] In villages without schools, the government often allows the villagers to raise money to open a school themselves, sometimes providing them with partial support. It is a common sight to see stalls set up by the main road, manned by villagers shaking collection-tins. The money raised may be intended for a school or for the local pagoda.

closer when we came from such different backgrounds. That's why I was always very careful to keep my distance. Of the ten times he came to see me, I'd only see him for five. The other times I used to think up some excuse. I had no room in my life for love affairs. I had to work to look after my parents and make sure my brothers and sisters could go to school.

Since I guessed he probably wanted to propose to me, I started to avoid him as much as I could. But it was difficult to hide from him since we both lived in the same town, went to the same university and even attended the same classes. I could avoid him when he visited my hostel, but in class or in practicals we couldn't escape seeing one other.

As I'd suspected he would, one day he proposed to me. I turned him down. I explained to him about my background, without mentioning that my father was an ice-cream seller. I explained to him that our lives were very different and I had a duty to look after my parents and make sure my brothers and sisters got an education. I explained I couldn't get in-volved with anyone while I was attending university.

But human psychology is a strange thing. Explaining all this to him just made me realise how much I cared about him. To start off with, I'd told myself that this was just an ordinary friendship. But when I rejected him, I realised there was more to it than that. It's strange, isn't it, how rejecting someone often makes you realise that really want them?

Anyway, in my fourth year I accepted his proposal. But I still didn't tell him about my father being an ice-cream vendor. It wasn't exactly lying. I just didn't come out with the whole truth. I was ashamed to tell him my father spent all his days pushing an ice-cream cart around, come rain or shine. And I was worried that if I told him this, it might make him change his opinion of me and he might leave me. I wasn't worried about him leaving me because he came from a rich upper-class family. I was worried because I really loved him. But I thought that it would all work out providing he was willing to brave it out with me.

He told me he couldn't wait until I'd finished my Masters, and he kept going on at me until eventually I agreed to get married. It was just a registry office ceremony. But his parents hadn't given their consent. And my father was very angry at me from the start. It really seemed to hurt him. He seemed to shrivel up. I suppose he was upset because his clev-erest daughter whom they all had been relying on to do well had gone and got married instead. One day when he'd been selling ice-cream all day in the rain, he came home and had a stroke which paralysed part of his body. He'd already broken off contact with me. But my sister, who'd finished her degree by then and had got a job, wrote me a letter. She was very angry with me, and it was just a short note which said that my father had had a stroke and that it was my fault since I had betrayed the family. It looked like she really hated me. Just look at the words she used: 'Betrayed the family'. That really upset me.

That was how my family took it. As for his family, they put an announcement in the paper saying they did not recognise our marriage. He said it didn't matter. He was their only son—the other three children were daughters—and he said that sooner or later they'd come round and accept us. I could live with the fact that his parents had rejected us. But I didn't like it. Both of our families had rejected our marriage and this made me very sad.

Once we got married, we had nowhere to live. We lived in the house of a friend of his who was the son of a high-ranking official. They had a fairly big house in a compound, but rather than living in the house, the friend lived over the garage in a sort of bachelor's flat. It was a garage, but it was quite comfortable. Downstairs was the garage and a sitting room and the friend lived upstairs. He had enough space to give us a room of our own.

We hadn't given any thought to our future before we got married. There wasn't much point in thinking about it. We knew we'd just have to take the rough with the smooth. We stayed with his friend for four or five months. Both he and his parents were very kind to us, giving us a roof over our heads.

Then, if you'll excuse my mentioning it, *Saya*, after about four or five months I fell pregnant. My husband seemed to become a bit depressed. He'd always been very cheerful, but now he started to become distracted, but he wouldn't tell me what the matter was. One day he announced that he didn't want to go on living like this and that he thought he would go off and get himself a job on board a ship. I didn't want him to leave me. I wanted him there so that we could face the rough and the smooth together. But since he didn't have a job, it was difficult for us to survive in the long run.

While we were living like this, my father died. My mother sent me a telegram asking me to come home. So I went home for the funeral. Alone. You can imagine how it was. Since I'd defied my parents by getting married, I thought I'd better go back on my own without my husband. So he stayed behind in Rangoon and carried on making arrangements to try and get on board a ship.

When I got home, my mother was weeping. My brothers wouldn't speak to me. My younger sisters hardly said a word to me and the two older sisters wouldn't talk to me at all. My mother told me that what I had done was cruel, but that she nonetheless would forgive me.

Returning home for my father's funeral was a turning point. I had been there a month or two when I received a letter from my husband. He said that he had got himself a job on board a ship and that as he was leaving immediately, he wasn't able to come to see me to say goodbye, and there was no point in me coming back to Rangoon. His parents had made the arrangements for him, he said, and he had to leave quickly. When I read his letter, I had my suspicions. I wasn't at all sure that he really had got a job on board a ship, or that he had to leave so soon. I wondered if his parents had fixed all this up simply in order to split us up.

Anyway, he did join ship. He was away for about two years. During that time, I didn't get a single letter from him. I thought he'd write to me as soon as he left, but after six months he still hadn't written and I began to give up hope. I thought that at least he'd write when our son was born. But he didn't.

Once our son was born, I gave up expecting him to write. Our son turned one. He'd been away over two years. Still no letters. I didn't even know where he was. One time I had to go to Rangoon so I looked up some of his friends who told me they thought he might be in Japan or Hong Kong, but they weren't too sure.

You can imagine I wasn't too happy. I came home depressed and humiliated. I'd not had a single letter from him. So I went back to Rangoon and registered at the labour office in the hope of getting a job. One of his friends helped me out, and took me around to find a job. I spent some time with him, but it was just because he was helping me out. My conscience was clear about it.

One time, I'd been for a job interview and on the way home we decided to go to the Thamada Cinema. The film was a well-known one and we thought we would go and see it to unwind. I often used to go to the cinema with my friends. But on that day, it was just him and me. As we came out of the cinema, we happened to run into my husband's sisters. I hadn't seen them since university. When his older sister saw us together, she spat on the pavement before getting into the car. The other two younger sisters were staring at us. We disappeared into the crowd. My companion didn't seem to have seen them.

I didn't get the job. So I went back home, where I'd left my son with my mother. But I couldn't stay there for long. I was itching to leave. I think I had what's called 'wanderlust'. If I'd been on my own, I would have upped sticks and left. But I had my son to think about.

One day I got a letter from a friend of mine in Shan State who said that the town she lived in was due to open a self-help high school and that there would be a job for me if I wanted to come. So I set off for Shan State with my son, and got a job as chemistry teacher. The salary was paid by the Parent-Teacher Association rather than the government but it was much the same salary as a government high-school teacher got.

Once I moved there, I felt a lot better. Maybe it was the change of scenery. Certainly there was plenty to feel relaxed about. The scenery was beautiful, the people were honest and simple, food was cheap and plentiful. Apart from being split up from my family and having a broken marriage, I had everything to be happy about. I still hadn't had a single letter from my husband. He could easily have found out where I was if he'd wanted to. I was upset that he'd left over two years ago and I'd not heard a word from him since then.

About six months after I arrived in that town, my son died of malaria. I then announced in the town that I was separated. About six months after my son died, I saw an announcement in the newspaper that my husband had re-married. It made me sad to see it. Now I had lost a son and a husband. In fact we had never officially divorced. Although he had broken off all communication when he left, we were still legally married.

When I saw the announcement in the newspaper, I wondered what I should do. I wondered if I should put an announcement in declaring myself to be his main wife. I wondered if I should go and see him. Maybe I should just sit tight. I couldn't decide. Eventually I decided I would just stay put in that town and close the book on that particular chapter of my life.

While I was living there, I met another man and we got married. But sometimes true life is stranger than fiction isn't it? Sometimes it's difficult to believe how coincidences can happen like this. You see, soon after I re-married, I read in the paper that my first husband had got divorced. Maybe his wife discovered he'd been married before. Or maybe they fell out since they both came from well-to-do families and they might have squabbled about money. I don't know what the reason was, but the fact was that they got divorced.

It would have been better if the two of us had kept out of one another's way now that we each had our second marriages. Instead, now that his second marriage had broken up, he came looking for me. When I saw him, it startled me, like seeing a ghost. I was shocked, partly because I hadn't expected to see him, and partly because he had changed so much. He was very run-down, skeletal. He'd become a drug addict. It probably happened while he was at sea. I discovered later that this was one of the factors which led to his divorce.

He turned up in my town and asked me to come back to him. Can you imagine the cheek of it? We had only been married a short time before he'd deserted me. Since then, I'd not had a single letter, a single bit of support from him. Then he'd come home and re-married. But now that his second wife had divorced him, he seemed to think that he could get me to come back to him. That I would just drop everything. It wasn't even as if I was on my own. I'd married again. I hadn't sorted the whole mess out beforehand and now it had become far more complicated.

277

He kept on asking me to come back to him. When I told him that I wasn't in a position to do so, he took me to court to make me come back. Then my second husband accused me of adultery. I was so ashamed. I'd never experienced anything so humiliating in all my life. And from the outside, it must have seemed very shameful. I had rolled up in town with a small baby. I'd said I was separated and got a job as a school-teacher. Then I'd re-married. Then my old husband had turned up and taken me to court. It was too shaming for words. I couldn't explain to everyone what had really happened. So instead, the whole town thought that I was a immoral woman.

The court case took far too long, more than a year. I didn't have the money to hire a lawyer, but in the end a lady lawyer from a big town nearby agreed to take the case on for free once she'd heard the details. She did what she could. But my second husband was determined. I almost felt scared to stay in town. In the end, some of the neighbourhood elders and the judges got together and sorted the case out outside the court and persuaded him to drop the court case.

Although it was solved, the outcome was pretty hopeless for me. My second husband was released from our marriage. He hated me. As for my first husband, I don't know if it was because of the drugs or what, but he told the elders he didn't want me back after all. My second husband was a simple honest man from the hills. He and his family despised me and divorced me in front of the elders. From his point of view, he was right to do so. I don't blame him for doing it. Even though my first husband had rejected me, there was no reason for him to have me back. I could understand how he would hate me after all the embarrassment I had put him through. As for my first husband, he went back to Rangoon, and died about a year later from alcohol poisoning after he'd tried to kick his drug habit.

My whole life had gone wrong. My family thought ill of me. My first husband and his family thought ill of me. My second husband and his family thought ill of me. I was very depressed. So depressed I even thought of killing myself. But I didn't because I was afraid of the five hundred and five miserable future existences that are promised to those that commit suicide.

So to get over the pain, I came to the Sagaing Hills where I met the mother abbess Daw Nyanatheingi. She told me about the teachings of Lord Buddha. She told me that according to those teachings, everything that had happened to me was part of my *karma*. She explained to me that you reap what you sow in your previous existences. There is no avoiding it. She explained all this to me every night as she taught me the *Dhamma*.

I find the *Dhamma*, the teachings of Buddha, to be very calming. Once I began to meditate in accordance with her instructions, I began to relax. She explained the *Satipitana* Sutra to me, one of the Buddha's teachings. That has released me from my sufferings. I no longer bear grudges or harbour resentment towards anyone. Now I meditate calmly in order to eventually free myself from *Samsara*, the cycle of re-birth.

I'm sure you know how good it feels to hear the sound of the brass gong as it rings out amongst all of life's other noises. The weeping, the laughing, the sighing and the last drawing of breath.

This is the last time I will tell anyone my story. I have vowed to myself that I will not repeat it again.

[March 1988]

MAP OF RANGOON

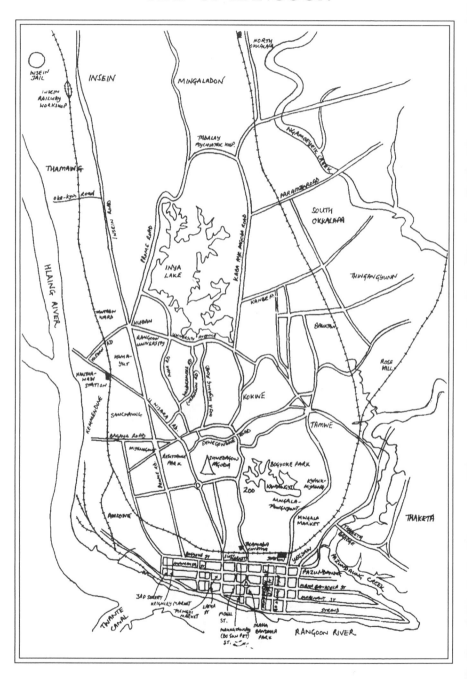

THE BURMESE CALENDAR

Lunar months		Approximate equivalent
Nattaw		December
Pyatho		January
Tabodwe		February
	hot season begins	
Tabaung		March
Tagu	(Thingyan New Year festival)	April
Kason		May
	monsoon begins	
Nayon		June
Waso	(start of Lent)	July
Wagaung		August
Tawthalin		September
Thadingyut	(end of Lent)	October
	cool season begins	
Tazaungmon		November

GLOSSARY

a-nyeint
originally consisted of dancing led by a female dancers interspersed with satirical and comic sketches by
comedians accompanied by a small Burmese orchestra. Nowadays, they are complex spectacles more like
the *zat-pwes* of larger troupes.

a-pyo-daw
female dancer at a *zat* who sings songs to assuage
the spirits and ward off problems in the performance.

a-yein
song and dance performance, performed by a swaying chorus of young girls, often at the New Year
Thingyan and other festivals. *Yein* means 'swaying
from a fixed point'.

Coringee
From Kalinga state, southern India, roughly corre-
sponding to the modern state of Orissa.

champac
ee sagawa

gaung-baung
traditional Burmese man's turban, made of salmon
coloured silk, nowadays only worn on formal occa-
sions

hti
ornamented 'umbrella' at the top of a pagoda.

jaggery
form of fudge made out of toddy palm juice. Sugary
liquid is extracted from the spathe or flower case before it opens. To tap this palm sap, the two parts of
the spathe are tied together at the tip, and then the
spathe is beaten with a mallet at regular intervals over
a few days. A thin slice of the spathe is then removed
and it is bent downwards to allow the liquid to drip
out and be collected. A palm only starts to produce
flowers after ten or twenty years but once mature,
there may be several spathes all producing simultaneously, at a rate of up to three litres per day per
spathe.

kamauk	bamboo hat with a broad brim worn by peasants
kyat	Burmese unit of currency. During the period 1987–1990, the official exchange rate for the kyat was approximately 6–8 *kyats* per US dollar. However, the real, or black-market exchange rate rose over the period from under forty to over sixty *kyats* per dollar.
kyay-thee-dan	hand-made traditional Burmese buttons made out of cloth knotted into a ball with a 3cm tail at one end.
longyi	men's or women's nether garment, similar to a sarong, consisting of a length of material sewn together on one edge to make a tube
mayan	ovoid fruit which turns yellow when ripe and may be sour or sweet, *Bouea burmanica*
mohinga	breakfast dish of rice noodles with a fish-flavoured gravy, served with eggs, coriander and lime
nat	guardian spirit
pinni	fawn homespun cloth, used to make jackets or shirts and regarded as nationalist dress
Pitaka	teachings of Buddha. There are three books—the *tripitaka*.
pukka	'full-fledged', permanent, solid, genuine
pya	one hundredth of a *kyat*
sagawa	the *champac* or *Michelia champaca*. A tree of the rhododendron family native to India, Assam and Burma where it grows in the plains and lower hills and is often grown along roads. It has lustrous evergreen oval leaves about 25cm long, smooth grey bark and is about 30 metres tall. The flowers are yellow, orange or white with narrow 6 cm petals that bloom in spring. They are highly scented and used to make the East Indian perfume *champak*. Scarlet or brown seeds cluster along a long stalk. The wood polishes

well and is used for making furniture, boats, drums and Buddha images.

Saya, Sayagyi, Sayama	terms of respect, meaning sir, master, teacher, boss or doctor (*Sayama* is used for women)
shin-byu	novitiation ceremony for young boys entering the monastery for a temporary period
standard, e.g. 10th standard	school classes, equivalent to the US grades. Primary school is up to 4th standard, middle school from 5th to 7th, and high school from 8th to 10th standard, National exams are held at 8th and 10th standard. High school graduates must pass the tenth standard exam to enter university. The minimum age for taking the exam is 16. Students who fail the year twice must drop out of school but can retake the exams privately.
thanakha	tree, *Limonia acidissima*, the perfumed bark of which is ground up with water and used by Burmese women as a yellow-white cosmetic and sunscreen
Vipassana	insight meditation
viss	unit of weight equivalent to 3.65 pounds or 1.65 kilograms. There are 100 *kyats* or *ticals* in a *viss*, and 100 *pyas* in a kyat. One *kyat* or *tical* is equivalent to 16.5 grams or 0.58 ounces.
yawgi	women who stay usually temporarily in nunneries to meditate. They dress in brown but do not have to shave their heads. (Also *yogi*)
zat, zat-pwe	dramatic performances, or the troupe giving the performance, led by a male actor/dancer. They usually last all night, and featuring singing, dancing. and dramatisations of classical Burmese stories and *Jatakas* as well as modern plays
zayat	public resthouse on the wayside or on the platform of a pagoda or within a monastery.